Religion in American History and Politics:
25 Core Documents

Religion in American History and Politics: 25 Core Documents

Edited by

Sarah Morgan Smith, Ellen Dietz Tucker and David Tucker

Ashbrook Press

Library of Congress Cataloging-in-Publication Data

Religion in American History and Politics;
Edited by Sarah Morgan Smith, Ellen Dietz Tucker, and David Tucker

p.   cm.
Includes Index
1. United States – Politics and government.

ISBN 978-1-878802-32-3 (pbk.)

Ashbrook Center at Ashland University
401 College Avenue
Ashland, Ohio 44805
www.ashbrook.org

About the Ashbrook Center

The Ashbrook Center, an independent center at Ashland University, restores and strengthens the capacities of the American people for constitutional self-government. Ashbrook teaches students and teachers across our country why America is exceptional and what America represents in the long history of the world. Ashbrook creates informed patriots.

Ashbrook is the nation's largest university-based educator in the enduring principles and practice of free government in the United States, offering programs and resources for students, teachers, and citizens. Dedicated in 1983 by President Ronald Reagan, the Ashbrook Center is governed by its own board and responsible for raising all of the funds necessary for its many programs.

Visit us online at Ashbrook.org, TeachingAmericanHistory.org, and 50coredocs.org.

Contents

Introduction

This volume draws together twenty-five primary documents through which readers may trace central themes in the long, complex story of religion and politics in American history. As the first publication of the Ashbrook Center's program in Religion in American History and Politics (RAHP), the collection aims to broaden a discussion too often limited to church-state relations. We hope to illuminate a larger dynamic: not only the influence of religion on American politics and culture, but also the influence of America on the religious convictions and practices of her citizens.

As this reciprocal relationship between religion and politics has unfolded, Americans have wrestled with certain recurrent questions. Is America a nation with a God-given mission to establish free government at home and abroad? Are religious belief and practice among its citizens necessary for the republic to survive and flourish? In what ways and to what degree should religion attempt to reform the morals and manners of Americans? Do such reform movements pose any dangers to republican government? Are there circumstances under which republicanism—or, at least, majoritarianism—might present a threat to religion or require religious believers to practice civil disobedience? Can all religious traditions accommodate American principles? Can the adherents of every faith successfully engage in republican self-government?

From the beginning, religion played an important role in shaping Americans' identity and purpose: colonization efforts were undertaken in the name of God, with the evangelization of the native peoples or the chance to establish a society in accordance with Biblical ideals included among the many ends of settlement (Documents 1 & 2). Many colonists were attracted to North America because of the potential for greater religious freedom than they had experienced in Europe. Yet prior to the American Revolution, all but a handful of the colonies had some form of religious establishment, some level of integration between church and state (Document 2). In the decades following the Revolution, the diversity of religious settlements in the individual states moved slowly in the direction of disestablishment, and religious liberty became increasingly a fact. What exactly the separation of church and state meant remained in question, however, as it does now. Yet, even as Americans came to the broad agreement that the institutions of church and state were to be separate, they did not agree that religion and politics could or should be. The documents illustrate this as they trace two major themes: the development and decline of the American Protestant synthesis, and the ongoing link between religion and social or civil reform and even dissent.

The American Protestant synthesis united reason, republican government, science and Reformed Christianity in a powerful combination that undergirded the Protestant establishment in the United States (see documents 3, 7, 10 and 11). This establishment exerted broad influence in America, not least through its dominance of American education (through most of the nineteenth century virtually all colleges were religious institutions presided over by ordained ministers). In brief, the synthesis held that the Reformation had restored the authority of human reason, and this eventually led to the restoration of reason's authority in politics and science. The Declaration ("the laws of nature and of nature's God") expressed the synthesis. The fundamental premise of the synthesis was that science and revelation could not contradict each other, because God was the author of both nature and the Bible. Moral, political and scientific progress went hand in hand.

The fundamental premise of the synthesis and thus the synthesis itself came increasingly into question after the Civil War, as developments in science seemed harder and harder to reconcile with the Bible. At the same time that developments in geology, for example, challenged the account in Genesis, technical criticism of the Biblical text raised questions about the Bible itself. This new thinking very often came to the United States with students returning from graduate study abroad, principally in Germany. Evolution as an explanation of the origins and changes among living things, in the years following the publication of Darwin's *On the Origin of Species* (1859), increasingly formed part of this new thinking, but only part of it. (Documents 14 and 16 deal with these developments.)

As the Protestant synthesis fell apart, Protestantism split into fundamentalist and modernist camps. The fundamentalists adhered to the moral and political aspects of the synthesis, particularly because they saw the changes in American society in the first decades of the twentieth century as evidence not of moral progress but of moral decline. The modernists adhered to the scientific aspects of the synthesis, continuing to promote progress, arguing in some cases that revelation was itself progressive and still, in fact, ongoing. For these progressives, the supreme virtue was tolerance, which they accused the fundamentalists of lacking. A tolerant attitude allowed new kinds of thought and behavior to emerge. And if new thought and behavior did not emerge, how could there be progress, how could God continue to reveal himself? We may understand the fundamentalists to be asking the progressives in turn, if revelation itself is progressive, by what standard are we to distinguish progress, which is presumably good, from mere change, which may be bad? (Documents 18-20 deal with these issues.) The fundamentalist-modernist split still largely defines religion in the United States and continues to shape our political life.

The other major theme illuminated in this volume is the role of religion in both motivating and shaping social and political change in the colonies and, later, states (Documents 1, 4, 8, 9, 10, 16, 17, 22, 23). From John Winthrop's almost utopian vision of a community grounded in Christian love (Document 1) to the more pragmatic observation, embodied in colonial legal codes, that religion tempers the vicious elements of human behavior (Document 2), early Americans were convinced that a religiously inspired sense of divine justice provided the best of all possible encouragements to personal and from there, social, order. A sense of divine justice properly understood would also lead some Americans to resist state power when it appeared to overstep its natural limit or threaten the public good (Document 4).

As American society advanced into the western territories in the 19th century, the issue of morality in public life became increasingly important. Lincoln's "Temperance Address" (Document 10) and Beecher's "Plea for the West" (Document 8) present two variations on this theme: Lincoln critiqued religiously inspired approaches to reform in the name of preserving a spirit of moderation and amity in civil reform, whereas Beecher linked the preservation of American liberty directly to the spread of religious institutions and teaching. Although for many, religious arguments gave powerful incentives to moral reform and prevented moral disorder, such arguments always carried the potential for reckless zealotry that others viewed as more politically dangerous than the vices against which it was aimed.

On the other hand, as the influence of modern scientism and relativism on American religious institutions grew, many of those institutions became much less active in their pursuit of social change. Latter-day reformers like Addams (Document 17), King (Document 22) and Schaeffer (Document 23) each attempted to counteract this tendency, calling on Americans to "revive" the idealistic elements of their religious roots and apply them to the problems of modernization, urbanization, and industrialization. Schaeffer's "Christian Manifesto," in particular, is a call to arms and a reminder of the counter-cultural thrust of much religious teaching. All three documents show the important role of dissent in correcting and directing the public opinion of the nation on policy questions with moral dimensions.

The stories just briefly recounted are told in greater detail and with more nuance in the documents themselves. The introductions to the documents provide some context for understanding them. Whenever possible, we have used footnotes to document quotations and allusions, and to identify little-known persons and concepts mentioned but not explained in the documents. We have modernized spelling, punctuation, and capitalization except for that of Document 2. Matter inserted in the documents for clarity is within brackets. We have also provided in Appendix A some study questions to promote analysis and discussion. In addition, in Appendix B, we have provided suggestions for further reading.

These 25 documents do not, of course, tell the whole story of religion in American history and politics. For that reason, we plan additional document collections on the following topics:

RAHP: The Prophetic Voice
RAHP: Religious Liberty
RAHP: Key Court Decisions
RAHP: Religion and Science
RAHP: Women's Voices
RAHP: Private Reflections

Over time, our goal is to develop a library of documents that reflects the depth and rich variety of American religious experiences and the ways in which such experiences relate to other ongoing social and political developments. Some of these documents will come from the pens of clerics or other formal spiritual leaders; some will be written by statesmen and legislators in the heat of public crises; some will be the private reflections of individual citizens speaking in neither a ministerial nor a political capacity about their own religious experience. All, we hope, will open new pathways for investigating the course of American history in the conviction that as we learn to better understand the past, we are better equipped to face and shape our civic future.

The editors would like to thank Roger Beckett and the staff of the Ashbrook Center for their support. We particularly appreciate the editorial assistance of Lisa Ormiston and the transcription work of Brooke Branson, Madeleine Emholtz, and Brennan Kunkel.

Religion in American History and Politics:
25 Core Documents

Document 1

"A Model of Christian Charity"
John Winthrop
1630

In this brief discourse, which is believed to have been delivered as a lecture to the group of colonists about to depart for the Massachusetts Bay Colony, John Winthrop (1588-1649) lays out a vision for building a godly commonwealth.

Winthrop, a devout Puritan, was a lawyer, not a minister, and his training shines through in both the structure and content of his argument. From the primary premise that God has ordained a variety of conditions among men–some to be rich, some to be poor, and so forth–he derives the traditional Christian ideal of unity realized through diversity to offer a vision of a political community based in the radical ideal of "brotherly affection." Based on the extraordinary demands of colonization, Winthrop urged his listeners to willingly be generous with their resources—both tangible and intangible—considering the good of their neighbor to be integral to their own good. The colonists—who were fleeing royal persecution for their religious beliefs—had to recognize that they were drawn together for a purpose far beyond their own liberty, or even security. They were, Winthrop predicted, in the first statement of American millennialism, to become God's new Israel, and their success or failure would prove to all the world the truth or falsehood of their religious claims.

CHRISTIAN CHARITY.

A Model hereof.

GOD ALMIGHTY in his most holy and wise providence, hath so disposed of the condition of mankind, as in all times some must be rich, some poor, some high and eminent in power and dignity; others mean and in submission.

The Reason hereof.

1 *Reason.* First, to hold conformity with the rest of his works, being delighted to show forth the glory of his wisdom in the variety and difference of the creatures, and the glory of his power in ordering all these differences for the preservation and good of the whole; and the glory of his greatness, that as it is the glory of princes to have many officers, so this great king will have many stewards, counting himself more honored in dispensing his gifts to man by man, than if he did it by his own immediate hands.

2 *Reason.* Secondly, that he might have the more occasion to manifest the work of his Spirit: first upon the wicked in moderating and restraining them: so that the rich and mighty should not eat up the poor, nor the poor and despised rise up against their superiors and shake off their yoke. Secondly, in the regenerate, in exercising his graces in them, as in the great ones, their love, mercy, gentleness, temperance etc., in the poor and inferior sort, their faith, patience, obedience, etc.

3 *Reason.* Thirdly, that every man might have need of others, and from hence they might be all knit more nearly together in the bonds of brotherly affection. From hence it appears plainly that no man is made more honorable than another or more wealthy etc., out of any particular and singular respect to himself, but for the glory of his creator and the common good of the creature, man. Therefore, God still reserves the property of these gifts to himself as Ezek. 16:17—he there calls wealth, *his gold and his silver,*[1] and Prov. 3:9—he claims their service as his due, *honor the Lord with thy riches, etc.*[2] All men being thus (by divine providence) ranked into two sorts, rich and poor; under the first are comprehended all such as are able to live comfortably by their own means duly improved; and all others are poor according to the former distribution.

... There is a time when a Christian must sell all and give to the poor, as they did in the Apostles' times. There is a time also when Christians (though they give not all yet) must give beyond their ability.... Likewise, a community of peril calls for extraordinary liberality, and so doth community in some special service for the church. Lastly, when there is no other means whereby our Christian brother may be relieved in his distress, we must help him beyond our ability rather than tempt God in putting him upon help by miraculous or extraordinary means.

---

[1] Ezekiel 16:17.
[2] Proverbs 3:9.

This duty of mercy is exercised in three kinds: giving, lending and forgiving.

Quest[ion]. What rule shall a man observe in giving in respect of the measure?

Ans[wer]. If the time and occasion be ordinary, he is to give out of his abundance. *Let him lay aside as God hath blessed him.*[3] If the time and occasion be extraordinary, he must be ruled by them: taking this withal, that then a man cannot likely do too much, especially if he may leave himself and his family under probable means of comfortable subsistence.

Object[ion]. A man must lay up for posterity, the fathers lay up for posterity and children, and *he is worse than an infidel that provideth not for his own.*[4]

Ans[wer]. For the first, it is plain that it being spoken by way of comparison, it must be meant of the ordinary and usual course of fathers, and cannot extend to times and occasions extraordinary. For the other place, the Apostle speaks against such as walked inordinately, and it is without question that he is worse than an infidel who through his own sloth and voluptuousness shall neglect to provide for his family....

Quest[ion]. What rule must we observe in lending?

Ans[wer]. Thou must observe whether thy brother hath present or probable or possible means of repaying thee, if there be none of those, thou must give him according to his necessity, rather than lend him as he requires; if he hath present means of repaying thee, thou art to look at him not as an act of mercy, but by way of Commerce, wherein thou art to walk by the rule of justice; but if his means of repaying thee be only probable or possible, then is he an object of thy mercy, thou must lend him, though there be danger of losing it, Deut. 15:7. *If any of thy brethren be poor* etc., *thou shalt lend him sufficient....*[5]

Quest[ion]. What rule must we observe and walk by in cause of community of peril?

Ans[wer]. The same as before, but with more enlargement towards others and less respect towards ourselves and our own right. Hence it was that in the primitive Church they sold all, had all things in common, neither did any man say that which he possessed was his own.[6] Likewise in their return out of the

---

[3] 1 Corinthians 16:2.
[4] 1 Timothy 5:8.
[5] Deuteronomy 15:7-8.
[6] As recounted in Acts 2:44-45.

captivity, because the work was great for the restoring of the church and the danger of enemies was common to all, Nehemiah directs the Jews to liberality and readiness in remitting their debts to their brethren, and disposing liberally to such as wanted, and stand not upon their own dues which they might have demanded of them.[7] Thus did some of our Forefathers in times of persecution in England, and so did many of the faithful of other churches, whereof we keep an honorable remembrance of them; and it is to be observed that both in Scriptures and latter stories of the churches that such as have been most bountiful to the poor saints, especially in those extraordinary times and occasions, God hath left them highly commended to posterity....

... The definition which the Scripture gives us of love is this: *Love is the bond of perfection.* First it is a bond or ligament. Secondly it makes the work perfect. There is no body but consists of parts, and that which knits these parts together, gives the body its perfection, because it makes each part so contiguous to others as thereby they do mutually participate with each other, both in strength and infirmity, in pleasure and pain. To instance in the most perfect of all bodies; Christ and his Church make one body; the several parts of this body considered apart before they were united, were as disproportionate and as much disordering as so many contrary qualities or elements, but when Christ comes, and by his spirit and love knits all these parts to himself and each to other, it is become the most perfect and best proportioned body in the world, Eph. 4:16: *Christ, by whom all the body being knit together by every joint for the furniture thereof, according to the effectual power which is in the measure of every perfection of parts, a glorious body without spot or wrinkle;*[8] the ligaments hereof being Christ, or his love, for Christ is love, 1 John 4:8. So this definition is right. *Love is the bond of perfection.*

... The next consideration is how this love comes to be wrought. Adam in his first estate was a perfect model of mankind in all their generations, and in him this love was perfected in regard of the habit. But Adam rent himself from his Creator, rent all his posterity also one from another; whence it comes that every man is borne with this principle in him: to love and seek himself only, and thus a man continueth till Christ comes and takes possession of the soul

---

[7] As recounted in Nehemiah 5.

[8] Winthrop here summarizes his reading of Ephesians 4 and 5, in part paraphrasing 4:13-16, which describes the church as a body made of many parts, each member learning to fill a particular role, all striving together in love to become the earthly embodiment of Christ, "the perfect man." He is also remembering 5:27, which likens the church to a body made perfect by Christ's atoning sacrifice.

and infuseth another principle, love to God and our brother, and this latter having continual supply from Christ, as the head and root by which he is united, gets the predomining in the soul, so by little and little expels the former. 1 John 4:7: *love cometh of God and every one that loveth is borne of God,*[9] so that this love is the fruit of the new birth, and none can have it but the new creature.

... From the former Considerations arise these conclusions. First, this love among Christians is a real thing, not imaginary. Secondly, this love is as absolutely necessary to the being of the body of Christ, as the sinews and other ligaments of a natural body are to the being of that body. Thirdly, this love is a divine, spiritual, nature; free, active, strong, courageous, and permanent; undervaluing all things beneath its proper object and of all the graces, this makes us nearer to resemble the virtues of our heavenly father....

It rests now to make some application of this discourse, by the present design, which gave the occasion of writing of it. Herein are four things to be propounded; first the persons, secondly the work, thirdly the end, fourthly the means.

1. For *the persons*. We are a company professing ourselves fellow members of Christ, in which respect only though we were absent from each other many miles, and had our employments as far distant, yet we ought to account ourselves knit together by this bond of love, and, live in the exercise of it, if we would have comfort of our being in Christ....

2. For the *work* we have in hand. It is by a mutual consent, through a special overvaluing providence and a more than an ordinary approbation of the churches of Christ, to seek out a place of cohabitation and consortship under a due form of Government both civil and ecclesiastical. In such cases as this, the care of the public must over sway all private respects, by which, not only conscience, but mere civil policy, doth bind us. For it is a true rule that particular estates cannot subsist in the ruin of the public.

3. The end is to improve our lives to do more service to the Lord; the comfort and increase of the body of Christ, whereof we are members; that ourselves and posterity may be the better preserved from the

---

[9] 1 John 4:7, "Beloved, let us love one another: for love is of God; and every one that loveth is born of God, and knoweth God."

common corruptions of this evil world, to serve the Lord and work out our Salvation under the power and purity of his holy ordinances.

4. For the means whereby this must be effected: they are twofold, a conformity with the work and end we aim at. These we see are extraordinary, therefore we must not content ourselves with usual ordinary means. Whatsoever we did, or ought to have, done, when we lived in England, the same must we do, and more also, where we go. That which the most in their churches maintain as truth in profession only, we must bring into familiar and constant practice; as in this duty of love, we must love brotherly without dissimulation, we must love one another with a pure heart fervently. We must bear one another's burdens. We must not look only on our own things, but also on the things of our brethren. Neither must we think that the Lord will bear with such failings at our hands as he dothe from those among whom we have lived....

... Thus stands the cause between God and us. We are entered into covenant with Him for this work. We have taken out a commission. The Lord hath given us leave to draw our own articles. We have professed to enterprise these and those accounts, upon these and those ends. We have hereupon besought Him of favor and blessing. Now if the Lord shall please to hear us, and bring us in peace to the place we desire, then hath he ratified this covenant and sealed our Commission, and will expect a strict performance of the articles contained in it; but if we shall neglect the observation of these articles which are the ends we have propounded, and, dissembling with our God, shall fall to embrace this present world and prosecute our carnal intentions, seeking great things for ourselves and our posterity, the Lord will surely break out in wrath against us; be revenged of such a [sinful] people and make us know the price of the breaches of such a covenant.

Now the only way to avoid this shipwreck, and to provide for our posterity, is to follow the counsel of Micah, *to do justly, to love mercy, to walk humbly with our God.*[10] For this end, we must be knit together, in this work, as one man. We must entertain each other in brotherly affection. We must be willing to abridge ourselves of our superfluities, for the supply of other's necessities. We must uphold a familiar commerce together in all meekness, gentleness, patience and liberality. We must delight in each other; make other's conditions our own; rejoice together, mourn together, labor and suffer together, always having before our eyes our commission and community in the

---

[10] Micah 6:8.

work, as members of the same body. So shall we *keep the unity of the spirit in the bond of peace.*[11] The Lord will be our God, and delight to dwell among us, as his own people, and will command a blessing upon us in all our ways. So that we shall see much more of his wisdom, power, goodness and truth, than formerly we have been acquainted with. We shall find that the God of Israel is among us, when ten of us shall be able to resist a thousand of our enemies; when he shall make us a praise and glory that men shall say of succeeding plantations, "the Lord make it likely that of *New England.*" For we must consider that we shall be as a city upon a hill. The eyes of all people are upon us. So that if we shall deal falsely with our God in this work we have undertaken, and so cause him to withdraw his present help from us, we shall be made a story and a by-word through the world. We shall open the mouths of enemies to speak evil of the ways of God, and all professors for God's sake. We shall shame the faces of many of God's worthy servants, and cause their prayers to be turned into curses upon us till wee be consumed out of the good land whither we are a going.

I shall shut up this discourse with that exhortation of Moses, that faithful servant of the Lord, in his last farewell to Israel, Deut. 30: *Beloved there is now set before us life and good, Death and evil, in that we are commanded this day to love the Lord our God, and to love one another, to walk in his ways and to keep his Commandments and his Ordinance and his laws,* and the articles of our Covenant with him, that *we may live and be multiplied, and that the Lord our God may blesse us in the land whither we go to possess it. But if our hearts shall turn away, so that we will not obey, but shall be seduced, and worship and serve other Gods,* our pleasure and profits, *and serve them;* it is propounded unto us this day, *we shall surely perish out of the good land whither we pass over this vast sea to possess it;*[12]

Therefore let us choose life—that we, and our seed may live, by obeying His voice and cleaving to Him, for He is our life and our prosperity.[13]

---

[11] Ephesians 4:3.

[12] Winthrop quotes Deuteronomy 30:15-18, inserting what he understands to be the contemporary application of "other gods".

[13] A summary of Deuteronomy 30:19-20.

Document 2

Laws, Rights, and Liberties Related to Religion in Early America
1610-1682

When they settled in North America, English colonists brought their religious beliefs with them. In most instances, this was accomplished not only as a matter of social or cultural transmission, but by acts of legislative authority. Only Pennsylvania, Delaware, Rhode Island and (possibly) New Jersey failed to establish a particular denomination at some point during the colonial period: in the other colonies, religious establishments were the norm, and generally seen as for the benefit of both church and state as institutions, as well as in accordance with the public good. The excerpts from the laws presented here have been selected for their ability to illustrate colonial attitudes about the relationship between religion and political life: note that all of them—even those which are more "tolerant" of religious variety—presume that religion is a necessary component of civil order.

Articles, Laws, and Orders, Divine, Politic, and Martial for the Colony in Virginia (c. 1610)

1.   First, since we owe our highest and supreme duty—our greatest, and all our allegiance—to Him, from whom all power and authority is derived, and flows as from the first, and only fountain; and [since], being especial soldiers impressed in this sacred cause, we must alone expect our success from Him—who is only the blesser of all good attempts, the King of Kings, the Commander of Commanders, and Lord of Hosts—I do strictly command and charge all Captains and Officers...to have a care that the Almighty God bee duly and daily served, and that they call upon their people to hear Sermons, as that also they diligently frequent Morning and Evening prayer themselves by their own exemplar and daily life, and duties herein, encouraging others thereunto, and that such, who shall often and willfully absent themselves, be duly punished according to the martial law in that case provided.

2. That no man speak impiously or maliciously, against the holy and blessed Trinity, or any of the three persons, that is to say, against God the Father, God the Son, and God the holy Ghost, or against the known Articles of the Christian faith, upon pain of death....

5. No man shall speak any word, or do any act, which may tend to the derision, or despising of God's holy word upon pain of death: Nor shall any man unworthily demean himself unto any Preacher, or Minister of the same, but generally hold them in all reverent regard, and dutiful entreaty, otherwise he the offender shall openly be whipt three times, and ask public forgiveness in the assembly of the congregation three several Sabbath Days.

6. Every man and woman duly twice a day upon the first tolling of the Bell shall (upon the working days) repair unto the Church, to hear divine Service upon pain of losing his or her day's allowance[1] for the first omission; for the second to be whipt; and for the third to be condemned to the Galleys[2] for six Months. Likewise no man or woman shall dare to violate or break the Sabbath by any gaming, public or private abroad, or at home, but duly sanctify and observe the same, both himself and his family, by preparing themselves at home with private prayer, that they may be the better fitted for the public, according to the commandments of God, and the orders of our Church, as also every man and woman shall repair in the morning to the divine service, and Sermons preached upon the Sabbath day, and in the afternoon to divine service, and Catechizing, upon pain for the first fault to lose their provision, and allowance for the whole week following, for the second to lose the said allowance, and also to be whipt, and for the third to suffer death.

7. All Preachers or Ministers within this our Colony, or Colonies, shall in the Forts, where they are resident, after divine Service, duly preach every Sabbath day in the forenoon, and Catechize in the afternoon, and weekly say the divine service, twice every day, and preach every Wednesday; likewise every Minister where he is resident, within the same Fort, or Fortress, Townes or Towne, shall choose unto him, four of the most religious and better disposed as well to inform of the abuses and neglects of the people in their duties, and service to God, as also to the due reparation, and keeping of the Church handsome, and fitted with all reverent observances thereunto belonging: likewise every Minister shall keep a faithful and true Record, or Church Book of all Christenings, Marriages, and deaths of such our people, as

---

[1] In the early years, Jamestown was governed as a collective society in which individuals received their food and other provisions from a common store.

[2] That is, to be imprisoned.

shall happen within their Fort, or Fortresses, Townes or Towne at any time, upon the burthen of a neglectful conscience, and upon pain of losing their entertainment.[3]

Maryland Toleration Act (September 21, 1649)

Forasmuch as in a well governed and Christian Commonwealth, matters concerning Religion and the honor of God ought in the first place to be taken into serious consideration and endeavored to be settled, be it therefore ordered and enacted by the Right Honorable Cecilius Lord Baron of Baltemore absolute Lord and Proprietary of this Province with the advice and consent of this General Assembly:

That whatsoever person or persons within this Province and the Islands thereunto belonging shall from henceforth blaspheme God, that is Curse him, or deny our Savior Jesus Christ to be the son of God, or shall deny the holy Trinity the father son and holy Ghost, or the Godhead of any of the said Three persons of the Trinity or the Unity of the Godhead, or shall use or utter any reproachful Speeches, words or language concerning the said Holy Trinity, or any of the said three persons thereof, shall be punished with death and confiscation or forfeiture of all his or her lands and goods to the Lord Proprietary and his heirs.

And be it also enacted by the authority and with the advice and assent aforesaid, that whatsoever person or persons shall from henceforth use or utter any reproachful words or Speeches concerning the blessed Virgin Mary the Mother of our Savior or the holy Apostles or Evangelists or any of them shall in such case for the first offence forfeit to the said Lord Proprietary and his heirs Lords and Proprietaries of this Province the sum of five pound Sterling or the value thereof to be levied on the goods and chattels of every such person so offending, but in case such offender or offenders, shall not then have goods and chattels sufficient for the satisfying of such forfeiture, or that the same be not otherwise speedily satisfied that then such offender or offenders shall be publically whipped and be imprisoned during the pleasure of the Lord Proprietary or the Lieutenant or chief Governor of this Province for the time being.

... And be it also further enacted by the same authority advice and assent that whatsoever person or persons shall from henceforth upon any occasion of offence or otherwise in a reproachful manner or way declare all or denominate

---

[3] That is, their salary and living expenses.

any person or persons whatsoever inhabiting, residing, trafficking, trading or commercing within this Province or within any the ports, harbors, creeks or havens to the same belonging an heretic, schismatic, idolater, Puritan, Independent, Presbyterian, popish priest, Jesuit, Jesuited papist, Lutheran, Calvinist, Anabaptist, Brownest,[4] Antinomian,[5] Barrowist,[6] Roundhead,[7] Separatist,[8] or any other name or term in a reproachful manner relating to matter of Religion shall for every such Offence forfeit and loose the sum of ten shillings sterling or the value thereof… half paid unto the person and persons of whom such reproachful words are or shall be spoken or uttered, and the other half thereof to the Lord Proprietary and his heirs Lords and Proprietaries of this Province.

…And whereas the enforcing of the conscience in matters of Religion hath frequently fallen out to be of dangerous Consequence in those commonwealths where it hath been practiced, And for the more quiet and peaceable government of this Province, and the better to preserve mutual Love and amity amongst the inhabitants thereof, be it therefore also by the Lord Proprietary with the advice and consent of this Assembly ordained and enacted (except as in this present Act is before declared and set forth) that no person or persons whatsoever within this Province, or the Islands, ports, harbors, creeks, or havens thereunto belonging professing to believe in Jesus Christ, shall from henceforth be any ways troubled, molested or discountenanced for or in respect of his or her religion nor in the free exercise thereof within this Province or the islands thereunto belonging nor any way compelled to the belief or exercise of any other religion against his or her consent, so as they be not unfaithful to the Lord Proprietary, or molest or

---

[4] So named after Robert Browne (1550-1633), an English clergyman who separated from the Church of England to found a Protestant sect organized on congregational principles.

[5] A pejorative term applied to those whose theology puts such emphasis on justification by faith as to suggest that Christians are under no obligation to obey moral laws.

[6] So named after Henry Barrowe (c. 1550–1593), a follower of Browne who maintained his separatist position even after Browne recanted. Barrowe was executed for his Separatist beliefs.

[7] So named because of the simple, close-cropped hair style preferred by the Puritans, "Roundheads" were adherents of the Parliamentary party during and after the English Civil War (1641-51).

[8] Separatists advocated separating from the Church of England rather than attempting to reform it.

conspire against the civil government established or to be established in this Province under him or his heirs. And that all and every person and persons that shall presume contrary to this Act and the true intent and meaning thereof directly or indirectly either in person or estate willfully to wrong, disturb, trouble, or molest any person whatsoever within this Province professing to believe in Jesus Christ for or in respect of his or her religion or the free exercise thereof within this Province other than is provided for in this Act that such person or persons so offending, shall be compelled to pay treble damages to the party so wronged or molested, and for every such offence shall also forfeit 20s sterling in money or the value thereof, half thereof for the use of the Lord Proprietary, and his heirs Lords and Proprietaries of this Province, and the other half for the use of the party so wronged or molested as aforesaid....

Preface to the Lawes and Liberties Concerning the Inhabitants of the Massachusetts (1648)

TO OUR BELOVED BRETHREN AND NEIGHBORS

The Inhabitants of the Massachusetts, the Governor, Assistants and Deputies assembled in the General Court of that Jurisdiction with grace and peace in our Lord Jesus Christ. So soon as God had set up political government among his people Israel he gave them a body of laws of judgement both in civil and criminal causes. These were brief and fundamental principles, yet withal so full and comprehensive as out of them clear deductions were to be drawn to all particular cases in future times. For a Common-wealth without laws is like a ship without rigging and steerage. Nor is it sufficient to have principles or fundamentals, but these are to be drawn out into so many of their deductions as the time and condition of that people may have use of. And it is very unsafe & injurious to the body of the people to put them to learn their duty and liberty from general rules, nor is it enough to have laws except they be also just. Therefore among other privileges which the Lord bestowed upon his peculiar people, these he calls them specially to consider of, that God was nearer to them and their laws were more righteous than other nations. God was said to be amongst them or near to them because of his Ordnances established by himself, and their laws righteous because himself was their Law-giver: yet in the comparison are implied two things, first that other nations had something of God's presence amongst them. Secondly that there was also somewhat of equity in their laws, for it pleased the Father (upon the Covenant of Redemption with his Son) to restore so much of his image to lost man as whereby all nations are disposed to worship God, and to advance righteousness: Which appears in that of the Apostle[9] (Rom. 1:21). They knew God &c: and in the 2:14: They did by nature the things contained in the law of God. But the nations corrupting his ordinances (both of Religion, and Justice) God withdrew his presence from them proportionally whereby they were given up to abominable lusts (Rom. 2:21). Whereas if they had walked according to that light & law of nature might have been preserved from such moral evils and might have enjoyed a common blessing in all their natural and civil Ordinances: now, if it might have been so with the nations who were so much strangers to the Covenant of Grace, what advantage have they who have interest in this Covenant, and may enjoy the special presence of God in the purity and native simplicity of all his Ordinances by which he is so near to his own people. This hath been no small privilege, and advantage to us in New-England that our Churches, and civil state have been planted, and grown up (like two twins) together like that of Israel in the wilderness by which we were put in mind (and had opportunities put into our hands) not only to gather our Churches, and set up the Ordinances of Christ Jesus in them according to the Apostolic pattern[10] by such light as the Lord graciously afforded us: but also withall to frame our civil Polity, and laws according to the rules of his most holy word whereby each do help and strengthen other (the Churches the civil authority, and the civil authority the Churches) and so both prosper the better without such emulation, and contention for privileges or priority as have proved the misery (if not ruin) of both in some other places.

For this end about nine years we used the help of some of the Elders of our Churches to compose a model of the Judicial laws of Moses[11] with such other cases as might be referred to them, with intent to make sure of them in composing our laws, but not to have them published as the laws of this Jurisdiction: nor were they voted in Court. For that book entitled *The Liberties*

---

[9] The Apostle Paul, who wrote the letter to the Romans.

[10] The Puritans wanted to "purify" the practice of the Church of England of all remnants of Catholicism; the only ceremonies they found acceptable were those specifically mentioned in the New Testament descriptions of the early church.

[11] Minister John Cotton (1585-1652) was the principal author of this document, a version of which was later published in London and incorrectly assumed to have been adopted by the colony as a set of laws, when, as the preface makes clear, it was only intended to serve as a reference for the colony's magistrates as they undertook the codification of their own legal system.

&c:[12] published about seven years since (which contains also many laws and orders both for civil & criminal causes) is commonly [though without ground] reported to be our Fundamentals[13] that we own as established by authority of this Court, and that after three years' experience & general approbation: and accordingly we have inserted them into this volume under the several heads to which they belong yet not as fundamentals, for divers of them have since been repealed, or altered, and more may justly be (at least) amended hereafter as further experience shall discover defects or inconveniences for Nihil simul natum et perfectum.[14]

...If any of you meet with some law that seems not to tend to your particular benefit, you must consider that laws are made with respect to the whole people, and not to each particular person: and obedience to them must be yielded with respect to the common welfare, not to thy private advantage, and as thou yield obedience to the law for common good, but to thy disadvantage: so another must observe some other law for them good, though to his own damage; thus must we be content to bear one another's burden and so fulfill the Law of Christ.

That distinction which is put between the Laws of God and the laws of men, becomes a snare to many as it is misapplied in the ordering of their obedience to civil Authority; for when the Authority is of God and that in way of an Ordinance (Rom. 13:1) and when the administration of it is according to deductions, and rules gathered from the word of God, and the clear light of nature in civil nations, surely there is no human law that tends to common good (according to those principles) but the same is mediately a law of God, and that in way of an Ordinance which all are to submit unto and that for conscience' sake (Rom. 13:5).

---

[12] A reference to the Massachusetts *Body of Liberties* (1641) prepared by minister and layer Nathaniel Ward (1578-1652). This was essentially a list of legal rights and privileges belonging to the citizens of the colony, some of which had been enacted into positive law, and others of which were drawn from the English common law tradition.

[13] A reference to fundamental law, or laws that cannot be abrogated. The authors of the preface are therefore tacitly asserting their ability to amend or alter the rights enumerated in the *Body of Liberties.*

[14] "Nothing is invented and perfected at the same moment." The phrase comes from the English jurist Edward Coke: see *First Part of the Institutes of the Lawes of England* (London: Companie of Stationers, 1628), p. 230a.

[The following laws are listed under the heading "Ecclesiastical" in the original]

1. All the people of God within this Jurisdiction who are not in a Church way and be orthodox in judgement and not scandalous in life shall have full liberty to gather themselves into a Church estate, provided they do it in a Christian way with due observation of the rules of Christ revealed in his word. Provided also that the General Court doth not, nor will hereafter approve of any such companies of men as shall join in any pretended way of Church fellowship unless they shall acquaint the Magistrates and the Elders of the neighbor Churches where they intend to join, & have their approbation therein....

3. Every Church hath free liberty to exercise all the Ordinances of God according to the rules of the Scripture.

4. Every Church hath free liberty of election and ordination of all her Officers from time to time. Provided they be able, pious and orthodox.

5. Every Church hath also free liberty of admission, recommendation, dismission & expulsion or deposal of their Officers and members upon due cause, with free exercise of the discipline and censures of Christ according to the rules of his word....

8. The Elders of churches also have liberty to meet monthly, quarterly or otherwise in convenient numbers and places, for conference and consultations about Christian and church questions and occasions.

9. All Churches also have liberty to deal with any their members in a church way that are in the hands of justice, so it be not to retard and hinder the course thereof.

10. Every Church hath liberty to deal with any Magistrate, Deputy of court, or other officer whatsoever that is a member of theirs, in a church way in case of apparent and just offence, given in their places, so it be done with due observance and respect.

11. We also allow private meetings for edification in Religion amongst Christians of all sorts of people so it be without just offence, both for number, time, place and other circumstances....

13. Forasmuch as the open contempt of God's word and Messengers thereof is the desolating sin of civil States and Churches and that the preaching of the word by those whom God doth send, is the chief ordinary means ordained of God for the converting, edifying and saving the souls of the Elect through the presence and power of the Holy-Ghost, thereunto promised: and that the ministry of the word, is set up by God in his Churches, for those holy

ends: and according to the respect or contempt of the same and of those whom God hath set apart for his own work & employment, the weal or woe of all Christian States is much furthered and promoted; it is therefore ordered and decreed, That if any Christian (so called) within this jurisdiction shall contemptuously behave himself toward the Word preached or the Messengers thereof called to dispense the same in any Congregation; when he doth faithfully execute his service and office therein, according to the will and word of God, either by interrupting him in his preaching, or by charging him falsely with any error which he hath not taught in the open face of the Church: or like a son of Korah[15] cast upon his true doctrine or himself any reproach, to the dishonor of the Lord Jesus who hath sent him and to the disparagement of that his holy Ordinance, and making God's ways contemptible and ridiculous: that every such person or persons (whatsoever censure the Church may pass) shall for the first scandal be ... reproved openly by the Magistrate at some lecture ....

The frame of the government of the province of Pennsylvania in America (1682)
—William Penn

THE PREFACE

... This the Apostle[16] teaches in diverse of his epistles: "The law (says he) was added because of transgression." In another place, "Knowing that the law was not made for the righteous man, but for the disobedient and ungodly, for sinners, for unholy and profane, for murderers, for whoremongers, for them that defile themselves with mankind, and for man-stealers, for liars, for perjured persons,"[17] &c.; but this is not all, he opens and carries the matter of government a little further: "Let every soul be subject to the higher powers; for there is no power but of God. The powers that be are ordained of God: whosoever therefore resisteth the power, resisteth the ordinance of God. For

---

[15] The story of Korah is told in Numbers 16. Korah led a brief revolt against the authority of Moses and Aaron during the period when the Israelites, having escaped from Egypt, lived in the wilderness. Korah and his followers filled leading roles among the Israelites, making sacrifices in the tabernacle, but did not have authority to teach and lead the whole people, as Moses and Aaron did. After they asked for this authority, Moses publicly reproved them, and God punished them, miraculously opening a rift in the ground that swallowed them up.

[16] Paul.

[17] 1 Timothy 1:9-10.

rulers are not a terror to good works, but to evil: wilt thou then not be afraid of the power? Do that which is good, and thou shalt have praise of the same." "He is the minister of God to thee for good." "Wherefore ye must needs be subject, not only for wrath, but for conscience' sake."[18]

This settles the divine right of government beyond exception, and that for two ends: first, to terrify evil doers: secondly, to cherish those that do well; which gives government a life beyond corruption, and makes it as durable in the world, as good men shall be. So that government seems to me a part of religion itself, a thing sacred in its institution and end. For, if it does not directly remove the cause, it crushes the effects of evil, and is as such, (though a lower, yet) an emanation of the same Divine Power, that is both author and object of pure religion; the difference lying here, that the one is more free and mental, the other more corporal and compulsive in its operations: but that is only to evil doers; government itself being otherwise as capable of kindness, goodness and charity, as a more private society. They weakly err, that think there is no other use of government, than correction, which is the coarsest part of it: daily experience tells us, that the care and regulation of many other affairs, more soft, and daily necessary, make up much of the greatest part of government; and which must have followed the peopling of the world, had Adam never fell, and will continue among men, on earth, under the highest attainments they may arrive at, by the coming of the blessed *Second Adam,*[19] the Lord from heaven. Thus much of government in general, as to its rise and end.

...Wherefore governments rather depend upon men, than men upon governments. Let men be good, and the government cannot be bad; if it be ill, they will cure it. But, if men be bad, let the government be never so good, they will endeavor to warp and spoil it to their turn. I know some say, let us have good laws, and no matter for the men that execute them: but let them consider, that though good laws do well, good men do better: for good laws may want good men, and be abolished or evaded by ill men; but good men will never want good laws, nor suffer[20] ill ones. It is true, good laws have some awe upon ill ministers, but that is where they have not power to escape or abolish them, and the people are generally wise and good: but a loose and depraved people (which is the question) love laws and an administration like themselves. That,

---

[18] Romans 13:1-5.

[19] A reference to Christ, 1 Corinthians 15:45.

[20] The words "want" and "suffer" here carry the older meanings of "lack" and "allow," respectively.

therefore, which makes a good constitution, must keep it, viz: men of wisdom and virtue, qualities, that because they descend not with worldly inheritances, must be carefully propagated by a virtuous education of youth; for which after ages will owe more to the care and prudence of founders, and the successive magistracy, than to their parents, for their private patrimonies ....

Pennsylvania: An Act for Freedom of Conscience (1682)

Whereas the glory of almighty God and the good of mankind is the reason and end of government and, therefore, government in itself is a venerable ordinance of God. And forasmuch as it is principally desired and intended by the Proprietary and Governor and the freemen of the province of Pennsylvania and territories thereunto belonging to make and establish such laws as shall best preserve true Christian and civil liberty in opposition to all unchristian, licentious, and unjust practices, whereby God may have his due, Caesar his due,[21] and the people their due, from tyranny and oppression on the one side and insolence and licentiousness on the other, so that the best and firmest foundation may be laid for the present and future happiness of both the Governor and people of the province and territories aforesaid and their posterity.

Be it, therefore, enacted by William Penn, Proprietary and Governor, by and with the advice and consent of the deputies of the freemen of this province and counties aforesaid in assembly met and by the authority of the same, that these following chapters and paragraphs shall be the laws of Pennsylvania and the territories thereof.

Chap. i. Almighty God, being only Lord of conscience, father of lights and spirits, and the author as well as object of all divine knowledge, faith, and worship, who can only enlighten the mind and persuade and convince the understandings of people, in due reverence to his sovereignty over the souls of mankind:

Be it enacted, by the authority aforesaid, that no person now or at any time hereafter living in this province, who shall confess and acknowledge one almighty God to be the creator, upholder, and ruler of the world, and who professes him or herself obliged in conscience to live peaceably and quietly under the civil government, shall in any case be molested or prejudiced for his

---

[21] An allusion to a saying of Jesus quoted in all the synoptic gospels: Matthew 22:21, Mark 12:17, and Luke 20:25. In each version of the story, Jesus resolves a dilemma posed by the Roman requirement that the Jews pay taxes to Caesar.

or her conscientious persuasion or practice. Nor shall he or she at any time be compelled to frequent or maintain any religious worship, place, or ministry whatever contrary to his or her mind, but shall freely and fully enjoy his, or her, Christian liberty in that respect, without any interruption or reflection. And if any person shall abuse or deride any other for his or her different persuasion and practice in matters of religion, such person shall be looked upon as a disturber of the peace and be punished accordingly.

But to the end that looseness, irreligion, and atheism may not creep in under pretense of conscience in this province, be it further enacted, by the authority aforesaid, that, according to the example of the primitive Christians and for the ease of the creation, every first day of the week, called the Lord's day, people shall abstain from their usual and common toil and labor that, whether masters, parents, children, or servants, they may the better dispose themselves to read the scriptures of truth at home or frequent such meetings of religious worship abroad as may best suit their respective persuasions.

Chap. ii. And be it further enacted by, etc., that all officers and persons commissioned and employed in the service of the government in this province and all members and deputies elected to serve in the Assembly thereof and all that have a right to elect such deputies shall be such as profess and declare they believe in Jesus Christ to be the son of God, the savior of the world, and that are not convicted of ill-fame or unsober and dishonest conversation and that are of twenty-one years of age at least.

Chap. iii. And be it further enacted, etc., that whosoever shall swear in their common conversation by the name of God or Christ or Jesus, being legally convicted thereof, shall pay, for every such offense, five shillings or suffer five days imprisonment in the house of correction at hard labor to the behoove of the public and be fed with bread and water only during that time.

Chap. v. And be it further enacted, etc., for the better prevention of corrupt communication, that whosoever shall speak loosely and profanely of almighty God, Christ Jesus, the Holy Spirit, or the scriptures of truth, and is legally convicted thereof, shall pay, for every such offense, five shillings or suffer five days imprisonment in the house of correction at hard labor to the behoove of the public and be fed with bread and water only during that time.

Chap. vi. And be it further enacted, etc., that whosoever shall, in their conversation, at any time curse himself or any other and is legally convicted thereof shall pay for every such offense five shillings or suffer five days imprisonment as aforesaid.

Document 3

A Man of Reason/A Divine and Supernatural Light
Cotton Mather/Jonathan Edwards
1718/1734

Cotton Mather (1663-1728) and Jonathan Edwards (1703-1758) were prominent New England ministers whose shared religious background helps illuminate the tension between reason and inspiration or 'enthusiasm' that would eventually lead to the Great Awakening. In these two sermons preached less than twenty years apart, we see a subtle shift in emphasis on the subject of human reason and its role in religion, and, subsequently, on the relationship of the church to the broader society.

Mather is responding to what he sees as the "host of unreasonable things" threatening to undermine the good order of society; he thus begins by arguing that reason is the innate—and unique—capacity of mankind to recognize certain universal truths, whether in science or morality. From this initial proposition, he argues both that reason can provide man with certain basic religious insights, and that since to be unreasonable is to be unhuman, all men have a duty to act in accordance with reason, both in civil and religious matters. Although Mather is careful to assert that there are things that must be taken on faith as "above reason," he nevertheless seems fully confident that his listeners can reason their way toward faith, as the final paragraph makes clear.

Edwards, on the other hand, puts much less confidence in human reason. Although he recognizes and respects man's natural capacity for reason as both a divine gift and a means by which men can acquire knowledge of God's nature and God's purposes for mankind (note the subtitle, with its appeal to reason), he argues strenuously that this alone is insufficient. In much the same way that we cannot fully appreciate the sweetness of honey until we taste it, he asserts that men cannot truly experience faith until they receive the "divine light" of inspiration. Since this is an entirely internal and individual experience, it is unsurprising that Edwards only vaguely addresses the outward manifestations of faith.

A Man of Reason: A Brief ESSAY to Demonstrate That all MEN should hearken to REASON and What a World of EVIL would be prevented of the World, if Men would once come so REASONABLE

Boston, 1718
Cotton Mather

Hear now my REASONING.

— Job 13:6

...

They were wise men, and they were good men, whom the afflicted Job has to do withal; and they were men of reason too. But it was a very sensible part of his affliction that they dealt unreasonably with him. He does accordingly take pains to convince them of their unreasonableness. His discourse is introduced with this preface; "Hear now my Reasoning." The word signifies a reasonable demonstration; such a demonstration as ought to be brought by a man, that would hope[fully] convince another man; an irrefragable, an unanswerable argument. . . . I conclude, every man, will pay so much homage to reason, as to grant me my doctrine, with which I do now again come upon you;

That he that would approve himself a Reasonable Man, must hearken to Reason.

That we may prosecute this doctrine to some effect, we may first settle the matter, in two self-evident propositions.

1. There is a reasonable spirit in man, and the inspiration of the Almighty has given him an understanding; and there are certain principles of reason, which every man does naturally and ordinarily bring with him into the world.

There is in every man an admirable spirit. In that spirit, there is a faculty called reason. 'Tis that faculty which is called the Spirit of Man, which is the Candle of the Lord (Prov. 20:27). By the light of this precious and wondrous candle it is, that we discern the connection and relation of things to one another. There are certain ideas imprinted on the Spirit of Man, by the GOD, who Forms the Spirit of Man within him. It is an Irrational, as well as an unscriptural opinion, that we have no ideas in our minds, but what are introduced from abroad, by observation. There are a rich clutter of ideas which we are born withal, and which are only awakened, and brought into exercise by observation. The ideas which I mean, are those, which we call, the principles of reason. According to these principles, the reason of men, does pronounce on things that are plainly brought unto it. Reason proceeds according to these common and innate principles, in passing a judgment on what is plainly laid before it. Reason judges of what is mathematically true or false. But this is not all; it judges as often, and as clearly, what is morally good, or what is morally evil; what is right and what is wrong, in morality too. Indeed, there are very many, who do not actually discern, what is morally good or evil, right or wrong; but so there are many, who do not actually discern mathematical truth from falsehood.

...

There is a foolish and cursed opinion, which has taken root, in a debauched generation of men; who pretend indeed that they magnify reason...but they go really to extinguish reason, and chase it out of the world. The opinion is, that nothing is good or evil, right or wrong, antecedent unto the compact of humane society upon it: That all the difference between good and evil, right and wrong, lies in the agreement of humane society thereupon. These wicked Sons of the Leviathan do confute themselves. For they themselves must own, that antecedently unto all compact, it is good and right, that a compact should be kept; it is evil and wrong to break a compact, else they say nothing.... In brief; there is an eternal difference between good and evil; between right and wrong. 'Tis constituted by GOD: GOD has inwrought those principles in the reasonable spirit of man, which will necessitate him to acknowledge this difference, when it is evidently set before him.

II. There is all possible reason (excuse the pleonasm of the expression) why every man should hearken to reason, or do nothing against the principles of reason. There are many principles of reason; But, I take this to be the very first of them; that a man ought to act according to them....

...

First; The man who does not hearken to reason, does rebel against the glorious GOD, which has placed man under the guidance of reason.... We have to do with GOD, as often as we have right reason calling upon us.... And I will now say, we never transgress any law of reason, but we do at the same time, transgress the law of GOD.... The voice of reason, is the voice of GOD. GOD speaks, as often as reason and wisdom utters its voice. GOD who has furnished us with reason, has required us, to be obedient unto the dictates of reason. To man, He says, Let reason be thy Guide; never go against thy well-enlightened reason. We have received this order from GOD our maker: Show your selves men (Isaiah 46:8). That is to say, act reasonably; do like reasonable men....

Secondly. The man who does not hearken to reason, is very unthankful to GOD, for endowing, enriching, ennobling of him with reason.... Reason, 'tis a noble thing; It makes man a noble creature. It is the glory of man; it is the glorious Image of GOD upon him. Reason, 'tis that wherein we excel the beasts of the field. Thou, reason, dwellest with prudence; and thou findest out the knowledge of witty inventions; counsel is thine, and sound wisdom and strength. By thee, man is able to rule over other men, as well as over the beasts of the earth: Thou art the sword in the hand of all the judges of the Earth... . To do unreasonably is to do most unthankfully. When a Man will not hearken to reason, he despises the particular advantage of mankind....

Thirdly. The Man who does not hearken to Reason, does the part of a brute, yea, he does worse than a brute, that is destitute of Reason. We read of brutish men; and of those who are as brute beasts (Jude 10): Men, who are far as they can, quite the order of men, and rank themselves with brutes[1]....

Fourthly, There is a conscience in the case. The man that will not hearken to reason, goes against the light of his conscience. There is a conscience in man, which commends unto him, what is reasonable; which condemns him to suffer the vengeance of GOD, if he do that which is not reasonable. We read, Rom. 2:15: There is the work of the law written in their hearts, their conscience also bearing witness. What is conscience, but, reason submitting to the judgment of GOD? When a man will not hearken to reason, he is one of those, who (Job 24:13) rebel against the light. The conscience of man, forewarns him, and assures him, of a punishment reserved in another world....

The reason of my speaking these things is, that I may come out the better armed for the expedition which I am now to make, against a host of unreasonable things, which are every day doing among us.... There are certain maxims of reason, which I am now to set before you. But they shall be every one of them, glorious maxims of religion....

First. *Hear now my reasoning*: We are to distinguish between what is against reason and what is above reason. We must not call a thing unreasonable, merely because unto us, it is incomprehensible. We must not so hearken to reason, as to make an idol of reason: or to admit nothing at a revelation from GOD, but what we can fathom, with our little reason....read, "Canst thou by searching find out GOD? Canst thou find out the Almighty unto perfection?" (Job. 11:7). Even so; canst thou by searching find out the mysteries in the religion of GOD? Canst thou find out the great mysteries of godliness unto perfection? It must not be pretended unto!

---

[1]Mather is not quoting Jude 10 exactly in this reference, but rather giving an interpretive gloss on the text for the purposes of illustrating his own point.

...

This reason will do. It will demonstrate it unto us, that the Scriptures are the Word of GOD, & the Book of Truth. If you will hearken to reason, you must confess, that writings full of such holiness, and wisdom, and grandeur, and exquisite contrivance and Heavenly Intention, as compose our Bible, must needs be of divine original. But there are many things in the Scriptures which are, above reason. Our shallow reason must not be set up, as the measure of what is to be received, as a faithful saying, and worthy of all acceptation. Faith, faith is here to interpose. Reason, stand thou by, with an humble reverence, an awful silence. In the Scriptures, there is nothing against reason, tho' there be some things above reason.

It must also be remembered, that by our fall from GOD, the strength of reason is much impaired in us; the eye of reason is darkened, is depraved, is miserably wounded. We are prone to take some things, as according to reason, which are not so. If then there be any thing prescribed in the Sacred Scriptures, which our carnal reason, may be ready to cavil at, say not, I can't see reason for this…. But if there be Scripture for any thing, lay this down for a maxim, there is reason for it. Perhaps we can't see the reason: but reason says, the Scripture is a revelation from GOD: And reason says, what GOD has revealed must be reasonable. But then also, vain man, do not imagine, that thy light within, or the light of reason, is a sufficient guide without the Scripture, to bring thee unto salvation: much more, to make a Christ, and a God of that light, it is a dangerous idolatry. We must hearken to right reason: but beware, lest we ascribe too much, to our own broken faculties.

Secondly. Hear now my reasoning, there is a Golden Rule of reason, which well-applied, would wonderfully rectify the conversation of mankind: Even that rule, for a man to do unto others, as he would own it reasonable for others to do unto him…. Yea; but it is a rule engraved by the hand of GOD, upon the reason of mankind. There is no reasonable man, but what will fall down before this rule, and say, 'tis an excellent rule! Happy, happy would the world be, if this rule might bear rule in the world. You may as easily bring a man to own this rule, as to own that three and four make seven. And the man that will say, 'tis unjust for another man to do so and so unto me, but it is not unjust… to do the same unto him,… prove himself as great a sot, as he that shall say, three and four make seven, but four and three won't do so….

Thirdly, Hear now my reasoning. It stands to reason, that…. If a thing be decried as a folly, or a baseness, in a man of another party, 'tis but reason, that it should be decried in one of our own party too…. If sinners of an inferior quality must be punished for their misdemeanors, 'tis but reason, that the bigger sort of sinners also should not pass unpunished. There is no reason, for laws to be cobwebs, only to catch the little flies, and let the greater birds break through them.

Fourthly. Hear now my reasoning. It is but reason, that a man should not be condemned, without any hearing of what may be pleaded for him.... It is not the manner of the reasonable, to condemn a man as a criminal, without first hearing, or knowing, what may be said in his defense. If this one demand of reason might be hearkened unto, what would become of the defamations, with which we commonly keep wounding one another!

Fifthly. Hear now my reasoning: Methinks, 'tis no more than reason that men should curb their passion, and not let that usurp the place of reason. If men are of a boisterous, raging, raving (I will not say, temper, but rather) distemper, there is little of reason to be expected in their doings. The bridle of reason is cast off, and passion, headstrong passion, will precipitate them, into very unreasonable exorbitances and enormities....

Lastly. Behold, an engine, to batter all impiety! Hear now my reasoning. It is from a prodigious hardness of heart, if men will not be reasoned out of all impiety. Of all ungodly men, we read, Psalm 14:4: They have no knowledge; they act, as if they had no reason in them. We may strike all impiety, with the lightning of reason as well as with the thunder of Scripture.... There are certain principles of religion, which must be acknowledged by the reason of all men, as much as any principles of the Mathematics. A reasonable creature, you may compel him to acknowledge, that two and two make four; or, that a square is double to a triangle, of equal base and height. The proportions in Arithmetic and Geometry, he must needs acknowledge them. You may as easily compel him, to acknowledge, that there is a GOD, who must be adored and obeyed: you may compel him, to acknowledge, that he ought not to offer unto his neighbor, anything which if he himself were in the state of that neighbor, he would count an injury. Now, upon transgressions on these two points, there turns all the wickedness of the world.

I must then arraign all wickedness before the bar of reason.... My hearers; you are dying; you are dying; you will die speedily; you may die suddenly.... You make ready for death, by repenting of all sin, and renouncing all your sinful vanities; by embracing of the Great GOD, for your GOD, His CHRIST for your complete and only Redeemer; by resolving upon a life of serious PIETY. Till you are thus made ready, you are every day in a danger, wherein a reasonable man would not sleep a night, for a thousand worlds! Awake, O Reason, awake! And Oh! That men would reasonably consider, that they are a dying, and what they would choose and wish, when they come to die.... Hear now my reasoning. Something should be done about the matter, effectually done, and immediately done. I beseech you, delay not the doing of it....

A Divine and Supernatural Light, Immediately Imparted to the Soul by the Spirit of God, Shown to be Both Scriptural and Rational Doctrine

Boston, 1734
Jonathan Edwards

> And Jesus answered and said unto him, "Blessed art thou, Simon Barjona: for flesh and blood hath not revealed it unto thee, but my Father which is in heaven."

— Matthew 16:17

CHRIST says these words to Peter upon occasion of his professing his faith in him as the Son of God. Our Lord was inquiring of his disciples, who men said he was.... Simon Peter, whom we find always zealous and forward, was the first to answer: he readily replied to the question, *Thou art Christ, the Son of the living God.*

Upon this occasion, Christ says as he does *to* him, and *of* him in the text: in which we may observe,

1. That Peter is pronounced blessed on this account. *Blessed art thou*— "Thou art a happy man, that thou art not ignorant of this, that I am *Christ, the Son of the living God....* Happy art thou, that art so distinguished as to know the truth in this matter."

2. The evidence of this his happiness declared; *viz.,* that God, and he *only,* had *revealed it* to him. This is an evidence of his being *blessed....*

What had passed in the preceding discourse naturally occasioned Christ to observe this; because the disciples had been telling how others did not know him, but were generally mistaken about him, and divided and confounded in their opinions of him: but Peter had declared his assured faith, that he was the *Son of God.* Now it was natural to observe, how it was not *flesh and blood* that had *revealed it to him,* but God: for if this knowledge were dependent on natural causes or means, how came it to pass that they, a company of poor fishermen, illiterate men, and persons of low education, attained to the knowledge of the truth; while the Scribes and Pharisees, men of vastly higher advantages, and greater knowledge and sagacity in other matters, remained in ignorance? This could be owing only to the gracious distinguishing influence and revelation of the Spirit of God. Hence, what I would make the subject of my present discourse from these words, is this:

DOCTRINE

That there is such a thing as a spiritual and divine light immediately imparted to the soul by God, of a different nature from any that is obtained by natural means.

And on this subject I would

I. Show what this divine light is.

II. How it is given immediately by God, and not obtained by natural means.

III. Show the truth of the doctrine.

And then conclude with a brief improvement.[2]

I. I would show what this spiritual and divine light is. And in order to it, would show, *First,* In a few things what it is not. And here,

1. Those convictions that natural men may have of their sin and misery, is not this spiritual and divine light. Men in a natural condition may have convictions of the guilt that lies upon them, and of the anger of God, and their danger of divine vengeance.... Conscience is a principle natural to men; and the work that it doth naturally, or of itself, is to give an apprehension of right and wrong, and to suggest to the mind the relation that there is between right and wrong, and a retribution....

2. This spiritual and divine light does not consist in any impression made upon the imagination. It is no impression upon the mind, as though one saw any thing with the bodily eyes: it is no imagination or idea of an outward light or glory, or any beauty of form or countenance, or a visible luster or brightness of any object....

3. This spiritual light is not the suggesting of any new truths or propositions not contained in the word of God.... It reveals no new doctrine, it suggests no new proposition to the mind, it teaches no new thing of God, or Christ, or another world, not taught in the Bible, but only gives a due apprehension of those things that are taught in the word of God.

---

[2] An application of the doctrine of the sermon to the practical circumstances of life.

4.   'Tis not every affecting view that men have of the things of religion that is this spiritual and divine light. Men by mere principles of nature are capable of being affected with things that have a special relation to religion as well as other things .... .

But I proceed to show, *Secondly*, Positively what this spiritual and divine light is. And it may be thus described: a true sense of the divine excellency of the things revealed in the word of God, and a conviction of the truth and reality of them thence arising.... A spiritual and saving conviction of the truth and reality of these things, arises from such a sight of their divine excellency and glory; so that this conviction of their truth is an effect and natural consequence of this sight of their divine glory.

There is therefore in this spiritual light

1.   A true sense of the divine and superlative excellency of the things of religion; a real sense of the excellency of God and Jesus Christ, and of the work of redemption, and the ways and works of God revealed in the gospel.... He that is spiritually enlightened truly apprehends and sees it, or has a sense of it. He does not merely rationally believe that God is glorious, but he has a sense of the gloriousness of God in his heart. There is not only a rational belief that God is holy, and that holiness is a good thing, but there is a sense of the loveliness of God's holiness. There is not only a speculatively judging that God is gracious, but a sense how amiable God is upon that account, or a sense of the beauty of this divine attribute .... .

Thus there is a difference between having an *opinion*, that God is holy and gracious, and having a *sense* of the loveliness and beauty of that holiness and grace. There is a difference between having a rational judgment that honey is sweet, and having a sense of its sweetness. A man may have the former, that knows not how honey tastes; but a man cannot have the latter unless he has an idea of the taste of honey in his mind.... The former rests only in the head, speculation only is concerned in it; but the heart is concerned in the latter. When the heart is sensible of the beauty and amiableness of a thing, it necessarily feels pleasure in the apprehension. It is implied in a person's being heartily sensible of the loveliness of a thing, that the idea of it is sweet and pleasant to his soul; which is a far different thing from having a rational opinion that it is excellent.

2.   There arises from this sense of divine excellency of things contained in the word of God, a conviction of the truth and reality of them; and that either directly or indirectly.

First, Indirectly, and that two ways.

    a.   … The mind of man is naturally full of prejudices against the truth of divine things: it is full of enmity against the doctrines of the gospel; which is a disadvantage to those arguments that prove their truth, and causes them to lose their force upon the mind. But when a person has discovered to him the divine excellency of Christian doctrines, this destroys the enmity, removes those prejudices, and sanctifies the reason, and causes it to lie open to the force of arguments for their truth … .

    b.   It not only removes the hinderances of reason, but positively helps reason … . It engages the attention of the mind, with the fixedness and intenseness to that kind of objects; which causes it to have a clearer view of them, and enables it more clearly to see their mutual relations, and occasions it to take more notice of them.

Secondly, A true sense of the divine excellency of the things of God's word doth more directly and immediately convince of the truth of them; and that because the excellency of these things is so superlative. There is a beauty in them that is so divine and godlike, that is greatly and evidently distinguishing of them from things merely human, or that men are the inventors and authors of; a glory that is so high and great, that when clearly seen, commands assent to their divinity and reality … .

Such a conviction of the truth of religion as this, arising, these ways, from a sense of the divine excellency of them, is that true spiritual conviction that there is in saving faith. And this original of it, is that by which it is most essentially distinguished from that common assent, which unregenerate men are capable of.

II. I proceed now to the *second* thing proposed, *viz.*, to show how this light is immediately given by God, and not obtained by natural means. And here,

    1.   It is not intended that the natural faculties are not made use of in it. The natural faculties are the subject of this light: and they are the subject in such a manner, that they are not merely passive, but active in it; the acts and exercises of man's understanding are concerned and made use of in it. God, in letting in this light into the soul, deals with man according to his nature, or as a rational creature; and makes use of his human faculties. But yet this light is not the less immediately from God for that; though the faculties are made use of, it is as the subject and not as the cause; and that acting of the faculties in it, is not the cause, but is either implied in the thing itself (in the light that is

imparted) or is the consequence of it. As the use that we make of our eyes in beholding various objects, when the sun arises, is not the cause of the light that discovers those objects to us.

2. ...

3. When it is said that this light is given immediately by God, and not obtained by natural means, hereby is intended, that it is given by God without making use of any means that operate by their own power...but it is not as mediate causes to produce this effect. There are not truly any second causes of it; but it is produced by God immediately. The word of God is no proper cause of this effect: it does not operate by any natural force in it. The word of God is only made use of to convey to the mind the subject matter of this saving instruction: and this indeed it doth convey to us by natural force or influence. It conveys to our minds these and those doctrines; it is the cause of the notion of them in our heads, but not of the sense of the divine excellency of them in our hearts.

I come now, III. To show the truth of the doctrine; that is, to show that there is such a thing as that spiritual light that has been described, thus immediately let into the mind by God. And here I would show briefly, that this doctrine is both *scriptural* and *rational.*

First, It is scriptural.... We are there abundantly taught, that the saints differ from the ungodly in this, that they have the knowledge of God, and a sight of God, and of Jesus Christ.... This knowledge, or sight of God and Christ, cannot be a mere speculative knowledge; because it is spoken of as a seeing and knowing, wherein they differ from the ungodly.... And this light and knowledge is always spoken of as immediately given of God...the arbitrary operation, and gift of God, bestowing this knowledge on whom he will, and distinguishing those with it, that have the least natural advantage or means for knowledge, even babes, when it is denied to the wise and prudent.

Secondly, This doctrine is rational.

1. It is rational to suppose, that there is really such an excellency in divine things, that is so transcendent and exceedingly different from what is in other things, that, if it were seen, would most evidently distinguish them. We cannot rationally doubt but that things that are divine, that appertain to the Supreme Being, are vastly different from things that are human.... Unless we would argue, that God is not remarkably distinguished in glory from men....

2. If there be such a distinguishing excellency in divine things; it is rational to suppose that there may be such a thing as seeing it. What should hinder but that it may be seen? It is no argument, that there is no such thing as such a distinguishing excellency, or that, if there be, that it cannot be seen, that some do not see it, though they may be discerning men in temporal matters.... It is not rational to suppose, that those whose minds are full of spiritual pollution, and under the power of filthy lusts, should have any relish or sense of divine beauty or excellency; or that their minds should be susceptive of that light that is in its own nature so pure and heavenly....

3. It is rational to suppose, that this knowledge should be given immediately by God, and not be obtained by natural means.... It is rational to suppose that God would reserve that knowledge and wisdom, that is of such a divine and excellent nature, to be bestowed immediately by himself, and that it should not be left in the power of second causes. Spiritual wisdom and grace is that highest and most excellent gift that ever God bestows on any creature: in this the highest excellency and perfection of a rational creature consists. It is also immensely the most important of all divine gifts: it is that wherein man's happiness consists, and on which his everlasting welfare depends. How rational is it to suppose that God, however he has left meaner goods and lower gifts to second causes, and in some sort in their power, yet should reserve this most excellent, divine, and important of all divine communications, in his own hands, to be bestowed immediately by himself, as a thing too great for second causes to be concerned in!

...

I will conclude with a very brief improvement[3] of what has been said.

First, This doctrine may lead us to reflect on the goodness of God, that has so ordered it, that a saving evidence of the truth of the gospel is such, as is attainable by persons of mean capacities and advantages, as well as those that are of the greatest parts and learning.... Persons with but an ordinary degree of knowledge, are capable, without a long and subtle train of reasoning, to see the

---

[3] See footnote 2 above.

divine excellency of the things of religion: they are capable of being taught by the Spirit of God, as well as learned men....

Secondly, This doctrine may well put us upon examining ourselves, whether we have ever had this divine light...let into our souls. If there be such a thing indeed, and it be not only a notion or whimsy of persons of weak and distempered brains, then doubtless it is a thing of great importance, whether we have thus been taught by the Spirit of God....

Thirdly, All may hence be exhorted earnestly to seek this spiritual light. To influence and move to it, the following things may be considered.

1.   This is the most excellent and divine wisdom that any creature is capable of. It is more excellent than any human learning; it is far more excellent than all the knowledge of the greatest philosophers or statesmen....

2.   This knowledge is that which is above all others sweet and joyful. Men have a great deal of pleasure in human knowledge, in studies of natural things; but this is nothing to that joy which arises from this divine light shining into the soul.... There is nothing so powerful as this to support persons in affliction, and to give the mind peace and brightness in this stormy and dark world.

3.   This light is such as effectually influences the inclination, and changes the nature of the soul.... This light, and this only, will bring the soul to a saving close with Christ. It conforms the heart to the gospel, mortifies its enmity and opposition against the scheme of salvation therein revealed: it causes the heart to embrace the joyful tidings, and entirely to adhere to, and acquiesce in the revelation of Christ as our Savior: it causes the whole soul to accord and symphonize with it, admitting it with entire credit and respect, cleaving to it with full inclination and affection; and it effectually disposes the soul to give up itself entirely to Christ.

This light, and this only, has its fruit in a universal holiness of life. No merely notional or speculative understanding of the doctrines of religion will ever bring to this. But this light, as it reaches the bottom of the heart, and changes the nature, so it will effectually dispose to a universal obedience. It shows God's worthiness to be obeyed and served. It draws forth the heart in a sincere love to God, which is the only principle of a true, gracious, and universal obedience; and it convinces of the reality of those glorious rewards that God has promised to them that obey him.

Document 4

A Discourse Concerning Unlimited Submission and Non-resistance to the Higher Powers

Jonathan Mayhew

1750

Boston

This sermon by Jonathan Mayhew (1720-1766) was delivered on the hundredth anniversary of the execution of Charles I during the English Revolution, and in the context of what seemed to be renewed efforts by the Crown to assert religious uniformity in the colonies. In commemorating the history of the regicide, Mayhew reminded his audience of the long English dissenting tradition in which the Christians are held to have not only a right but a duty to resist governments whenever they fail to secure the public good. In doing so, Mayhew tacitly asserted the right of individual conscience to prevail over other social obligations—a position that even he recognized had the potential to lead to political chaos. Mayhew dismisses these concerns on the grounds that the truth of a principle does not depend upon its likelihood for abuse—a position that even if true, does little to address the practical consequences of disorderly or illegitimate political resistance. Nevertheless, in the context of the brewing turmoil between the crown and the colonies in the 1750s, Mayhew's sermon was an immediate publishing success both at home and in London. Indeed, reflecting on the origins of the American Revolution in his retirement, John Adams credited Mayhew's sermon with helping to shape public opinion on the need for—and the legitimacy of—political resistance.

Mayhew's sermon text, Romans 13:1-7, is printed below:

Let every soul be subject unto the higher powers. For there is no power but of God: the powers that be are ordained of God. 2 Whosoever therefore resisteth the power, resisteth the ordinance of God: and they that resist shall receive to themselves damnation. 3 For rulers are not a terror to good works, but to the evil. Wilt thou then not be afraid of the power? Do that which is good, and thou shalt have praise of the same: 4 for he is the minister of God to thee for good. But if thou do that which is evil, be afraid; for he beareth not the sword in vain: for he is the minister of God, a revenger to execute wrath upon him that doeth evil. 5 Wherefore ye must needs be subject, not only for wrath, but also for conscience sake. 6 For this cause pay ye tribute also: for they are God's ministers, attending continually upon this very thing. 7 Render therefore to all their dues: tribute to whom tribute is due; custom to whom custom; fear to whom fear; honor to whom honor.

…Let us now trace the apostle's reasoning in favor of submission to the higher powers, a little more particularly and exactly. For by this it will appear, on one hand, how good and conclusive it is, for submission to those rulers who exercise their power in a proper manner: And, on the other, how weak and trifling and unconnected it is, if it be supposed to be meant by the apostle to show the obligation and duty of obedience to tyrannical, oppressive rulers, in common with others of a different character.

The apostle enters upon his subject thus—"Let every soul be subject unto the higher powers; for there is no power but of God: the powers that be, are ordained of God." Here he urges the duty of obedience from this topic of argument, that civil rulers, as they are supposed to fulfill the pleasure of God, are the ordinance of God. But how is this an argument for obedience to such rulers as do not perform the pleasure of God, by doing good; but the pleasure of the devil, by doing evil ; and such as are not, therefore, God's ministers, but the devil's! "Whosoever, therefore, resisteth the power, resisteth the ordinance of God; and they that resist, shall receive to themselves damnation."

Here the apostle argues, that those who resist a reasonable and just authority, which is agreeable to the will of God, do really resist the will of God himself; and will, therefore, be punished by him. But how does this prove, that those who resist a lawless, unreasonable power, which is contrary to the will of God, do therein resist the will and ordinance of God? Is resisting those who resist God's will, the same thing with resisting God? Or shall those who do so, receive to themselves damnation! "For rulers are not a terror to good works, but to the evil. Wilt thou then not be afraid of the power? Do that which is good; and thou shalt have praise of the same. For he is the minister of God to thee for good." Here the apostle argues more explicitly than he had before done, for revering, and submitting to magistracy, from this consideration, that such as really perform the duty of magistrates, would be enemies only to the evil actions of men, and would befriend and encourage the good; and so be a common blessing to society.

But how is this an argument, that we must honor, and submit to such magistrates as are not enemies to the evil actions of men, but to the good; and such as are not a common blessing, but a common curse, to society! "But if thou do that which is evil, be afraid: For he is the minister of God, a revenger, to execute wrath upon him that doth evil." Here the apostle argues from the nature and end of magistracy, that such as did evil, (and such only) had reason to be afraid of the higher powers; it being part of their office to punish evil doers, no less than to defend and encourage such as do well. But if magistrates are unrighteous; if they are respecters of persons; if they are partial in their administration of justice; then those who do well, have as much reason to be afraid, as those that do evil: there can be no safety for the good, nor any peculiar ground of terror to the unruly and injurious. So that in this case, the main end of civil government will be frustrated. And what reason is there for submitting to that government, which does by no means answer the design of government? "Wherefore ye must needs lie subject not only for wrath, but also for conscience sake." Here the apostle argues the duty of a cheerful and conscientious submission to civil government, from the nature and end of magistracy as he had before laid it down, i.e. as the design of it was to punish evil doers, and to support and encourage such as do well; and as it must, if so exercised, be agreeable to the will of God. But how does what he here says, prove the duty of a cheerful and conscientious subjection to those who forfeit, the character of rulers? To those who encourage the bad, and discourage the good?

The argument here used no more proves it to be a sin to resist such rulers, than it does, to resist the devil that he may flee from us. For one is as truly the minister of God as the other. "For, for this cause pay you tribute also; for they are God's ministers, attending continually upon this very thing." Here the apostle argues the duty of paying taxes, from this consideration that those who perform the duty of rulers, are continually attending upon the public welfare. But how does this argument conclude for paying taxes to such princes as are continually endeavoring to ruin the public? And especially when such payment would facilitate and promote this wicked design! "Render therefore to all their dues; tribute, to whom tribute is due; custom, to whom custom; fear, to whom fear; honor, to whom honor." Here the apostle sums up what he had been saying concerning the duty of subjects to rulers. And his argument stands thus—"Since magistrates who execute their office well, are common benefactors to society, and may, in that respect, be properly styled the ministers and ordinance of God; and since they are constantly employed in the service of the public, it becomes you to pay them tribute and custom; and to reverence, honor, and submit to them in the execution of their respective offices." This is apparently good reasoning. But does this argument conclude for the duty of paying tribute, custom, reverence, honor and obedience to such persons as (although they bear the title of rulers) use all their power to hurt and injure the public? Such as are not God's ministers, but Satan's? Such as do not take care of, and attend upon the public interest, but their own, to the ruin of the public? that is, in short, to such as have no natural and just claim at all to tribute, custom, reverence, honor and obedience? It is to be hoped that those who have any regard to the apostle's character as an inspired writer, or even as a man of common understanding, will not present him as reasoning in such a loose incoherent manner; and drawing conclusions which have not the least relation to his premises. For what can be more absurd than an argument thus framed? "Rulers are, by their office, bound to consult the public welfare and the good of society: therefore you are bound to pay them tribute, to honor, and submit to them, even when they destroy the public welfare, and are a common pest to society, by acting in direct contradiction to the nature and end of their office."

Thus, upon a careful review of the apostle's reasoning in this passage, it appears that his arguments to enforce submission, are of such a nature, as to conclude only in favor of submission to such rulers as he himself describes; i.e. such as rule for the good of society, which is the only end of their institution. Common tyrants, and public oppressors, are not entitled to obedience from their subjects, by virtue of anything here laid down by the inspired apostle.

I now add farther, that the apostle's argument is so far from proving it to be the duty of people to obey, and submit to such rulers as act in contradiction to the public good, and so to the design of their office, that it proves the direct contrary. For, please to observe—that if the end of all civil government, be the good of society; if this be the thing that is aimed at in constituting civil rulers; and if the motive and argument for submission to government, be taken from the apparent usefulness of civil authority, it follows, that when no such good end can be answered by submission, there remains no argument or motive to enforce it; if instead of this good end's being brought about by submission, a contrary end is brought about, and the ruin and misery of society effected by it; here is a plain and positive reason against submission in all such cases, should they ever happen. And therefore, in such cases, a regard to the public welfare, ought to make us withhold from our rulers that obedience and subjection which it would, otherwise, be our duty to render to them.

If it be our duty, for example, to obey our king, merely for this reason, that he rules for the public welfare, (which is the only argument the apostle makes use of) it follows, by a parity of reason, that when he turns tyrant, and makes his subjects his prey to devour and to destroy, instead of his charge to defend and cherish, we are bound to throw off our allegiance to him, and to resist; and that according to the tenor of the apostle's argument in this passage. Not to discontinue our allegiance, in this case, would be to join with the sovereign in promoting the slavery and misery of that society, the welfare of which, we ourselves, as well as our sovereign, are indispensably obliged to secure and promote, as far as in us lies. It is true the apostle puts no case of such a tyrannical prince; but by his grounding his argument for submission wholly upon the good of civil society; it is plain he implicitly authorizes, and even requires us to make resistance, whenever this shall be necessary to the public safety and happiness. Let me make use of this easy and familiar similitude to illustrate the point in hand—Suppose God requires a family of children, to obey their father and not to resist him; and enforces his command with this argument; that the superintendence and care and authority of a just and kind parent, will contribute to the happiness of the whole family; so that they ought to obey him for their own sakes more than for his: Suppose this parent at length runs distracted, and attempts, in his mad fit, to cut all his children's throats: Now, in this case, is not the reason before assigned, why these children should obey their parent while he continued of a sound mind, namely, their common good, a reason equally conclusive for disobeying and resisting him, since he is become delirious, and attempts their ruin? It makes no alteration in argument, whether this parent, properly speaking, loses his reason, or does while he retains his understanding, that which is as fatal in its consequences, as any thing he could do, were he really deprived of it. This similitude needs no formal application.

But it ought to be remembered, that if the duty of universal obedience and non-resistance to our king or prince, can be argued from this passage, the same unlimited submission under a republican, or any other form of government; and even to all the subordinate powers in any particular state, can be proved by it as well: which is more than those who allege it for the mentioned purpose, would be willing should be inferred from it. So that this passage does not answer their purpose; but really overthrows and confutes it. This matter deserves to be more particularly considered.—The advocates for unlimited submission and passive obedience, do, if I mistake not, always speak with reference to kingly or monarchical government, as distinguished from all other forms; and, with reference to submitting to the will of the king, in distinction from all subordinate officers, acting beyond their commission, and the authority which they have received from the crown. It is not pretended that any person besides kings, have a divine right to do what they please, so that no one may resist them, without incurring the guilt of factiousness and rebellion. If any other supreme powers oppress the people, it is generally allowed, that the people may get redress, by resistance, if other methods prove ineffectual. And if any officers in a kingly government, go beyond the limits of that power which they have derived from the crown, (the supposed original source of all power and authority in the state) and attempt, illegally, to take away the properties and lives of their fellow subjects, they may be forcibly resisted, at least till application can be made to the crown. But as to the sovereign himself, he may not be resisted in any case; nor has any of his officers, while they confine themselves within the bounds which he prescribed to them. This is, I think, a true sketch of the principles of those who defend the doctrine of passive obedience and non-resistance.

Now there is nothing in scripture which supports this scheme of political principles. As to the passage under consideration, the apostle here speaks of civil rulers in general: of all persons in common, vested with authority for the good of society, without any particular reference to one form of government, more than to another; or to the supreme power in any particular state, more than to subordinate powers. The apostle does not concern himself with the different forms of government. This he supposes left entirely to human prudence and discretion. Now the consequence of this is, that unlimited and passive obedience is no more enjoined in this passage, under monarchical government; or to the supreme power in any state, than under all other species of government, which answer the end of government; or, to all the subordinate degrees of civil authority, from the highest to the lowest. Those, therefore, who would from this passage infer the guilt of resisting kings, in all cases whatever, though acting ever so contrary to the design of their office, must, if they will be consistent, go much farther, and infer from it the guilt of resistance under all other forms of government; and of resisting any petty officer in the state though acting beyond his commission, in the most arbitrary, illegal manner possible. The argument holds equally strong in both cases.

All civil rulers, as such, are the ordinance and ministers of God; and they are all, by the nature of their office, and in their respective spheres and stations, bound to consult the public welfare. With the same reason therefore, that any deny unlimited and passive obedience to be here enjoined under a republic or aristocracy, or any other established form of civil government; or to subordinate powers, acting in an illegal and oppressive manner; (with the same reason) others may deny, that such obedience is enjoined to a king or monarch, or any civil power whatever. For the apostle says nothing that is peculiar to kings; what he says, extends equally to all other persons whatever, and vested with any civil office. They are all, in exactly the same sense, the ordinance of God; and the ministers of God; and obedience is equally enjoined to be paid to them all. For, as the apostle expresses it, "there is NO POWER but of God: And we are required to render to ALL their DUES; and not MORE than their DUES." And what these dues are, and to whom they are to be rendered, the apostle sayeth not; but leaves to the reason and consciences of men to determine.

Thus it appears, that the common argument, grounded upon this passage, in favor of universal and passive obedience, really overthrows itself, by proving too much, if it proves any thing at all; namely, that no civil officer is, in any case whatever, to be resisted, though acting in express contradiction to the design of his office; which no man, in his senses, ever did, or can assert.

If we calmly consider the nature of the thing itself, nothing can well be imagined more directly contrary to common sense, than to suppose that millions of people should be subjected to the arbitrary, precarious pleasure of one single man; (who has naturally no superiority over them in point of authority) so that their estates, and every thing that is valuable in life, and even their lives also, shall be absolutely at his disposal, if he happens to be wanton and capricious enough to demand them. What unprejudiced man can think, that God made ALL to be thus subservient to the lawless pleasure and frenzy of ONE, so that it shall always be a sin to resist him! Nothing but the most plain and express revelation from heaven could make a sober, impartial man believe such a monstrous, unaccountable doctrine, and, indeed, the thing itself, appears so shocking, so out of all proportion, that it may be questioned, whether all the miracles that ever were wrought, could make it credible, that this doctrine really came from God.

At present, there is not the least syllable in scripture which gives any countenance to it. The hereditary, indefeasible, divine right of kings, and the doctrine of non-resistance, which is built upon the supposition of such a right, are altogether as fabulous and chimerical, as transubstantiation; or any of the most absurd reveries of ancient or modern visionaries. These notions are fetched neither from divine revelation, nor human reason; and if they are derived from neither of those sources, it is not much matter from whence they come, or whither they go. Only it is a pity that such doctrines should be propagated in society, to raise factions and rebellions, as we see they have, in fact, been both in the last, and in the present REIGN.

But then, if unlimited submission and passive obedience to the higher powers, in all possible cases, be not a duty, it will be asked, "how far are we obliged to submit? If we may innocently disobey and resist in some cases, why not in all? Where shall we stop? What is the measure of our duty? This doctrine tends to the total dissolution of civil government; and to introduce such scenes of wild anarchy and confusion, as are more fatal to society than the worst of tyranny."

After this manner, some men object; and, indeed, this is the most plausible thing that can be said in favor of such an absolute submission as they plead for. But the worst (or rather the best) of it, is, that there is very little strength or solidity in it. For similar difficulties may be raised with respect to almost every duty of natural and revealed religion.—To instance only in two, both of which are near akin, and indeed exactly parallel, to the case before us. It is unquestionably the duty of children to submit to their parents; and of servants, to their masters. But no one asserts, that it is their duty to obey, and submit to them, in all supposable cases; or universally, a sin to resist them. Now does this tend to subvert the just authority of parents and masters? Or to introduce confusion and anarchy into private families? No. How then does the same principle tend to unhinge the government of that larger family, the body politic? We know, in general, that children and servants are obliged to obey their parents and masters respectively. We know also, with equal certainty, that they are not obliged to submit to them in all things, without exception; but may, in some cases, reasonably, and therefore innocently, resist them. These principles are acknowledged upon all hands, whatever difficulty there may be in fixing the exact limits of submission.

Now there is at least as much difficulty in stating the measure of duty in these two cases, as in the case of rulers and subjects. So that this is really no objection, at least no reasonable one, against resistance to the higher powers: Or, if it is one, it will hold equally against resistance in the other cases mentioned.—It is indeed true, that turbulent, vicious-minded men, may take occasion from this principle, that their rulers may, in some cases, be lawfully resisted, to raise factions and disturbances in the state; and to make resistance where resistance is needless, and therefore, sinful. But is it not equally true, that children and servants of turbulent, vicious minds, may take occasion from this principle, that parents and masters may, in some cases be lawfully resisted, to resist when resistance is unnecessary, and therefore, criminal? Is the principle in either case false in itself, merely because it may be abused; and applied to legitimate disobedience and resistance in those instances, to which it ought not to be applied? According to this way of arguing, there will be no true principles in the world; for there are none but what may be wrested and perverted to serve bad purposes, either through the weakness or wickedness of men....

The next question which naturally arises, is, whether this resistance which was made to the king by the Parliament, was properly rebellion, or not? The answer to which is plain, that it was not; but a most righteous and glorious stand, made in defense of the natural and legal rights of the people, against the unnatural and illegal encroachments of arbitrary power. Nor was this a rash and too sudden opposition: The nation had been patient under the oppressions of the crown, even to long suffering;—for a course of many years; and there was no rational hope of redress in any other way.—Resistance was absolutely necessary, in order to preserve the nation from slavery, misery and ruin. And who so proper to make this resistance, as the Lords and Commons;—the whole representative body of the people;—guardians of the public welfare; and each of which, was, in point of legislation, vested with an equal, co-ordinate power, with that of the crown? Here were two branches of the legislature against one;—two of which, had law and equity, and the constitution on their side, against one which was impiously attempting to overturn law and equity, and the constitution; and to exercise a wanton licentious sovereignty over the properties, consciences and lives of all the people:—Such a sovereignty as some inconsiderately ascribe to the Supreme Governor of the world.—I say, inconsiderately; because God himself does not govern in an absolutely arbitrary and despotic manner. The power of this Almighty King (I speak it not without caution and reverence; the power of this Almighty King) is limited by law; not, indeed, by acts of parliament, but by the eternal law as of truth, wisdom and equity; and the everlasting tables of right reason; tables that cannot be repealed, or thrown down and broken like those of Moses....

Document 5

Excerpts from Founding Documents
1776-1798

The following excerpts express some of the contending views of religion and politics characteristic of the Founding. Jefferson, who thought a great deal about the relationship between politics and religion, even contended with himself. In Notes on the State of Virginia, *the only book that Jefferson published, when speaking of nature, Jefferson stressed its law abiding, unvarying character; yet when speaking of morality and politics (the issue of slavery), he called upon divine intervention, that is, for God to intervene in the ordinary, orderly workings of the world. The Declaration of Independence also contains both views of God's relationship to the world and politics, referring to the Creator, the Supreme Judge, as well as to Providence, but also to the laws of nature and of Nature's God. Again, in* Notes on the State of Virginia, *Jefferson wrote that the only firm basis for liberty was the belief that it was a gift of God. This is a view echoed in Washington's Farewell Address, the Northwest Ordinance and Benjamin Rush's[1] discussion of education in the new republic. The Declaration, on the other hand, derives liberty by a rational argument from the premise of human equality. It is possible to overstress this difference, of course, since if God created men equal and gave them a capacity to reason, then we might say that the Declaration also presents liberty as the gift of God. Differences among the Founders appear sharpest, perhaps, in what Jefferson and Rush had to say about education. While Rush thought the Bible and religion should be the basis of a republican education, Jefferson argued to exclude the Bible in favor of the study of history and secular authors. All agreed that religious liberty was essential to free government (see Washington's letter to the Touro Synagogue, Document 6), but Jefferson's views represented those who were most inclined to separate religion and politics.*

---

[1] Rush (1746–1813) signed the Declaration of Independence and was a political leader, social reformer and educator.

Declaration of Independence

IN CONGRESS, July 4, 1776.

The unanimous Declaration of the thirteen united States of America,

When in the Course of human events, it becomes necessary for one people to dissolve the political bands which have connected them with another, and to assume among the powers of the earth, the separate and equal station to which the Laws of Nature and of Nature's God entitle them, a decent respect to the opinions of mankind requires that they should declare the causes which impel them to the separation.

We hold these truths to be self-evident, that all men are created equal, that they are endowed by their Creator with certain unalienable Rights, that among these are Life, Liberty and the pursuit of Happiness.—That to secure these rights, Governments are instituted among Men, deriving their just powers from the consent of the governed,— That whenever any Form of Government becomes destructive of these ends, it is the Right of the People to alter or to abolish it, and to institute new Government, laying its foundation on such principles and organizing its powers in such form, as to them shall seem most likely to effect their Safety and Happiness. Prudence, indeed, will dictate that Governments long established should not be changed for light and transient causes; and accordingly all experience hath shewn, that mankind are more disposed to suffer, while evils are sufferable, than to right themselves by abolishing the forms to which they are accustomed. But when a long train of abuses and usurpations, pursuing invariably the same Object evinces a design to reduce them under absolute Despotism, it is their right, it is their duty, to throw off such Government, and to provide new Guards for their future security. —Such has been the patient sufferance of these Colonies; and such is now the necessity which constrains them to alter their former Systems of Government. The history of the present King of Great Britain is a history of repeated injuries and usurpations, all having in direct object the establishment of an absolute Tyranny over these States....

...We, therefore, the Representatives of the United States of America, in General Congress, Assembled, appealing to the Supreme Judge of the world for the rectitude of our intentions, do, in the Name, and by Authority of the good People of these Colonies, solemnly publish and declare, That these United Colonies are, and of Right ought to be Free and Independent States; that they are Absolved from all Allegiance to the British Crown, and that all political connection between them and the State of Great Britain, is and ought to be totally dissolved; and that as Free and Independent States, they have full Power to levy War, conclude Peace, contract Alliances, establish Commerce, and to do all other Acts and Things which Independent States may of right do. And for the support of this Declaration, with a firm reliance on the protection of divine Providence, we mutually pledge to each other our Lives, our Fortunes and our sacred Honor.

Notes on the State of Virginia (1787)

Thomas Jefferson

Query VI, A Notice of the Mines and other Subterranean Riches; Its Trees, Plants, Fruits, etc

...Near the eastern foot of the North mountain are immense bodies of schist, containing impressions of shells in a variety of forms. I have received petrified shells of very different kinds from the first sources of the Kentucky, which bear no resemblance to any I have ever seen on the tide-waters. It is said that shells are found in the Andes, in South-America, fifteen thousand feet above the level of the ocean. This is considered by many, both of the learned and unlearned, as a proof of an universal deluge. To the many considerations opposing this opinion, the following may be added. The atmosphere, and all its contents, whether of water, air, or other matters, gravitate to the earth; that is to say, they have weight. Experience tells us, that the weight of all these together never exceeds that of a column of mercury of 31 inches height, which is equal to one of rain-water of 35 feet high. If the whole contents of the atmosphere then were water, instead of what they are, it would cover the globe but 35 feet deep; but as these waters, as they fell, would run into the seas, the superficial measure of which is to that of the dry parts of the globe as two to one, the seas would be raised only 52 ½ feet above their present level, and of course would overflow the lands to that height only. In Virginia this would be a very small proportion even of the champaign country, the banks of our tide-waters being frequently, if not generally, of a greater height. Deluges beyond this extent then, as for instance, to the North mountain or to Kentucky, seem out of the laws of nature. But within it they may have taken place to a greater or less degree, in proportion to the combination of natural causes which may be supposed to have produced them. History renders probable some instances of a partial deluge in the country lying round the Mediterranean sea. It has been often supposed, and is not unlikely, that that sea was once a lake. While such, let us admit an extraordinary collection of the waters of the atmosphere from the other parts of the globe to have been discharged over that and the countries whose waters run into it. Or without supposing it a lake, admit such an extraordinary collection of the waters of the atmosphere, and an influx of waters from the Atlantic ocean, forced by long continued Western winds. That lake, or that sea, may thus have been so raised as to overflow the low lands adjacent to it, as those of Egypt and Armenia, which, according to a tradition of the Egyptians and Hebrews, were overflowed about 2300 years before the Christian era; those of Attica,[2] said to have been overflowed in the time of Ogyges,[3] about 500 years later; and those of Thessaly, in the time of Deucalion, still 300 years posterior. But such deluges as these will not account for the shells found in the higher lands. A second opinion has been entertained, which is, that, in times anterior to the records either of history or tradition, the bed of the ocean, the principal residence of the shelled tribe, has, by some great convulsion of nature, been heaved to the heights at which we now find shells and other remains of marine animals. The favorers of this opinion do well to suppose the great events on which it rests to have taken place beyond all the eras of history; for within these, certainly none such are to be found: and we may venture to say further, that no fact has taken place, either in our own days, or in the thousands of years recorded in history, which proves the existence of any natural agents, within or without the bowels of the earth, of force sufficient to heave, to the height of 15,000 feet, such masses as the Andes. The difference between the power necessary to produce such an effect, and that which shuffled together the different parts of Calabria in our days,[4] is so immense, that, from the existence of the latter we are not authorized to infer that of the former.

M. de Voltaire has suggested a third solution of this difficulty (Quest. encycl. Coquilles).[5] He cites an instance in Touraine, where, in the space of 80 years, a particular spot of earth had been twice metamorphosed into soft stone, which had become hard when employed in building. In this stone shells of various kinds were produced, discoverable at first only with the microscope,

---

[2] The region of Greece centered around Athens.

[3] Mythological king of ancient Greece whose name is associated with Greek accounts of the Great Flood.

[4] On February 5, 1783, an earthquake of an estimated magnitude of 7.5 or 8 devastated the southeastern portion of Italy called Calabria. This and aftershocks in the month following dramatically changed the topography of the region.

[5] The entry on "Shells" in Voltaire's *Questions on the Encyclopedia*.

but afterwards growing with the stone. From this fact, I suppose, he would have us infer, that, besides the usual process for generating shells by the elaboration of earth and water in animal vessels, nature may have provided an equivalent operation, by passing the same materials through the pores of calcareous earths and stones: as we see calcareous dropstones generating every day by the percolation of water through lime-stone, and new marble forming in the quarries from which the old has been taken out; and it might be asked, whether it is more difficult for nature to shoot the calcareous juice into the form of a shell, than other juices into the forms of crystals, plants, animals, according to the construction of the vessels through which they pass? There is a wonder somewhere. Is it greatest on this branch of the dilemma; on that which supposes the existence of a power, of which we have no evidence in any other case; or on the first, which requires us to believe the creation of a body of water, and its subsequent annihilation? The establishment of the instance, cited by M. de Voltaire, of the growth of shells unattached to animal bodies, would have been that of his theory. But he has not established it. He has not even left it on ground so respectable as to have rendered it an object of enquiry to the literati of his own country. Abandoning this fact, therefore, the three hypotheses are equally unsatisfactory; and we must be contented to acknowledge, that this great phenomenon is as yet unsolved. Ignorance is preferable to error; and he is less remote from the truth who believes nothing, than he who believes what is wrong.

Query XIV, The Administration of Justice and the Description of the Laws

... The general objects of this law ["to diffuse knowledge more generally through the mass of the people"] are to provide an education adapted to the years, to the capacity, and the condition of every one, and directed to their freedom and happiness. Specific details were not proper for the law. These must be the business of the visitors entrusted with its execution. The first stage of this education being the schools of the hundreds, wherein the great mass of the people will receive their instruction, the principal foundations of future order will be laid here. Instead therefore of putting the Bible and Testament into the hands of the children, at an age when their judgments are not sufficiently matured for religious enquiries, their memories may here be stored with the most useful facts from Grecian, Roman, European and American history. The first elements of morality too may be instilled into their minds; such as, when further developed as their judgments advance in strength, may teach them how to work out their own greatest happiness, by showing them that it does not depend on the condition of life in which chance has placed them, but is always the result of a good conscience, good health, occupation, and freedom in all just pursuits.

Query XVII, Religion

... The error seems not sufficiently eradicated, that the operations of the mind, as well as the acts of the body, are subject to the coercion of the laws. But our rulers can have authority over such natural rights only as we have submitted to them. The rights of conscience we never submitted, we could not submit. We are answerable for them to our God. The legitimate powers of government extend to such acts only as are injurious to others. But it does me no injury for my neighbor to say there are twenty gods, or no god. It neither picks my pocket nor breaks my leg. If it be said, his testimony in a court of justice cannot be relied on, reject it then, and be the stigma on him. Constraint may make him worse by making him a hypocrite, but it will never make him a truer man. It may fix him obstinately in his errors, but will not cure them. Reason and free enquiry are the only effectual agents against error. Give a loose to them, they will support the true religion, by bringing every false one to their tribunal, to the test of their investigation. They are the natural enemies of error, and of error only. Had not the Roman government permitted free enquiry, Christianity could never have been introduced. Had not free enquiry been indulged, at the era of the reformation, the corruptions of Christianity could not have been purged away. If it be restrained now, the present corruptions will be protected, and new ones encouraged.... Reason and experiment have been indulged, and error has fled before them. It is error alone which needs the support of government. Truth can stand by itself.

Subject opinion to coercion: whom will you make your inquisitors? Fallible men; men governed by bad passions, by private as well as public reasons. And why subject it to coercion? To produce uniformity. But is uniformity of opinion desirable? No more than of face and stature. Introduce the bed of Procrustes then, and as there is danger that the large men may beat the small, make us all of a size, by lopping the former and stretching the latter. Difference of opinion is advantageous in religion. The several sects perform the office of a Censor morum[6] over each other. Is uniformity attainable? Millions of innocent men, women, and children, since the introduction of

---

[6] Censor of morals

Christianity, have been burnt, tortured, fined, imprisoned; yet we have not advanced one inch towards uniformity.

What has been the effect of coercion? To make one half the world fools, and the other half hypocrites. To support roguery and error all over the earth. Let us reflect that it is inhabited by a thousand millions of people. That these profess probably a thousand different systems of religion. That ours is but one of that thousand. That if there be but one right, and ours that one, we should wish to see the 999 wandering sects gathered into the fold of truth. But against such a majority we cannot effect this by force. Reason and persuasion are the only practicable instruments. To make way for these, free enquiry must be indulged; and how can we wish others to indulge it while we refuse it ourselves.

But every state, says an inquisitor, has established some religion. No two, say I, have established the same. Is this a proof of the infallibility of establishments? Our sister states of Pennsylvania and New York, however, have long subsisted without any establishment at all. The experiment was new and doubtful when they made it. It has answered beyond conception. They flourish infinitely. Religion is well supported; of various kinds, indeed, but all good enough; all sufficient to preserve peace and order: or if a sect arises, whose tenets would subvert morals, good sense has fair play, and reasons and laughs it out of doors, without suffering the state to be troubled with it. They do not hang more malefactors than we do. They are not more disturbed with religious dissensions. On the contrary, their harmony is unparalleled, and can be ascribed to nothing but their unbounded tolerance, because there is no other circumstance in which they differ from every nation on earth. They have made the happy discovery, that the way to silence religious disputes, is to take no notice of them. Let us too give this experiment fair play, and get rid, while we may, of those tyrannical laws. It is true, we are as yet secured against them by the spirit of the times. I doubt whether the people of this country would suffer an execution for heresy, or a three years imprisonment for not comprehending the mysteries of the Trinity. But is the spirit of the people an infallible, a permanent reliance? Is it government? Is this the kind of protection we receive in return for the rights we give up? Besides, the spirit of the times may alter, will alter. Our rulers will become corrupt, our people careless. A single zealot may commence persecutor, and better men be his victims. It can never be too often repeated, that the time for fixing every essential right on a legal basis is while our rulers are honest, and ourselves united. From the conclusion of this war we shall be going down hill. It will not then be necessary to resort every moment to the people for support. They will be forgotten, therefore, and their rights disregarded. They will forget themselves, but in the sole faculty of making money, and will never think of uniting to effect a due respect for their rights. The shackles, therefore, which shall not be knocked off at the conclusion of this war, will remain on us long, will be made heavier and heavier, till our rights shall revive or expire in a convulsion.

Query XVIII, Manners

It is difficult to determine on the standard by which the manners of a nation may be tried, whether *catholic*, or *particular*. It is more difficult for a native to bring to that standard the manners of his own nation, familiarized to him by habit. There must doubtless be an unhappy influence on the manners of our people produced by the existence of slavery among us....

...And can the liberties of a nation be thought secure when we have removed their only firm basis, a conviction in the minds of the people that these liberties are of the gift of God? That they are not to be violated but with his wrath? Indeed I tremble for my country when I reflect that God is just: that his justice cannot sleep for ever: that considering numbers, nature and natural means only, a revolution of the wheel of fortune, an exchange of situation, is among possible events: that it may become probable by supernatural interference! The Almighty has no attribute which can take side with us in such a contest. But it is impossible to be temperate and to pursue this subject through the various considerations of policy, of morals, of history natural and civil. We must be contented to hope they will force their way into every one's mind. I think a change already perceptible, since the origin of the present revolution. The spirit of the master is abating, that of the slave rising from the dust, his condition mollifying, the way I hope preparing, under the auspices of heaven, for a total emancipation, and that this is disposed, in the order of events, to be with the consent of the masters, rather than by their extirpation.

Northwest Ordinance (1787)

...**Sec. 14.** It is hereby ordained and declared by the authority aforesaid, That the following articles shall be considered as articles of compact between the original States and the people and States in the said territory and forever remain unalterable, unless by common consent, to wit:

Art. 1. No person, demeaning himself in a peaceable and orderly manner, shall ever be molested on account of his mode of worship or religious sentiments, in the said territory....

Art. 3. Religion, morality, and knowledge, being necessary to good government and the happiness of mankind, schools and the means of education shall forever be encouraged. The utmost good faith shall always be observed towards the Indians; their lands and property shall never be taken from them without their consent; and, in their property, rights, and liberty, they shall never be invaded or disturbed, unless in just and lawful wars authorized by Congress; but laws founded in justice and humanity, shall from time to time be made for preventing wrongs being done to them, and for preserving peace and friendship with them....

The Farewell Address (1796)

George Washington

... The name of American, which belongs to you in your national capacity, must always exalt the just pride of patriotism more than any appellation derived from local discriminations. With slight shades of difference, you have the same religion, manners, habits, and political principles. You have in a common cause fought and triumphed together; the independence and liberty you possess are the work of joint counsels, and joint efforts of common dangers, sufferings, and successes....,

... Of all the dispositions and habits which lead to political prosperity, religion and morality are indispensable supports. In vain would that man claim the tribute of patriotism, who should labor to subvert these great pillars of human happiness, these firmest props of the duties of men and citizens. The mere politician, equally with the pious man, ought to respect and to cherish them. A volume could not trace all their connections with private and public felicity. Let it simply be asked: Where is the security for property, for reputation, for life, if the sense of religious obligation desert the oaths which are the instruments of investigation in courts of justice? And let us with caution indulge the supposition that morality can be maintained without religion. Whatever may be conceded to the influence of refined education on minds of peculiar structure, reason and experience both forbid us to expect that national morality can prevail in exclusion of religious principle.

It is substantially true that virtue or morality is a necessary spring of popular government. The rule, indeed, extends with more or less force to every species of free government. Who that is a sincere friend to it can look with indifference upon attempts to shake the foundation of the fabric?

Promote then, as an object of primary importance, institutions for the general diffusion of knowledge. In proportion as the structure of a government gives force to public opinion, it is essential that public opinion should be enlightened....

Of the Mode of Education Proper in a Republic (1798)

Benjamin Rush

I proceed in the next place, to enquire, what mode of education we shall adopt so as to secure to the state all the advantages that are to be derived from the proper instruction of youth; and here I beg leave to remark, that the only foundation for a useful education in a republic is to be laid in Religion. Without this there can be no virtue, and without virtue there can be no liberty, and liberty is the object and life of all republican governments.

Such is my veneration for every religion that reveals the attributes of the Deity, or a future state of rewards and punishments, that I had rather see the opinions of Confucius or Mohamed inculcated upon our youth, than see them grow up wholly devoid of a system of religious principles. But the religion I mean to recommend in this place, is that of the New Testament.

It is foreign to my purpose to hint at the arguments which establish the truth of the Christian revelation. My only business is to declare, that all its doctrines and precepts are calculated to promote the happiness of society, and the safety and well being of civil government. A Christian cannot fail of being a republican. The history of the creation of man, and of the relation of our species to each other by birth, which is recorded in the Old Testament, is the best refutation that can be given to the divine right of kings, and the strongest argument that can be used in favor of the original and natural equality of all mankind. A Christian, I say again, cannot fail of being a republican, for every precept of the Gospel inculcates those degrees of humility, self-denial, and brotherly kindness, which are directly opposed to the pride of monarchy and the pageantry of a court. A Christian cannot fail of being useful to the republic, for his religion teacheth him, that no man "liveth to himself." And lastly, a Christian cannot fail of being wholly inoffensive, for his religion teacheth him, in all things to do to others what he would wish, in like circumstances, they should do to him.

Document 6

Letter to the Hebrew Congregation of Newport, Rhode Island

George Washington

1790

In 1790, George Washington visited Rhode Island to acknowledge the state's recent ratification of the Constitution and to promote passage of the Bill of Rights, the first ten amendments to the Constitution. As was the custom, when Washington visited Newport, he was met by a delegation of citizens, who read messages of welcome. One of those who welcomed Washington was Moses Seixas, the warden of the Touro Synagogue in Newport. In his welcome, Seixas gave thanks to "the Ancient of Days, the great preserver of men" that the Jews, previously "deprived ... of the invaluable rights of free Citizens" on account of their religion, now lived under a government "which to bigotry gives no sanction, to persecution no assistance." In his letter to the Synagogue responding to Seixas' welcome, Washington used some of Seixas' own words to describe with moving eloquence the religious liberty found in the new republic. It was of the utmost importance that Washington used his extraordinary moral authority to support this new and untried liberty.

Gentlemen:

While I received with much satisfaction your address replete with expressions of esteem, I rejoice in the opportunity of assuring you that I shall always retain grateful remembrance of the cordial welcome I experienced on my visit to Newport from all classes of citizens.

The reflection on the days of difficulty and danger which are past is rendered the more sweet from a consciousness that they are succeeded by days of uncommon prosperity and security.

If we have wisdom to make the best use of the advantages with which we are now favored, we cannot fail, under the just administration of a good government, to become a great and happy people.

The citizens of the United States of America have a right to applaud themselves for having given to mankind examples of an enlarged and liberal policy—a policy worthy of imitation. All possess alike liberty of conscience and immunities of citizenship.

It is now no more that toleration is spoken of as if it were the indulgence of one class of people that another enjoyed the exercise of their inherent natural rights, for, happily, the Government of the United States, which gives to bigotry no sanction, to persecution no assistance, requires only that they who live under its protection should demean themselves as good citizens in giving it on all occasions their effectual support.

It would be inconsistent with the frankness of my character not to avow that I am pleased with your favorable opinion of my administration and fervent wishes for my felicity.

May the children of the stock of Abraham who dwell in this land continue to merit and enjoy the good will of the other inhabitants—while every one shall sit in safety under his own vine and fig tree and there shall be none to make him afraid.[1]

May the father of all mercies scatter light, and not darkness, upon our paths, and make us all in our several vocations useful here, and in His own due time and way everlastingly happy.

---

[1] Micah 4:4 ("But they shall sit every man under his vine and under his fig tree; and none shall make *them* afraid: for the mouth of the LORD of hosts hath spoken *it*.") was one of the more popular Biblical passages during the Revolution. The preceding verse (Micah 4:3) is now better known: "And he shall judge among many people, and rebuke strong nations afar off; and they shall beat their swords into plowshares, and their spears into pruning hooks: nation shall not lift up a sword against nation, neither shall they learn war any more."

Document 7

An Address... Celebrating the Declaration of Independence

John Quincy Adams
July 4, 1821
Washington, DC.

When John Quincy Adams was Secretary of State, he was invited to give a speech to celebrate the anniversary of the Declaration of Independence in 1821. The speech is most famous for the words "Wherever the standard of freedom and independence has been unfurled, there will [America's] heart, her benedictions and her prayers be. But she goes not abroad in search of monsters to destroy." Yet these words were preceded by a less famous but more important exposition of the causes and meaning of the Declaration of Independence. In this detailed exposition, excerpted below, Adams argues that the United States was the first legitimate government in the history of mankind, an achievement, as he says, that "must forever stand alone." In addition to expressing what is now called American exceptionalism, Adams' speech epitomizes the moral and political view of the Protestant establishment that dominated the United States until late into the nineteenth century. In this view, the Declaration was made possible by the Reformation. Adams argues that the Reformation restored reason to its rightful place in religion, making its restoration in politics only a matter of time. That time came with the Declaration. Among other things, this understanding of the connection between the Reformation and the Declaration helps explain the longstanding animus of the Protestant establishment to Catholics. Not accepting the work of the Reformation, how could Catholics be citizens of a country essentially shaped by its spirit?

Fellow Citizens,

Until within a few days before that which we have again assembled to commemorate, our fathers, the people of this Union, had constituted a portion of the British nation; a nation, renowned in arts and arms, who, from a small Island in the Atlantic ocean, had extended their dominion over considerable parts of every quarter of the globe. Governed themselves by a race of kings, whose title to sovereignty had originally been founded on *conquest*, spell-bound, for a succession of ages, under that portentous system of despotism and of superstition which, in the name of the meek and humble Jesus, had been spread over the Christian world, the history of this nation had, for a period of seven hundred years, from the days of the conquest till our own, exhibited a conflict almost continued, between the oppressions of power and the claims of right. In the theories of the crown and the mitre, *man* had no rights. Neither the body nor the soul of the individual was his own....

The religious reformation was an improvement in the science of mind; an improvement in the intercourse of man with his Creator, and in his acquaintance with himself. It was an advance in the knowledge of his *duties* and his *rights*. It was a step in the progress of man, in comparison with which the magnet and gunpowder, the wonders of either India, nay the printing press itself, were but as the paces of a pigmy to the stride of a giant....

The corruptions and usurpations of the church were the immediate objects of these reformers; but at the foundation of all their exertions there was a single plain and almost self-evident principle—that man has a right to the exercise of his own reason. It was this principle which the sophistry and rapacity of the church had obscured and obliterated, and which the intestine divisions of that same church itself first restored. The triumph of reason was the result of inquiry and discussion. Centuries of desolating wars have succeeded and oceans of human blood have flowed, for the final establishment of this principle; but it was from the darkness of the cloister that the first spark was emitted, and from the arches of a university that it first kindled into day. From the discussion of religious rights and duties, the transition to that of the political and civil relations of men with one another was natural and unavoidable; in both, the reformers were met by the weapons of temporal power. At the same glance of reason, the tiara would have fallen from the brow of priesthood, and the despotic scepter would have departed from the hand of royalty, but for the sword, by which they were protected; that sword which, like the flaming sword of the Cherubims, turned every way to debar access to the tree of life.[2]

The double contest against the oppressors of church and state was too appalling for the vigor, or too comprehensive for the faculties of the reformers of the European continent. In Britain alone was it undertaken, and in Britain but partially succeeded.

---

[2] Genesis 3:24

It was in the midst of that fermentation of the human intellect, which brought right and power in direct and deadly conflict with each other, that the rival crowns of the two portions of the British Island were united on the same head. It was then, that, released from the fetters of ecclesiastical domination, the minds of men began to investigate the foundations of civil government. But the mass of the nation surveyed the fabric of their Institutions as it existed in fact. It had been founded in *conquest*; it had been cemented in *servitude*; and so broken and molded had been the minds of this brave and intelligent people to their actual conditions, that instead of solving civil society into its first elements in search of their rights, they looked back only to conquest as the origin of their liberties, and claimed their rights but as donations from their kings. This faltering assertion of freedom is not chargeable indeed upon the whole nation. There were spirits capable of tracing civil government to its first foundation in the moral and physical nature of man: but conquest and servitude were so mingled up in every particle of the social existence of the nation, that they had become vitally necessary to them, as a portion of the fluid, itself destructive of life, is indispensably blended with the atmosphere in which we live.

Fellow citizens, it was in the heat of this war of moral elements, which brought one Stuart to the block and hurled another from his throne, that our forefathers sought refuge from its fury, in the then wilderness of this Western World. They were willing exiles from a country dearer to them than life. But they were the exiles of liberty and of conscience: dearer to them even than their country. They came too, with *charters* from their kings; for even in removing to another hemisphere, they "cast longing, lingering looks behind,"[3] and were anxiously desirous of retaining ties of connection with their country, which, in the solemn compact of a charter, they hoped by the corresponding links of allegiance and protection to preserve. But to their sense of *right*, the charter was only the ligament between them, their country, and their king. Transported to a new world, they had relations with one another, and relations with the aboriginal inhabitants of the country to which they came; for which no royal charter could provide. The first settlers of the Plymouth colony, at the eve of landing from their ship, therefore, bound themselves together by a written covenant; and immediately after landing, purchased from the Indian natives the right of settlement upon the soil.

Thus was a social compact formed upon the elementary principles of civil society, in which conquest and servitude had no part. The slough of brutal

---

[3] An allusion to Thomas Gray's "Elegy Written in a Country Church-Yard."

force was entirely cast off; all was voluntary; all was unbiased consent; all was the agreement of soul with soul.

Other colonies were successively founded, and other charters granted, until in the compass of a century and a half, thirteen distinct British provinces peopled the Atlantic shores of the North American continent with two millions of freemen; possessing by their charters the rights of British subjects, and nurtured by their position and education, in the more comprehensive and original doctrines of human rights. From their infancy they had been treated by the parent state with neglect, harshness and injustice. Their charters had often been disregarded and violated; their commerce restricted and shackled; their interest wantonly or spitefully sacrificed; so that the hand of the parent had been scarcely ever felt, but in the alternate application of whips and scorpions.

When in spite of all these persecutions, by the natural vigor of their constitution, they were just attaining the maturity of political manhood, a British parliament, in contempt of the clearest maxims of natural equity, in defiance of the fundamental principle upon which British freedom itself had been cemented with British blood; on the naked, unblushing allegation of absolute and uncontrollable power, undertook by their act to levy, without representation and without consent, *taxes* upon the people of America for the benefit of the people of Britain. This enormous project of public robbery was no sooner made known, than it excited, throughout the colonies, one general burst of indignant resistance. It was abandoned, reasserted and resumed, until fleets and armies were transported, to record in the characters of fire, famine, and desolation, the transatlantic wisdom of British legislation, and the tender mercies of British consanguinity....

For the independence of North America, there were ample and sufficient causes in the laws of moral and physical nature. The tie of colonial subjection is compatible with the essential purposes of civil government, only when the condition of the subordinate state is from its weakness incompetent to its own protection. Is the greatest moral purpose of civil government, the administration of justice? And if justice has been truly defined, the constant and perpetual will of securing to every one his *right*, how absurd and impracticable is that form of polity, in which the dispenser of justice is in one quarter of the globe, and he to whom justice is to be dispensed is in another.... Are the essential purposes of civil government, to administer to the wants, and to fortify the infirmities of solitary man? To unite the sinews of numberless arms, and combine the councils of multitudes of minds, for the promotion of the well-being of all? The first moral element then of this composition is sympathy between the members of which it consists; the second is sympathy between the giver and the receiver of the law. The sympathies of men begin with the relations of domestic life. They are rooted in the natural relations of domestic life. They are rooted in the natural relations of husband and wife, of parent and child, of brother and sister; thence they spread through the social and moral propinquities of neighbor and friend, to the broader and more complicated relations of countryman and fellow-citizens; terminating only with the circumference of the globe which we inhabit, in the co-extensive charities incident to the common nature of man. To each of these relations, different degrees of sympathy are allotted by the ordinances of nature. The sympathies of domestic life are not more sacred and obligatory, but closer and more powerful, than those of neighborhood and friendship. The tie which binds us to our country is not more holy in the sight of God, but it is more deeply seated in our nature, more tender and endearing, than that common link which merely connects us with our fellow-mortal, man. It is a common government that constitutes our *country*. But in that association, all the sympathies of domestic life and kindred blood, all the moral ligatures of friendship and of neighborhood, are combined with that instinctive and mysterious connection between man and physical nature, which binds the first perceptions of childhood in a chain of sympathy with the last gasp of expiring age, to the spot of our nativity, and the natural objects by which it is surrounded. These sympathies belong and are indispensable to the relations ordained by nature between the individual and his country. They dwell in the memory and are indelible in the hearts of the first settlers of a distant colony. These are the feelings under which the children of Israel "sat down by the rivers of Babylon, and wept when they remembered Zion." These are the sympathies under which they "hung their harps upon the willow," and instead of songs of mirth, exclaimed, "If I forget thee, O Jerusalem, let my right hand forget her cunning."[4] But these sympathies can never exist for a country, which we have never seen. They are transferred in the hearts of succeeding generations, from the country of human institution, to the country of their birth; from the land of which they have only heard, to the land where their eyes first opened to the day. The ties of neighborhood are broken up, those of friendship can never be formed, with an intervening ocean; and the natural ties of domestic life, the all-subduing sympathies of love, the indissoluble bonds of marriage, the heart-riveted kindliness of consanguinity, gradually wither and perish in the lapse of a few generations. All the elements, which form the basis of that sympathy between the individual and his country, are dissolved.

---

[4] Psalm 137.

Long before the Declaration of Independence, the great mass of the people of America and of the people of Britain had become total strangers to each other.... The sympathies therefore most essential to the communion of country were, between the British and American people, extinct. Those most indispensable to the just relation between sovereign and subject, had never existed and could not exist between the British government and the American people. The connection was unnatural; and it was in the moral order no less than in the positive decrees of Providence, that it should be dissolved.

Yet, fellow-citizens, these are not the causes of the separation assigned in the paper which I am about to read. The connection between different portions of the same people and between a people and their government, is a connection of *duties* as well as *rights*. In the long conflict of twelve years which had preceded and led to the Declaration of Independence, our fathers had been not less faithful to their *duties*, than tenacious of their *rights*. Their resistance had not been rebellion. It was not a restive and ungovernable spirit of ambition, bursting from the bonds of colonial subjection; it was the deep and wounded sense of successive wrongs, upon which complaint had been only answered by aggravation, and petition repelled with contumely, which had driven them to their last stand upon the adamantine rock of human rights.

It was *then* fifteen months after the blood of Lexington and Bunker's hill, after Charlestown and Falmouth, fired by British hands, were but heaps of ashes, after the ear of the adder had been turned to two successive supplications to the throne; after two successive appeals to the people of Britain, as *friends, countrymen,* and *brethren,* to which no responsive voice of sympathetic tenderness had been returned.... Then it was that the thirteen United Colonies of North America, by their delegates in Congress assembled, exercising the first act of sovereignty by a right ever inherent in the people, but never to be resorted to, save at the awful crisis when civil society is solved into its first elements, declared themselves free and independent states; and two days afterwards, in justification of that act, issued this [Declaration].

[*Adams here read the Declaration of Independence*]

... The interest, which in this paper has survived the occasion upon which it was issued; the interest which is of every age and every clime; the interest which quickens with the lapse of years, spreads as it grows old, and brightens as it recedes, is in the principles which it proclaims. It was the first solemn declaration by a nation of the only *legitimate* foundation of civil government. It was the corner stone of a new fabric, destined to cover the surface of the globe. It demolished at a stroke the lawfulness of all governments founded upon conquest. It swept away all the rubbish of accumulated centuries of servitude.

It announced in practical form to the world the transcendent truth of the unalienable sovereignty of the people. It proved that the social compact was no figment of the imagination; but a real, solid, and sacred bond of the social union. From the day of this declaration, the people of North America were no longer the fragment of a distant empire, imploring justice and mercy from an inexorable master in another hemisphere. They were no longer children appealing in vain to the sympathies of a heartless mother; no longer subjects leaning upon the shattered columns of royal promises, and invoking the faith of parchment to secure their rights. They were a *nation*, asserting as of right, and maintaining by war, its own existence. A nation was born in a day.

> How many ages hence
> Shall this their lofty scene be acted o'er
> In states unborn, and accents yet unknown?[5]

It will be acted o'er, fellow-citizens, but it can never be repeated. It stands, and must forever stand alone, a beacon on the summit of the mountain, to which all the inhabitants of the earth may turn their eyes for a genial and saving light, till time shall be lost in eternity, and this globe itself dissolve, nor leave a wreck behind.[6] It stands forever, a light of admonition to the rulers of men; a light of salvation and redemption to the oppressed. So long as this planet shall be inhabited by human beings, so long as man shall be of social nature, so long as government shall be necessary to the great moral purposes of society, and so long as it shall be abused to the purposes of oppression, so long shall this declaration hold out to the sovereign and to the subject the extent and the boundaries of their respective rights and duties; founded in the laws of nature and of nature's God. Five and forty years have passed away since this Declaration was issued by our fathers; and here are we, fellow-citizens, assembled in the full enjoyment of its fruits, to bless the Author of our being for the bounties of his providence, in casting our lot in this favored land; to remember with effusions of gratitude the sages who put forth, and the heroes who bled for the establishment of this Declaration; and, by the communion of soul in the re-perusal and hearing of this instrument, to renew the genuine

---

[5] Shakespeare, *Julius Caesar*, Act 3, Scene 1, l. 112–114.
[6] Shakespeare, The Tempest, Act 4, Scene 1, I. 170-173.

Holy Alliance[7] of its principles, to recognize them as eternal truths, and to pledge ourselves and bind our posterity to a faithful and undeviating adherence to them….

---

[7] Adams here contrasts the Holy Alliance of the American people based on the principles of the Declaration with the so-called Holy Alliance of Russia, Prussia and Austria formed in 1815 against the spread of republicanism.

Document 8

A Plea for the West
Lyman Beecher
1835

Lyman Beecher (1775-1863), father of Edward Beecher (Document 9) and Henry Ward Beecher (Document 13), moved from New England (where he had struggled to uphold the traditional Calvinism of the Congregational Church against the encroachments of Unitarianism) to Cincinnati, Ohio in 1832 to assume the presidency of Lane Theological Seminary. Shortly thereafter he published this short tract urging Americans to support protestant educational institutions (like Lane) in order to secure the "religious and political destiny" of the nation, which, he argued, hinged upon the Western spread of a protestant evangelicalism with deeply Calvinist roots. Although many of his contemporaries derided the tenets of the reformed tradition, American liberty, Beecher argued, was deeply rooted in the Calvinist theology of New England with its tradition of principled resistance to arbitrary power (see Mayhew, Document 4). The spread of religion, education, and liberty were interconnected, Beecher asserted—and all were equally threatened by the growing influence of Catholicism in the United States, with its historic associations with monarchical and even despotic regimes.

Even in the context of the antebellum nativism in which anti-Catholicism was a seminal feature, Beecher was sensitive to the potential that his arguments would be dismissed as merely intolerant. Yet religious toleration—or what Beecher calls "charity"—does not require turning a blind eye to potential threats, he argues, for the simple reason that truth can always withstand the strongest scrutiny. Beecher's anti-Catholic rhetoric raises several important questions about the possible limits on religious liberty and the proper course of action for a republican nation to take when faced with a potential incompatibility between the principles undergirding its political order and the teachings of a particular religion.

...It is certain that the glorious things spoken of the church and of the world, as affected by her prosperity, cannot come to pass under the existing civil organization of the nations. Such a state of society as is predicted to pervade the earth, cannot exist under an arbitrary despotism, and the predominance of feudal institutions and usages. Of course, it is predicted that revolutions and distress of nations will precede the introduction of the peaceful reign of Jesus Christ on the earth. The mountains shall be cast down, and the valleys shall be exalted and he shall "overturn, and overturn, and overturn, till he whose right it is, shall reign King of nations King of saints."[1]

It was the opinion of Edwards[2] that the millennium would commence in America. When I first encountered this opinion, I thought it chimerical; but all providential developments since, and all the existing signs of the times, lend corroboration to it. But if it is by the march of revolution and civil liberty, that the way of the Lord is to be prepared, where shall the central energy be found, and from what nation shall the renovating power go forth? What nation is blessed with such experimental knowledge of free institutions, with such facilities and resources of communication, obstructed by so few obstacles, as our own? There is not a nation upon earth which, in fifty years, can by all possible reformation place itself in circumstances so favorable as our own for the free, unembarrassed applications of physical effort and pecuniary and moral power to evangelize the world.

But if this nation is, in the providence of God, destined to lead the way in the moral and political emancipation of the world, it is time she understood her high calling, and were harnessed for the work. For mighty causes, like floods from distant mountains, are rushing with accumulating power, to their consummation of good or evil, and soon our character and destiny will be stereotyped forever.

It is equally plain that the religious and political destiny of our nation is to be decided in the West. There is the territory, and there soon will be the population, the wealth, and the political power. The Atlantic commerce and manufactures may confer always some peculiar advantages on the East. But the West is destined to be the great central power of the nation, and under heaven, must affect powerfully the cause of free institutions and the liberty of the world…. It is equally clear, that the conflict which is to decide the destiny of

---

[1] A popular quotation linking the prophecy in Ezekiel 21:27 to the second coming of Christ.

[2] Jonathan Edwards, New England minister (see document 3), has often been credited with this position, although the nature of Edwards' millennialism has been the subject of significant scholarly debate. See John F. Wilson, "History, Redemption, and the Millennium," in *Jonathan Edwards and the American Experience*, Nathan O. Hatch and Harry S. Stout, eds. (Oxford, 1988), 131-141.

the West, will be a conflict of institutions for the education of her sons, for purposes of superstition, or evangelical light; of despotism, or liberty.

... The thing required for the civil and religious prosperity of the West, is universal education, and moral culture, by institutions commensurate to that result—the all-pervading influence of schools, and colleges, and seminaries, and pastors, and churches. When the West is well supplied in this respect, though there may be great relative defects, there will be, as we believe, the stamina and the vitality of a perpetual civil and religious prosperity.

By whom shall the work of rearing the literary and religious institutions of the West be done?

Not by the West alone. The West is able to do this great work for herself, —and would do it, provided the exigencies of her condition allowed to her the requisite time. The subject of education is nowhere more appreciated; and no people in the same time ever performed so great a work as has already been performed in the West. Such an extent of forest never fell before the arm of man in forty years, and gave place, as by enchantment, to such an empire of cities, and towns, and villages, and agriculture, and merchandise, and manufactures, and roads, and rapid navigation, and schools, and colleges, and libraries, and literary enterprise, with such a number of pastors and churches, and such a relative amount of religious influence, as has been produced by the spontaneous effort of the religious denominations of the West. The later peopled states of New-England did by no means come as rapidly to the same state of relative, intellectual and moral culture as many portions of the West have already arrived at, in the short period of forty, thirty, and even twenty years.

But this work of self-supply is not completed, and by no human possibility could have been completed by the West, in her past condition. No people ever did, in the first generation, fell the forest, and construct the roads, and rear the dwellings and public edifices, and provide the competent supply of schools and literary institutions. New-England did not. Her colleges were endowed extensively by foreign munificence, and her churches of the first generation were supplied chiefly from the mother country; and yet the colonists of New-England were few in number, compact in territory, homogeneous in origin, language, manners, and doctrines; and were coerced to unity by common perils and necessities; and could be acted upon by immediate legislation; and could wait also for their institutions to grow with their growth and strengthen with their strength. But the population of the great West is not so, but is assembled from all the states of the Union, and from all the nations of Europe, and is rushing in like the waters of the flood, demanding for its moral preservation the immediate and universal action of those institutions which discipline the mind, and arm the conscience and the heart. And so various are the opinions and habits, and so recent and imperfect is the acquaintance, and so sparse are the settlements of the West, that no homogeneous public sentiment can be formed to legislate immediately into being the requisite institutions. And yet they are all needed immediately, in their utmost perfection and power. A nation is being "born in a day," and all the nurture of schools and literary institutions is needed, constantly and universally, to rear it up to a glorious and unperverted manhood.

It is no implication of the West, that in a single generation, she has not completed this work. In the circumstances of her condition she could not do it; and had it been done, we should believe that a miraculous, and not a human power had done it.

Who then, shall co-operate with our brethren of the West, for the consummation of this work so auspiciously begun? Shall the South be invoked? The South have difficulties of their own to encounter, and cannot do it; and the middle states have too much of the same work to do, to volunteer their aid abroad.

Whence, then, shall the aid come, but from those portions of the Union where the work of rearing these institutions has been most nearly accomplished, and their blessings most eminently enjoyed. And by whom, but by those who in their infancy were aided; and who, having freely received, are now called upon freely to give, and who, by a hard soil and habits of industry and economy, and by experience are qualified to endure hardness as good soldiers and pioneers in this great work? And be assured that those who go to the West with unostentatious benevolence, to identify themselves with the people and interests of that vast community, will be adopted with a warm heart and an unwavering right hand of fellowship.

...Experience has evinced, that schools and popular education, in their best estate, go not far beyond the suburbs of the city of God. All attempts to legislate prosperous colleges and schools into being without the intervening influence of religious education and moral principle, and habits of intellectual culture which spring up in alliance with evangelical institutions, have failed. Schools wane, invariably, in those towns where the evangelical ministry is neglected, and the Sabbath is profaned, and the tavern supplants the worship of God. Thrift and knowledge in such places go out, while vice and irreligion come in.

But the ministry is a central luminary in each sphere, and soon sends out schools and seminaries as its satellites by the hands of sons and daughters of its own training. A land supplied with able and faithful ministers, will of course be filled with schools, academies, libraries, colleges, and all the apparatus for the perpetuity of republican institutions. It always has been so—it always will be.

But the ministry for the West must be educated at the West. The demands on the East, for herself and for pagan lands, forbid the East ever to supply our wants. Nor is it necessary. For the Spirit of God is with the churches of the West, and pious and talented young men are there in great numbers, willing, desiring, impatient to consecrate themselves to the glorious work. If we possessed the accommodations and the funds, we might easily send out a hundred ministers a year, a thousand ministers in ten years, around each of whom schools would arise, and instructors multiply, and churches spring up, and revivals extend, and all the elements of civil and religious prosperity abound.

[*At this point in the pamphlet, Beecher shifts his focus to the changing demographics of the West. He refers repeatedly to the rising number of Catholic immigrants in the region as a threat to its American character, due to their "ignorant" and "corrupting" influence.*]...It [*Beecher's concern with Catholic influence*] is nothing but a controversy about religion, it is said—a thing which has nothing to do with the liberty and prosperity of nations, and the sooner it is banished from the world the better.

As well might it be insisted that the sun has no influence on the solar system, or the moon on the tides. In all ages, religion, of some kind, has been the former of man's character and the mainspring of his action. It has done more to fill up the eventful page of history, than all moral causes beside. It has been the great agitator or tranquilizer of nations, the orb of darkness or of light to the world, the fountain of purity or pollution, the mighty power of riveting or bursting the chains of men. Atheists may rage and blaspheme, but they cannot expel religion of some kind from the world. Their epidemic madness, like the volcano, may at times break out, and obscure the sun, and turn the moon into blood, and extend from nation to nation the cup of God's displeasure, covering the earth with the slain and the fragments of demolished institutions. But it can reconstruct nothing. It must be temporary, or it would empty the earth of its inhabitants. It will be temporary, because so bright are the evidences of a superior power, and so frail and full of sorrow are men, and so guilty and full of fears, that if Christianity does not guide them to the true God and Jesus Christ, superstition will send them to the altars of demons.

But it is a contest, it is said, about religion—and religion and politics have no sort of connection. Let the religionists fight their own battles; only keep the church and state apart, and there is no danger.

It [*what will happen in the west as the number of Catholics increases*] is a union of church and state, which we fear, and to prevent which we lift up our voice: a union which never existed without corrupting the church and enslaving the people, by making the ministry independent of them and dependent on the state, and to a great extent a sinecure aristocracy of indolence and secular ambition, auxiliary to the throne and inimical to liberty. No treason against our free institutions would be more fatal than a union of church and state; none, when perceived, would bring on itself a more overwhelming public indignation, and which all Protestant denominations would resist with more loathing and abhorrence.

... But in republics the temptation and the facilities of courting an alliance with church power may be as great as in governments of less fluctuation. Amid the competitions of party and the struggles of ambition, it is scarcely possible that the clergy of a large denomination should be able to give a direction to the suffrage of their whole people, and not become for the time being the most favored denomination, and in balanced elections the dominant sect, whose influence in times of discontent may perpetuate power against the unbiased verdict of public opinion. The free circulation of the blood is not more essential to bodily health, than the easy, unobstructed movement of public sentiment in a republic. All combinations to forestall and baffle its movements tend to the destruction of liberty. Its fluctuations are indeed an evil; but the power to arrest its fluctuations and chain it down is despotism; and when it is accomplished by the bribed alliance of ecclesiastical influence in the control of suffrage, it appears in its most hateful and alarming form. It is true, that the discovery might produce a reaction, and sweep away the ecclesiastical intermeddlers. But in political crises, calamities may be inflicted in a day, which ages cannot repair; and who can tell, when the time comes, whether the power will be too strong for the fetters, or the fetters for the power? For none but desperate men will employ such measures for the acquisition of power; and when desperate men have gained power they will not relinquish it without a struggle.

... "But why so much excitement about the Catholic religion? Is not one religion just as good as another?"

There are some who think that Calvinism is not quite as good a religion as some others. I have heard it denounced as a severe, unsocial, self-righteous, uncharitable, exclusive, prosecuting system—"dealing damnation round the land"—compassing sea and land to make proselytes, and forming conspiracies to overturn the liberties of the nation by an unhallowed union of church and state. There have been those, too, who have thought it neither meddlesome nor persecution to investigate the facts in the case, and scan the republican tendencies of the Calvinistic system. Though it has always been on the side of liberty in its struggles against arbitrary power; though, through the Puritans, it breathed into the British constitution its most invaluable principles, and laid the foundations of the republican institutions of our nation, and felled the forests, and fought the colonial battles with Canadian Indians and French Catholics, when often our destiny balanced on a pivot and hung upon a hair; and though it wept, and prayed, and fasted, and fought, and suffered through the revolutionary struggle, when there was almost no other creed but the Calvinistic in the land; still it is the opinion of many, that its well-doings of the past should not invest the system with implicit confidence, or supersede the scrutiny of its republican tendencies. They do not think themselves required to let Calvinists alone; and why should they? We do not ask to be let alone, nor cry persecution when our creed or conduct is analyzed. We are not annoyed by scrutiny; we seek no concealment. We court investigation of our past history, and of all the tendencies of the doctrines and doings of the friends of the Reformation; and why should the Catholic religion be exempted from scrutiny? Has it disclosed more vigorous republican tendencies? Has it done more to enlighten the intellect, to purify the morals, and sanctify the hearts of men, and fit them for self-government? Has it fought more frequently or successfully the battles of liberty against despotism? or done more to enlighten the intellect, purify the morals, and sanctify the heart of the world, and prepare it for universal liberty?

I protest against that unlimited abuse with which it is thought quite proper to round off declamatory periods against the religion of those who fought the battles of the reformation and the battles of the revolution, and that sensitiveness and liberality which would shield from animadversion and spread the mantle of charity over a religion which never prospered but in alliance with despotic governments, has always been and still is the inflexible enemy of liberty of conscience and free inquiry, and at this moment is the main stay of the battle against republican institutions.

A despotic government and despotic religion may not be able to endure free inquiry, but a republic and religious liberty CANNOT EXIST WITHOUT IT. Where force is withdrawn, and millions are associated for self-government, the complex mass of opinions and interests can be reduced to system and order only by the collision and resolution of intellectual and moral forces.

To lay the ban of a fastidious charity on religious free inquiry, would terminate in unthinking apathy and the intellectual stagnation of the dark ages.

...It is an anti-republican charity, then, which would shield the Catholics, or any other religious denomination, from the animadversion of impartial criticism. Denominations, as really as books, are public property, and demand and are benefited by criticism. And if ever the Catholic religion is liberalized and assimilated to our institutions, it must be done, not by a sickly sentimentalism screening it from animadversion, but by subjecting it to the tug of controversy, and turning upon it the searching inspection of the public eye, and compelling it, like all other religions among us, to pass the ordeal of an enlightened public sentiment.

...Catholic powers are determined to take advantage of our halting by thrusting in professional instructors and underbidding us in the cheapness of education—calculating that for a morsel of meat we shall sell our birth-right. Americans, republicans, Christians, can you, will you, for a moment, permit your free institutions, blood bought, to be placed in jeopardy, for want of the requisite intellectual and moral culture?

One thing more only demands attention, and that is the extension of such intellectual culture, and evangelical light to the Catholic population, as will supersede implicit confidence, and enable and incline them to read, and think, and act for themselves. They are not to be regarded as conspirators against our liberties; their system commits its designs and higher movements, like the control of an army, to a few governing minds, while the body of the people may be occupied in their execution, unconscious of their tendency. I am aware of the difficulty of access, but kindness and perseverance can accomplish anything, and wherever the urgency of the necessity shall put in requisition the benevolent energy of this Christian nation—the work under the auspices of heaven will be done.

It is a cheering fact, also, that the nation is waking up—a blind and indiscriminate charity is giving place to sober observation, and a Christian feeling and language towards Catholics is taking the place of that which was petulant, and exceptionable. There is rapidly extending a just estimate of danger. Multitudes who till recently regarded all notices of alarm as without foundation, are now beginning to view the subject correctly, both in respect to the reality of the danger, and the means which are necessary to avert it, and both the religious and the political papers are beginning to lay aside the language of asperity and to speak the words of truth and soberness. Under such auspices we commit the subject to the guardianship of heaven, and the intelligent instrumentality of our beloved country.

Document 9

The Nature, Importance, and Means of Eminent Holiness Throughout the Church
Edward Beecher
1835

Edward Beecher (1803–1895) was a prominent minister and writer. The son of Lyman Beecher (document 8), the brother of Henry Ward Beecher (document 13) and Harriet Beecher Stowe, Beecher was an abolitionist and social reformer. In this sermon, he expresses the view that the millennium must come about on earth before Christ returns. This is the "intervening event" he speaks of "between the first coming of the Savior to redeem, and his final advent to judge the world." This view, referred to as post-millennialism (Christ will come after the millennium) was commonly held in antebellum America. It was a powerful force behind the "evangelical empire," the collection of religious organizations that sought to reform and evangelize America at that time. Beecher mentions a number of the causes (temperance, missions, Sabbath observance) these organizations served. Beecher also argues that such reform movements are not enough. To bring about the millennium and hasten Christ's return, Christians must aim at holiness. Not only must they be born again, they must recognize sin as vile and loathsome, crucify it, and aim for communion with God, sharing His views, certainty and emotions. This demand for holiness explains the fervency of the reformers, including the abolitionists, and thus is important for understanding American politics in the antebellum period. We reproduce here the complete text of the first of six sermons that Beecher published on holiness.

Published in *The American National Preacher* 10, 1&2 (June-July 1835).

Matt. 16:3: *Can ye not discern the signs of the times?*

Rom. 14:17: *For the kingdom of God is not meat and drink; but righteousness and peace, and joy in the Holy Ghost.*

Luke 17:20-21: *The kingdom of God cometh not with observation. Neither shall they say, Lo here! or lo there! for, behold, the kingdom of God is within you.*

Isaiah 52:1-2: *Awake, awake; put on thy strength, O Zion; put on thy beautiful garments, O Jerusalem, the holy city; for henceforth there shall no more come unto thee the uncircumcised and the unclean. Shake thyself from the dust; arise, and sit down, O Jerusalem; loose thyself from the bands of thy neck, O captive daughter of Zion.*

In the progress of the cause of God on earth, there are certain great crises, or turning points of destiny, full of deep interest to him and to the intelligent universe. Such was the coming of Christ, an event around which were concentrated the interests of the whole human race, and of the moral government of God in all ages.

The advent of such eras is announced beforehand, and preceded by signs. The event stands predicted on the prophetic page, throwing its light into the dark regions of futurity; and God himself, as the long-expected day draws near, so orders his providence that signs may be seen on every side. He holds up a standard to his people, and calls on them to behold it from afar.

When he does this, it is their duty to notice such signs, to be fully aware of their import, and to act accordingly; and to do this is rightly to discern the signs of the times.

To none are these great truths more applicable than to Christians of every denomination of the present age. By the sure word of prophecy a great event has been announced as near at hand. It is the regeneration of the world. An event which, like a lofty mountain summit, rises to view on the chart of prophecy, as the great intervening event between the first coming of the Savior to redeem, and his final advent to judge the world.

The advent of this day is also preceded by its appropriate signs, which may be clearly seen by all of unblinded vision, but to mention which, time will not now permit. And to a great extent these signs are seen and understood, and the people of God seem to be making preparation for correspondent action.

Beneath the inspiring influence of the Almighty, the universal church is aroused, excited, and agitated by the persuasion that a glorious advent of the kingdom of God is near at hand. The conversion of the world to God is no longer regarded as merely the glorious but distant vision of inspired prophets. As a vivid reality, and near even at the door, it rises in all its majesty and soul-exciting power before the mind, awakening intense desire, and urging to incessant effort. Under this influence the church is daily approaching nearer to a full conception of all that is involved in a deliberate, all-absorbing effort to accomplish the mighty whole.

The field is the world, and the plans of the present age are as comprehensive as the field, and the church seems determined not to rest until the gospel shall be preached to every creature. Nor is this all. A result is to be expected, and should be aimed at, unlike any thing ever seen or conceived of on earth before. Not merely to fill the earth with the knowledge of the Lord, not merely to preach the gospel to every creature, but to re-organize human society in accordance with the law of God. To abolish all corruptions in religion, and all abuses in the social system, and, so far as it has been erected on false principles, to take it down and erect it anew. Hence incessant efforts are made to extend the influence of the Christian system into all departments of life; and all institutions, usages, and principles, civil or religious, are exposed to a rigid and fiery scrutiny. Abuses are assailed, and the whole community is in a state of constant agitation. Nor is this state of things destined to cease till the heavens and the earth have been shaken at the advent of God; till the last remnant of rebellion has passed away from the earth, and the human race shall repose in peace beneath the authority of Him whose right is to reign.

How great the privilege, and how great the responsibility of living in an age like this; and to one who deeply feels the responsibility, and the shortness of life, how natural the enquiry—How can I do most to secure the end in view? My time is short, the work in great. I desire to enter into it with all my heart and soul, and to be supremely engaged in some department of action. Which shall I select?

The inquiry is appropriate. A man cannot be supremely devoted to all departments of action. He must lay out his main energies in some one. He needs and must have a ruling passion, an all-absorbing purpose of the soul, of power to draw all else into its current, and render all else subservient to itself. And the natural course is to select some one of the great enterprises of the present age, and throw into that all the energies of the soul. Nor is it difficult to find an enterprise large enough to absorb the whole soul. Any one is vast enough to give exercise to more than all the energies of the highest mind, and to him who meditates much and deeply on it, to fill the whole horizon of his vision, and to seem more intimately connected than any other with the salvation of the world. Thus to one the cause of Sabbath-schools may easily become the most important of all; to another, foreign and domestic missions; to another, the discussion and defense of doctrinal truth, and the exposure of error; to another, the cause of temperance; and to another, the circulation of tracts, or of the word of God. These and similar enterprises are, without doubt, great and glorious beyond conception. But neither one of them is or can become the leading and most important enterprise of the present age. Neither one of them can deserve to become the all-absorbing object of the soul, nor can safely so become.

This prominence belongs to one enterprise and only one. An enterprise at present not at all recognized as a great enterprise of the age, or as an enterprise at all; and on which public apathy is deep and general. Yet, on reflection, it must be seen to be the only one which deserves the first rank, and the only one to which it is safe to give supreme and all-absorbing power in the soul, so as to compel us to view all other subjects only in their relations to it. The enterprise to which I refer is this:

The immediate production of an elevated standard of personal holiness throughout the universal church—such a standard of holiness as God requires, and the present exigencies of the world demand.

That such a standard of holiness *ought* to exist, cannot be denied; that it will exist *hereafter*, is expected. But its indispensible necessity *now, this very day* is not felt as it ought to be, nor the possibility of producing it; and adequate efforts to secure it are not made. These things ought not so to be. The attention of the whole church should be at once aroused to the subject and fixed intently on it, and the work of producing such a standard of holiness deliberately undertaken, as the first great enterprise of the present day. That it is such is the obvious import of our text. It teaches us that the kingdom of God is a spiritual kingdom, that its advent depends on no secular power, and implies no worldly victories, no external splendor, no earthly dominions, but simply that reign of God over man which is the result of holiness in the soul. From this it is manifest that the kingdom of God can make no real progress except by an increase of holiness, and can never be fully established on earth till holiness prevails in its highest power. Of course, to secure such a prevalence of holiness ought to be the great business of the present day. Still further to illustrate this truth, I propose,

I. To consider what is implied in a standard of holiness adapted to the exigencies of the present age.

II. Show that to produce such a standard of holiness should be regarded as the most important enterprise of the age.

III. Show how this enterprise should be undertaken and conducted.

In general, we remark that the standard of holiness required by the present age should be distinguished by two great peculiarities—that it should *include all parts of a holy character*, and that these should be *fully developed* so as to exert a *high degree of power*. In other words, the exigencies of the age require a *complete, fully developed, and well-balanced* holy character. Let us now proceed to look in detail at the elementary parts of this.

1. Communion with God deserves a prominent place, as the foundation of all high attainments in holiness.

By communion with God I understand an interchange or reciprocal exercise of views and feelings between God and the soul, when, according to his promise, he draws near, and manifests himself to those who love him.

This is both a reasonable and intelligible state of mind. Men are so made that they can exchange with each other both views and emotions, and this is essential to the highest degree of love and mutual confidence. And the same is no less true of the relations that exist between men and God. He is a holy being, and has infinite intellect and emotions, and if emotions exist in us of a corresponding kind, there is a rational basis laid for union with him, not only in views but in emotions. Hence it is said, "every one that loveth is born of God, and knoweth God, and he that dwelleth in love dwelleth in God and God in him."[1] And all Christians familiarly speak of this state of mind as involving *a sense of the presence of God.* It was this state of mind which David desired when he longed, and thirsted and fainted after God, and which he actually enjoyed when he said, "thy loving kindness is better than life," and spoke of his soul as "satisfied with marrow and fatness"[2] while in a state of joyful communion with God, and when he exclaimed, "whom have I in heaven but thee, and there is none on earth that I desire besides thee."[3]

This is the very foundation of all high attainments in holiness. The great and fundamental principle of Christianity is, that the mind of unrenewed man is entirely corrupt and degraded. Even the mind of a renewed man has no self-restoring power. Left to itself, it would again subside into passions and purposes corrupt and only corrupt. Nor is there any way to restore it to perfect purity, but to bring it under the renovating influence of the pure and holy mind of God. In him are found the only causes adequate to produce this result— infinite power of exhibiting the truth, and infinite holy emotion to destroy the deadness and apathy of the soul. Both these influences are needed, and either without the other is ineffectual. And both reside in God alone. Hence the whole progress of the work of moral renovation depends entirely on putting the mind wholly under the influence of the illuminating intellect and holy emotions of Jehovah. He is our life. In him holy emotions glow, pure, intense,

---

[1] 1 John 4:7, 16.

[2] Psalm 63:5.

[3] Psalm 73:25.

unmixed. And when his glories beam upon the soul, and the elevating and invigorating power of his holiness is felt, then sinful emotions subside and die, and the soul is filled with all the fullness of God. But let him retire, and sin revives again, and we die. On this point I speak to those who have experienced in their own hearts the influence of holy communion with God. I may fail to describe the state of mind with metaphysical exactness. But do you not know, by your own experience, that the thing itself is a reality? The Bible also speaks on the subject with the utmost fullness. What else is meant by "dwelling in God, and God dwelling in us?" or by the promise, "ye shall know that ye are in me, and I in you?"[4] or by the promise, "I will love him, and manifest myself unto him?"[5]

But if communion with God is a reality, to increase it throughout the church is the foundation of all efforts to elevate the standard of holiness. It is by the life of God alone that the church can be made fully alive. The first great object then should be to remove all that prevents communion with God, to elevate our views and enlarge our desires on this subject and to bring the church of every denomination fully under the power of his own infinitely pure and almighty mind. Then, and then alone, may we hope that the church will truly begin to live. Then, and then only, will she be strong in the Lord and in the power of his might. Intimately connected with this, and originating from it is—

2. Faith. By this I mean such firm belief and clear and habitual views of divine and eternal things, as shall correct all false estimates of the worth of earthly joys, or the evils of earthly sufferings, and give to motives, derived from things unseen and eternal their full power upon the mind, as vivid and present realities. Man is made to shrink from present suffering and pain, and to desire present enjoyment. But he is also made to regard the future; and to gain a greater future good, or to avoid a greater future evil, he can cheerfully, if satisfied that it is necessary, sacrifice present pleasures or encounter present pain. And as the magnitude of the motive, and the firmness of his persuasion increase, so does his readiness to make sacrifices or endure sufferings. Hence, if the motives are infinite and the persuasion complete, finite pleasure or pain loses all its power to affect the soul. And such are the motives presented by the word of God: they are great beyond expression, and beyond imagination. The joy set before us is a far more exceeding and eternal weight of glory, and the evil to be shunned is the fierceness of the wrath of the Almighty God. When

---

[4] Beecher seems to refer to John 15: 4-5, 7.
[5] John 14:21.

such considerations gain the ascendancy the world loses its power. Its joys and its sorrows are estimated not in theory merely, but in practice, as less than nothing, and vanity. And under the influence of such a faith, the feeblest mortal can encounter and overcome all the terrors of earth and hell. And why should it not be so? It is a conflict between infinite and finite for mastery over the mind; and if they contend on equal grounds, must not the infinite of necessity prevail? And it is faith which puts the infinite on equal grounds with the finite. It clothes motives of eternity with the vividness and reality of objects of sense, and thus exposes the mind to their full power. This has been in all ages the great source of Christian energy and self-denial. Under its influence, missionaries and martyrs, prophets and apostles, have cheerfully passed their lives in toils and sufferings, and died in triumph, by the sword or at the stake, in excruciating torments. And should the primitive energy of this principle once more be restored to the church, no obstacles could resist her power.

Let it not, however, be supposed that such faith can originate from the independent and unaided reflection of the human mind. It is the gift of God, and is the result of intimate and habitual communion with him. To his mind, the realities of eternity have an absolute certainty, and he fully appreciates and feels their worth. Hence, as we have communion with him, he transfers his own views, and his own certainty, and his own emotions, to our minds. Eternity rises before us in all its grandeur and glory. The joys of heaven and the woes of hell become real, and the mind surrenders itself to the full and overpowering impression of the scene.

Such are the habits of faith needed in the present age. Such as imply a power to enter into the emotions of God, and walk daily in the light of heaven, and to mold the character, views, and habits, in accordance with the feelings and public sentiment of that blessed world. The natural result of such a state of mind would be,

3. Supreme devotedness to God and his cause. And in this respect also, the standard of holiness in the present age needs to be greatly raised. By the preceding states of mind, the great objects of choice are brought before us, presented in their true light, and contrasted with all else. In this, is implied the decision of the soul to employ all its energies for God, and in his cause. A decision first made when the sinner ceases to rebel, and submits to his Savior. The worth of his cause is infinite, and the obligations of a redeemed soul beyond all utterance or conception; and when, in the light of eternity, and under the full influence of divine love, these things are fully seen, what can longer divide the choice of the soul, or prevent a full consecration of all its powers and faculties to God? Such is the appropriate and natural result of a

true view of things, and when it takes place, all our wishes and interests will be entirely identified with those of God, so that we shall have no plans, no purposes, no ends of our own. And such will be our love to him, that the promotion of his glory and the advancement of his cause will become "entirely essential to our happiness." This is an important point—it is the great point to be urged in the present age. That Christians should no longer cherish a mere general determination to serve God on the whole, resulting in feebleness of heart, low degrees of liberality, and irregular and inefficient action, but give themselves and all they have away wholly to the Lord, and so identify all their interests with those of God. Are you in such a state of mind that you can be happy while God is dishonored and his cause declining on earth? Can you sleep at ease and enjoy the pleasures of life, whilst your fellow-men are sinking to woe eternal? Does wealth increase, or honors multiply, or worldly prosperity attend you, and do such things fill you with joy and satisfy all the cravings of your soul? Is there in you no aching void which such things can never fill? Where then is your love of God, and entire devotedness to his cause? He is still dishonored, and his cause languishes on earth; but you can be happy! Where, I ask again, is your supreme love to God, and devotedness to his cause? No: we shall never love God as we ought, until his glory and the progress of his cause, are "entirely and absolutely essential to our happiness," so that we can enjoy nothing on earth whilst these are neglected—so that ease and influence, and riches and honor, shall lose all their power to charm, so long as the main desire of the soul remains unsatisfied. This is a practical test; all can see its force; and all ought to be made to feel its power. It ought to be made the standard—and the only standard—of the degree of our devotedness to God. It ought to meet every eye as if written in letters of fire on the heavens above, and resound in every ear as if spoken from on high by the voice of the Almighty. In short, the church must be constantly tried by this test till it feels its full power, and is in truth, entirely, supremely, and universally devoted to God.

4. Moral sensibility to the evils of sin, is another point in which the standard of holiness needs to be greatly elevated.

A high degree of moral repulsion from sin is always a striking characteristic of a holy mind. Among the holy in heaven, we shall find not only right purposes and holy emotions, but the highest loathing of sin. Indeed, this is an essential characteristic of a holy mind, and no mind that has it not, can be in a healthy moral state. Sin is truly odious, loathsome, and repulsive. No natural pollution can for a moment be compared to it in this respect. And if our minds were in a proper moral state, we should shrink from it in all its forms, with loathing and horror unutterable. It is in this respect that the evil consequences of the fall are peculiarly manifest. In this respect it is, that men are dead in trespasses and sins. They have not ceased to be free agents, but all holy sensibility to the evil of sin is gone. They see that they are guilty of sin, but do not feel its moral pollution, and they have no spiritual energy to loathe and to renounce it. This is produced by the Spirit of God. The energy of his holy mind removes the torpor and apathy of our own, and gives to us some of his own moral sensibility to the evil of sin, and energy to renounce it. And it is only as this state of mind increases, that we can make any progress in eradicating the corrupt passions and propensities of our nature. But of this work a vast amount must be done, before we can make any progress toward eminent holiness: for in the attainment of such holiness, is implied, not only the formation of right principles, feelings, and purposes, but also the extinction of wrong ones, previously existing. We are commanded not only to put on the new man, but to put off the old man: not only to walk after the Spirit, but to crucify the flesh with the affections and lusts thereof:[6] and in the latter work lies no small part of the duty of a Christian. It is not enough that the main purpose of the soul be changed, and that a Christian be on the whole, *for* God and not *against* him, and that he organize his life on this general hypothesis. All this may be done, and yet unfathomable depths of wickedness remain unexplored, and unutterable energies of sin remain within, unsubdued. A change of heart is but the first blow which the old man receives, and though in its ultimate results it is a mortal wound, he is yet far from dead. The work of entirely crucifying and eradicating all remains of sin is yet to be performed. And it is an arduous work. No one who has not fully and deeply engaged in it, can tell the efforts and conflicts it requires. All men are inclined with unutterable strength of feeling to the indulgence of self-complacency in some form. But to come to the point of utter self-renunciation, self-loathing, and self-abhorrence, is diametrically opposed to all the strongest feelings of the soul. To do it is to die a moral death; and the proud heart recoils with agony from the point. It desires leave, at least, to glory in its humility; but to renounce all merit, to be fully sensible of one's utter vileness, guilt, and degradation, to believe, to own, acknowledge, and deeply feel it, and to be habitually humble and broken hearted, is the most arduous and difficult attainment of a Christian. But arduous and difficult as it is, it may be carried to an extent far beyond our highest conceptions, if we constantly aim at the standard of entire perfection: and no one should aim at anything lower. No one should aim at anything less than an entire and radical crucifixion of the old man, in all his members and parts, and to put on entire,

---

[6] Ephesians 4: 22-24; Colossians 3:9-10.

and in full proportion, the Lord Jesus Christ, and to make no provision for the flesh to serve the lusts thereof.

But how can this be done without an exquisite moral sensibility to the evil of all sin? To see our sins, and acknowledge that they are sins, is one thing; but to have moral energy to loathe, abhor, and renounce them, is quite another. But all victory over sin depends entirely on this. The whole process is one of self-loathing and abhorrence of sin, and determined, agonizing efforts to subdue it. And why should it not be? How can a soul so polluted and degraded as that of man, so full of apathy and moral death, be restored to holiness and life, in any other way?

It ought, then, to be a leading object of the present age, to produce a more exquisite moral sensibility to the evils of all sin. No sin should be deemed trivial or venial. All should be abhorred. There should be the feelings of heaven on this subject. The evils of moral pollution should be felt, and mourned over as they would be in heaven, before the throne of God, where every robe is pure and spotless. And if the church will commune with God as she ought, she can gain this also. His feelings are pure and unmixed, and can impart a healthy energy to our own. He can teach us to loathe all our sins, even as he does, to crucify them with unsparing severity, and to long after perfect purity with the intensity of his own desires.

Document 10

The Temperance Address
Abraham Lincoln
1842

Religiously inspired moral reform was a powerful force in American life and politics in the antebellum years, as Edward Beecher's sermon on holiness makes clear (Document 9). On Washington's birthday in 1842, in a church in Springfield, Illinois, Abraham Lincoln addressed a meeting of a new temperance society, the Washingtonian Society, which six alcoholics had started two years before in Baltimore, Maryland. The Washingtonians distinguished themselves from other temperance groups by working to make individual drunkards temperate, rather than by trying to reform society as a whole. They also avoided religious rhetoric, emphasizing the practical benefits of sobriety. This is one reason Lincoln states in his speech that he will address the rational causes of the success of the Washingtonians. As Lincoln's speech progresses, it becomes clear that he is talking about the abolition movement, as well as the temperance movement, and indeed about all religiously inspired reform. Using Biblical imagery and allusions, Lincoln's speech offers a detailed, if largely implicit, critique of such reform movements. One question Lincoln raised is whether the theology of the saved and damned central to the reform movements was compatible with a politics based on the equality of all men. We can also understand Lincoln to be questioning whether the spirit of religiously inspired moral reform is compatible with the sympathy among fellow citizens that Adams argued was necessary for republican government (Document 7). Given Lincoln's argument, we must read the rhetorical flourish at the end of his speech as an ironically intemperate praise—and thus critique—of temperance.

Although the Temperance cause has been in progress for near twenty years, it is apparent to all, that it is, *just now*, being crowned with a degree of success, hitherto unparalleled.

The list of its friends is daily swelled by the additions of fifties, of hundreds, and of thousands. The cause itself seems suddenly transformed from a cold abstract theory, to a living, breathing, active, and powerful chieftain, going forth "conquering and to conquer."[1] The citadels of his great adversary are daily being stormed and dismantled; his temple and his altars, where the rites of his idolatrous worship have long been performed, and where human sacrifices have long been wont to be made, are daily desecrated and deserted. The trump of the conqueror's fame is sounding from hill to hill, from sea to sea, and from land to land, and calling millions to his standard at a blast.

For this new and splendid success, we heartily rejoice. That that success is so much greater *now* than *heretofore*, is doubtless owing to rational causes; and if we would have it continue, we shall do well to inquire what those causes are. The warfare heretofore waged against the demon of Intemperance, has, some how or other, been erroneous. Either the champions engaged, or the tactics they adopted, have not been the most proper. These champions for the most part, have been Preachers, Lawyers, and hired agents.—Between these and the mass of mankind, there is a want of *approachability*, if the term be admissible, partially at least, fatal to their success. They are supposed to have no sympathy of feeling or interest, with those very persons whom it is their object to convince and persuade.

And again, it is so easy and so common to ascribe motives to men of these classes, other than those they profess to act upon. The *preacher*, it is said, advocates temperance because he is a fanatic, and desires a union of the Church and State; the *lawyer*, from his pride and vanity of hearing himself speak; and the *hired agent*, for his salary. But when one, who has long been known as a victim of intemperance, bursts the fetters that have bound him, and appears before his neighbors "clothed, and in his right mind,"[2] a redeemed specimen of long lost humanity, and stands up with tears of joy trembling in his eyes, to tell of the miseries once endured, *now* to be endured no more forever; of his once naked and starving children, now clad and fed comfortably; of a wife long weighed down with woe, weeping, and a broken heart, now restored to health, happiness and renewed affection; and how easily it all is done, once it is resolved to be done; however simple his language, there is a logic, and an eloquence in it, that few, with human feelings, can resist. They cannot say that *he* desires a union of church and state, for he is not a church member; they can not say *he* is vain of hearing himself speak, for his whole demeanor shows, he would gladly avoid speaking at all; they cannot say *he* speaks for pay, for he receives none, and asks for none. Nor can his sincerity in

---

[1]Revelation 6:2.
[2]Mark 5:15.

any way be doubted; or his sympathy for those he would persuade to imitate his example, be denied.

In my judgment, it is to the battles of this new class of champions that our late success is greatly, perhaps chiefly, owing.—But, had the old school champions themselves, been of the most wise selecting, was their *system* of tactics, the most judicious? It seems to me, it was not. Too much denunciation against dram sellers and dram drinkers was indulged in. This, I think, was both impolitic and unjust. It was *impolitic*, because, it is not much in the nature of man to be driven to any thing; still less to be driven about that which is exclusively his own business; and least of all, where such driving is to be submitted to, at the expense of pecuniary interest, or burning appetite. When the dram-seller and drinker, were incessantly told, not in the accents of entreaty and persuasion, diffidently addressed by erring man to an erring brother, but in the thundering tones of anathema and denunciation, with which the lordly Judge often groups together all the crimes of the felon's life, and thrusts them in his face just ere he passes sentence of death upon him, that *they* were the authors of all the vice and misery and crime in the land; that *they* were the manufacturers and material of all the thieves and robbers and murderers that infested the earth; that *their* houses were the workshops of the devil; and that *their persons* should be shunned by all the good and virtuous, as moral pestilences—I say, when they were told all this, and in this way, it is not wonderful that they were slow, *very slow*, to acknowledge the truth of such denunciations, and to join the ranks of their denouncers, in a hue and cry against themselves.

To have expected them to do otherwise than they did—to have expected them not to meet denunciation with denunciation, crimination with crimination, and anathema with anathema, was to expect a reversal of human nature, which is God's decree, and never can be reversed. When the conduct of men is designed to be influenced, *persuasion*, kind, unassuming persuasion, should ever be adopted. It is an old and a true maxim, "that a drop of honey catches more flies than a gallon of gall."—So with men. If you would win a man to your cause, *first* convince him that you are his sincere friend. Therein is a drop of honey that catches his heart, which, say what he will, is the great high road to his reason, and which, when once gained, you will find but little trouble in convincing his judgment of the justice of your cause, if indeed that cause really be a just one. On the contrary, assume to dictate to his judgment, or to command his action, or to mark him as one to be shunned and despised, and he will retreat within himself, close all the avenues to his head and his heart; and though your cause be naked truth itself, transformed to the heaviest lance, harder than steel, and sharper than steel can be made, and tho' you throw it with more than Herculean force and precision, you shall no more be able to pierce him, than to penetrate the hard shell of a tortoise with a rye straw.

Such is man, and so *must* he be understood by those who would lead him, even to his own best interest.

On this point, the Washingtonians greatly excel the temperance advocates of former times. Those whom *they* desire to convince and persuade, are their old friends and companions. They know they are not demons, nor even the worst of men. *They* know that generally, they are kind, generous, and charitable, even beyond the example of their more staid and sober neighbors. *They* are practical philanthropists; and *they* glow with a generous and brotherly zeal, that mere theorizers are incapable of feeling. Benevolence and charity possess *their* hearts entirely; and out of the abundance of their hearts, their tongues give utterance. "Love through all their actions runs, and all their words are mild."[3] In this spirit they speak and act, and in the same, they are heard and regarded. And when such is the temper of the advocate, and such of the audience, no good cause can be unsuccessful.

But I have said that denunciations against dram-sellers and dram-drinkers are *unjust* as well as impolitic. Let us see.

I have not enquired at what period of time the use of intoxicating drinks commenced; nor is it important to know.[4] It is sufficient that to all of us who now inhabit the world, the practice of drinking them, is just as old as the world itself,—that is, we have seen the one, just as long as we have seen the other. When all such of us, as have now reached the years of maturity, first opened our eyes upon the stage of existence, we found intoxicating liquor, recognized

---

[3]Paraphrase of line in a poem by the prolific British hymn writer Isaac Watts (1674–1748), "Let dogs delight to bark and bite," instructing children to be like "the blessed Virgin's son." Watts's hymns were well known in the United States.

[4]By denying the importance of the origin of intoxicating drinks, Lincoln may have been drawing attention to this question ironically. If so, his Biblically literate listeners may have thought appropriately of Genesis 9:20–27. These verses recount both the first episode of drunkenness in the Bible and the first occurrence of slavery. Noah grew a vineyard, got drunk on wine and lay naked. Ham, one of Noah's sons, saw him uncovered, for which Noah cursed him by making Ham's son, Canaan, a slave to Ham's brothers. This episode was used in nineteenth century America as a Biblical justification for slavery. But one could read it as linking drunkenness and slavery together, showing how the one arises from man's intractable sinfulness and the second from unwillingness to admit this sin. In the second to last paragraph of this address, Lincoln mentions both slavery and intemperance.

by every body, used by every body, and repudiated by nobody. It commonly entered into the first draught of the infant, and the last draught of the dying man. From the sideboard of the parson, down to the ragged pocket of the houseless loafer, it was constantly found. Physicians prescribed it in this, that, and the other disease. Government provided it for soldiers and sailors; And to have a rolling or raising, a husking or hoe-down, any where about without it was *positively insufferable*.

So too, it was every where a respectable article of manufacture and of merchandize. The making of it was regarded as an honorable livelihood; and he who could make most, was the most enterprising and respectable. Large and small manufactories of it were every where erected, in which all the earthly goods of their owners were invested. Wagons drew it from town to town— boats bore it from clime to clime, and the winds wafted it from nation to nation; and merchants bought and sold it, by wholesale and retail, with precisely the same feelings, on the part of the seller, buyer, and by-stander, as are felt at the selling and buying of flour, beef, bacon, or any other of the real necessaries of life. Universal public opinion not only tolerated, but recognized and adopted its use.

It is true, that even *then*, it was known and acknowledged, that many were greatly injured by it; but none seemed to think the injury arose from the *use* of a *bad thing*, but from the *abuse* of a *very good thing*. The victims of it were pitied, and compassionated, just as now are the heirs of consumptions, and other hereditary diseases. Their failing was treated as a *misfortune*, and not as a *crime*, or even as a *disgrace*.

If, then, what I have been saying be true, is it wonderful, that *some* should think and act *now* as *all* thought and acted *twenty years ago*? And is it *just* to assail, *contemn*, or despise them, for doing so? The universal sense of mankind, on any subject, is an argument, or at least an *influence* not easily overcome. The success of the argument in favor of the existence of an over-ruling Providence, mainly depends upon that sense; and men ought not, in justice, to be denounced for yielding to it in any case, for giving it up slowly, *especially*, where they are backed by interest, fixed habits, or burning appetites.

Another error, as it seems to me, into which the old reformers fell, was, the position that all habitual drunkards were utterly incorrigible, and therefore, must be turned adrift, and damned without remedy, in order that the grace of temperance might abound to the temperate *then*, and to all mankind some hundred years *thereafter*. There is in this something so repugnant to humanity, so uncharitable, so cold-blooded and feelingless, that it never did, nor ever can enlist the enthusiasm of a popular cause. We could not love the man who taught it—we could not hear him with patience. The heart could not throw open its portals to it. The generous man could not adopt it. It could not mix with his blood. It looked so fiendishly selfish, so like throwing fathers and brothers overboard, to lighten the boat for our security—that the noble-minded shrank from the manifest meanness of the thing.

And besides this, the benefits of a reformation to be effected by such a system, were too remote in point of time, to warmly engage many in its behalf. Few can be induced to labor exclusively for posterity; and none will do it enthusiastically. Posterity has done nothing for us; and theorize on it as we may, practically we shall do very little for it, unless we are made to think, we are, at the same time, doing something for ourselves. What an ignorance of human nature does it exhibit, to ask or expect a whole community to rise up and labor for the *temporal* happiness of *others*, after *themselves* shall be consigned to the dust, a majority of which community take no pains whatever to secure their own eternal welfare, at a no greater distant day? Great distance, in either time or space, has wonderful power to lull and render quiescent the human mind. Pleasures to be enjoyed, or pains to be endured, *after* we shall be dead and gone, are but little regarded, even in our *own* cases, and much less in the cases of others.

Still, in addition to this, there is something so ludicrous in *promises* of good, or *threats* of evil, a great way off, as to render the whole subject with which they are connected, easily turned into ridicule. "Better lay down that spade you're stealing, Paddy,—if you don't you'll pay for it at the day of judgment." "By the powers, if ye'll credit me so long, I'll take another, jist."

By the Washingtonians, this system of consigning the habitual drunkard to hopeless ruin, is repudiated. *They* adopt a more enlarged philanthropy. *They* go for present as well as future good. *They* labor for all *now* living, as well as all *hereafter* to live. They teach hope to all—despair to none. As applying to *their* cause, *they* deny the doctrine of unpardonable sin. As in Christianity it is taught, so in this *they* teach, that

> "While the lamp holds out to burn,
>
> The vilest sinner may return."[5]

And, what is a matter of most profound gratulation, they, by experiment upon experiment, and example upon example, prove the maxim to be no less true in the one case than in the other. On every hand we behold those, who but

---

[5]Isaac Watts, Hymn 88, Hymns and Spiritual Songs, Book I.

yesterday, were the chief of sinners, now the chief apostles of the cause. Drunken devils are cast out by ones, by sevens, and by legions; and their unfortunate victims, like the poor possessed, who was redeemed from his long and lonely wanderings in the tombs,[6] are publishing to the ends of the earth, how great things have been done for them.

To these *new* champions, and this *new* system of tactics, our late success is mainly owing; and to *them* we must mainly look for the final consummation. The ball is now rolling gloriously on, and none are so able as *they* to increase its speed, and its bulk—to add to its momentum, and its magnitude. Even though unlearned in letters, for this task, none are so well educated. To fit them for this work, they have been taught in the true school. *They* have been in *that* gulf, from which they would teach others the means of escape. *They* have passed that prison wall, which others have long declared impassable; and who that has not shall dare to weigh opinions with *them*, as to the mode of passing.

But if it be true, as I have insisted, that those who have suffered by intemperance *personally*, and have reformed, are the most powerful and efficient instruments to push the reformation to ultimate success, it does not follow, that those who have not suffered, have no part left them to perform. Whether or not the world would be vastly benefitted by a total and final banishment from it of all intoxicating drinks, seems to me not *now* an open question. Three-fourths of mankind confess the affirmative with their *tongues*, and, I believe, all the rest acknowledge it in their *hearts*.

Ought *any*, then, to refuse their aid in doing what the good of the *whole* demands? Shall he, who cannot do *much*, be for that reason, excused if he do *nothing*? "But," says one, "what good can I do by signing the pledge? I never drink even without signing." This question has already been asked and answered more than millions of times. Let it be answered once more. For the man to suddenly, or in any other way, to break off from the use of drams, who has indulged in them for a long course of years, and until his appetite for them has become ten or a hundred fold stronger, and more craving, than any natural appetite can be, requires a most powerful moral effort. In such an undertaking, he needs every moral support and influence, that can possibly be brought to his aid, and thrown around him. And not only so; but every moral prop, should be taken from whatever argument might rise in his mind to lure him to his backsliding. When he casts his eyes around him, he should be able to see, all that he respects, all that he admires, and all that [he?] loves, kindly and

---

[6]Mark 5:3

anxiously pointing him onward; and none beckoning him back, to his former miserable "wallowing in the mire."[7]

But it is said by some, that men will *think* and *act* for themselves; that none will disuse spirits or anything else, merely because his neighbors do; and that *moral influence* is not that powerful engine contended for. Let us examine this. Let me ask the man who could maintain this position most stiffly, what compensation he will accept to go to church some Sunday and sit during the sermon with his wife's bonnet upon his head? Not a trifle, I'll venture. And why not? There would be nothing irreligious in it: nothing immoral, nothing uncomfortable. Then why not? Is it not because there would be something egregiously unfashionable in it? Then it is the influence of *fashion*; and what is the influence of fashion, but the influence that *other* people's actions have on our own actions, the strong inclination each of us feels to do as we see all our neighbors do? Nor is the influence of fashion confined to any particular thing or class of things. It is just as strong on one subject as another. Let us make it as unfashionable to withhold our names from the temperance cause as for husbands to wear their wives' bonnets to church, and instances will be just as rare in the one case as the other.

"But," say some, "we are no drunkards; and we shall not acknowledge ourselves such by joining a reformed drunkard's society, whatever our influence might be." Surely no Christian will adhere to this objection. If they believe, as they profess, that Omnipotence condescended to take on himself the form of sinful man, and, as such, to die an ignominious death for their sakes, surely they will not refuse submission to the infinitely lesser condescension, for the temporal, and perhaps eternal salvation, of a large, erring, and unfortunate class of their own fellow creatures. Nor is the condescension very great.

In my judgment, such of us as have never fallen victims, have been spared more from the absence of appetite, than from any mental or moral superiority over those who have. Indeed, I believe, if we take habitual drunkards as a class, their heads and their hearts will bear an advantageous comparison with those of any other class. There seems ever to have been a proneness in the brilliant, and warm-blooded to fall into this vice. The demon of intemperance ever seems to have delighted in sucking the blood of genius and of generosity. What one of us but can call to mind some dear relative, more promising in youth than all his fellows, who has fallen a sacrifice to his rapacity? He ever seems to have gone forth, like the Egyptian angel of death, commissioned to slay if not

---

[7] 2 Peter 2:2.

the first, the fairest born of every family. Shall he now be arrested in his desolating career? In that arrest, all can give aid that will; and who shall be excused that *can*, and will not? Far around as human breath has ever blown, he keeps our fathers, our brothers, our sons, and our friends, prostrate in the chains of moral death. To all the living every where we cry, "come sound the moral resurrection trump, that these may rise and stand up, an exceeding great army"—"Come from the four winds, O breath! and breathe upon these slain, that they may live."[8]

If the relative grandeur of revolutions shall be estimated by the great amount of human misery they alleviate, and the small amount they inflict, then indeed, will this be the grandest the world shall ever have seen. Of our political revolution of '76 we all are justly proud. It has given us a degree of political freedom, far exceeding that of any other nation of the earth. In it the world has found a solution of the long mooted problem, as to the capability of man to govern himself. In it was the germ which has vegetated, and still is to grow and expand into the universal liberty of mankind.

But with all these glorious results, past, present, and to come, it had its evils too. It breathed forth famine, swam in blood and rode in fire; and long, long after, the orphan's cry, and the widow's wail, continued to break the sad silence that ensued. These were the price, the inevitable price, paid for the blessings it bought.

Turn now, to the temperance revolution. In *it*, we shall find a stronger bondage broken; a viler slavery, manumitted; a greater tyrant deposed. In *it*, more of want supplied, more disease healed, more sorrow assuaged. By *it* no orphans starving, no widows weeping. By it, none wounded in feeling, none injured in interest. Even the dram-maker and dram seller, will have glided into other occupations so gradually, as never to have felt the change; and will stand ready to join all others in the universal song of gladness.

And what a noble ally this, to the cause of political freedom. With such an aid, its march cannot fail to be on and on, till every son of earth shall drink in rich fruition, the sorrow quenching draughts of perfect liberty. Happy day, when, all appetites controlled, all passions subdued, all matter subjected, *mind*, all conquering *mind*, shall live and move the monarch of the world. Glorious consummation! Hail, fall of Fury! Reign of Reason, all hail!

And when the victory shall be complete—when there shall be neither a slave nor a drunkard on the earth—how proud the title of that *Land*, which may truly claim to be the birthplace and the cradle of both those revolutions,

---

[8]Ezekiel 37:9.

that shall have ended in that victory. How nobly distinguished that People, who shall have planted, and nurtured to maturity, both the political and moral freedom of their species.

This is the one hundred and tenth anniversary of the birthday of Washington. We are met to celebrate this day. Washington is the mightiest name of earth—*long since* mightiest in the cause of civil liberty; *still* mightiest in moral reformation. On that name an eulogy is expected. It cannot be. To add brightness to the sun, or glory to the name of Washington, is alike impossible. Let none attempt it. In solemn awe pronounce the name, and in its naked deathless splendor, leave it shining on.

Document 11

"Baconianism and the Bible"
Benjamin Morgan Palmer
1852

Palmer's address shows that the relationship between science and revelation was an issue well before Darwin published Origin of Species. *In antebellum America, geology was already casting doubt on the literal truth of the story of creation in the Bible because recent discoveries had caused scientists to conclude that the earth was much older than the Biblical account suggested. In the face of these growing doubts, Palmer argued that there could not be any conflict between revelation and science because God was the author of both the Bible and nature. He reinforced this assertion by arguing that it was the Bible, restored to its authority by the Reformation, that made modern science possible. Francis Bacon (1561–1626) reformed science—indeed, invented modern or true science—just as Luther and Calvin reformed religion because true science and true religion share a number of fundamental principles and characteristics, according to Palmer. Once the reformation established these, true science could flourish. For example, both religion and science should be more than idle chatter (as they were in the Middle Ages, Palmer contends); they should result in charitable or productive acts, such as clothing the naked, feeding the hungry, and healing the sick.*

Palmer's account should be read in conjunction with John Quincy Adams's explanation of the causes and consequences of the Declaration of Independence (Document 7). Adams argued that the reformation was necessary for the development of free government; Palmer that it was necessary for the development of true science. The practical effects of reformed religion, its support for human freedom and its encouragement of a useful, productive life, were central elements of the Protestant synthesis that dominated America until late in the nineteenth century. When reading Palmer's assertion that "one infinite, designing and governing mind presides over all the phenomena of nature," we should recall the passage in Beecher's sermon on Holiness (Document 9) in which he says that when we attain holiness God transfers His certainty to us. Taken together, these claims help us understand the power of the social reform movement in antebellum America. It believed it had cosmic support; that mind could govern human society as it governed the universe. This is the view against which Lincoln contended in the

Temperance Address (Document 10). He argued in that speech, in effect, that while the rule of mind over nature may be a metaphysical truth, it is not for that reason also a practical or political truth.

The substance of an address delivered before the Ecumenean and
Philanthropic Societies of Davidson College, N.C.

We[1] live in an age distinguished by the wide diffusion of scientific knowledge. This results from the independent labors of two distinct classes of minds. Beside the great masters of thought, whose inventive genius gives birth to systems of philosophy, has sprung up a race of interpreters, who translate the mystic Cabala[2] of the learned into the common dialect of mankind ... .

The second class, to whom this dissemination of knowledge must be ascribed, will embrace a nobler order of minds, whose aim is not to translate great thoughts, but to reproduce them in other forms. They are not engaged in the discovery, but in the application, of truths. They find science occupied with experiment and hypothesis as instruments to establish some theoretic principle; but the principle, when demonstrated, they embody in some practical invention....

The profound thinkers, who open the sluices of human knowledge...never regard their first generalizations as final truths, but as successive rounds in the ascending ladder of science—processes for the elimination of mysteries still concealed. They authenticate no conclusions, till the widest induction has been reached, and the last analysis has been made. Nor, on the other hand, do theologians, who have measured the full argument of inspiration, flout or dread the growing discoveries of science. He who gave the Bible built the universe, and His voice must be heard in the utterances of both. If science lifts a theory against the inspired record, they calmly wait till a larger induction shall blend these discords into the melody of truth.... Philosophers know the history of science too well as a long record of conjectures to be verified, and of mistakes to be corrected: a wholesome recollection of which forbids the too positive assertion of hostile theories

---

[1] Excerpted from the printed version in *Southern Presbyterian Review*, 6(1852), 226–253.

[2] Cabala or Kabbalah is a mystical explanation of the relationship between eternity and the temporal universe.

which may soon require to be vacated. Theologians know Christianity not only as a record, but as a life. For eighteen centuries, she has turned the edge of every sword and blunted the point of every spear, that have rung upon her harness. Even when struck with the leprosy of error, her inherent life has thrown off the hideous scales and "her flesh has come again like the flesh of a little child."[3] What has this invulnerable and immortal system to dread in the encounter with human wisdom?...

These preliminary observations open a pathway into the present discourse. This alleged opposition of science and revelation, we wish to confront with one great historical fact: *that the only philosophy which has given to the world a true physical and intellectual science, is itself the product of Protestant Christianity.* This fact, if established, concludes debate.... If in the scriptures we find the genesis of that philosophy which gives the world its only true science, there can be no antagonism in the case. It will devolve upon us, therefore, to show the radical deficiency of the science and psychology possessed by the ancients, until the inductive method was fully expounded by Sir Francis Bacon; and then to show the historical and logical connection between his philosophy and the Christian scriptures....

But what is science in its broadest import?... It is when the various processes of observation and arrangement, of hypothesis and experiment, of induction and generalization, have been successfully gone through; and when the secret powers, both near and remote, which underlie the outward and tangible, have been detected, that science, in robes of majesty, ascends the throne she may never abdicate. The Greek philosophy was entirely barren of fruits like these. In its whole course, no universal and pervading laws were proclaimed, such as those which have immortalized the names of Kepler and of Newton. It had therefore no key to unlock the cabinet in which Nature treasures her mysteries, and the baffled curiosity of mankind labored vainly in the search of her undiscovered secrets....

The great vice of their physical science was the unchastened use of the speculative faculty. Not content with the relative knowledge of properties and qualities and the fundamental laws under which these are developed, they indulged the presumptuous hope of penetrating, by one transcendental effort of thought, into the essence of matter.... The inevitable result of which was a laborious trifling with words of equivocal import, and overwhelming the facts of science with petty and barren speculations....

---

[3] 2 Kings 5:14.

As in physics, men ceased to inquire about properties in the presumptuous hope to compass the knowledge of essence: so in metaphysics, the search was after abstract being and the whole science of ontology, to the neglect and disparagement of the facts of their inward consciousness. How opposed this psychology and its method of inquiry are to that productive philosophy which has been advocated by the English and Scotch metaphysicians, it is almost superfluous to remark. Bacon taught the true method of inquiry in all science to be inductive, the reverse of that a priori method pursued by the ancients. This mighty Reformer called men off from transcendental inquiries to observe and to classify facts; to ascend carefully through more comprehensive generalizations, till the most general axioms are arrived at....

But if these barren results alone repay our gloomy search into the ancient systems which at least were fresh with the dew of original thought, what must we expect from the middle ages, when philosophy in her dotage drivels in all the absurdities of the schoolmen?[4] During the long interval between Archimedes and Galileo, no solid contribution was made to science. Mind, though sufficiently active, was occupied with studies so utterly trivial as to exhaust it of productive power.... In metaphysical reasoning, all calm and patient thought was drowned in the din and clatter of dialectic wrangling. The barbarous scholastic jargon stuns the ear, and the brain whirls in the struggle to recognize as entities what before were only abstract conceptions. Substantial forms and essences, quantities and qualities and quiddities, formalities, realities, and individualities, dance in fantastic motion before the mind, like sprites and fairies in a mid-summer's night dream....

Compare now with these chaffy speculations the extension and rich discoveries of modern science. It is needless to enumerate them, for they lie all around us, and are in contact with the humblest minds:—blessings not within the monopoly of wealth, but freely dispensed to the poor, whose comforts they increase, and the laborer, whose toils they abridge. As one has described it, it is "the philosophy of utility, the philosophy of lightning rods, of steam engines, safety lamps, spinning jennies, and cotton gins—the philosophy which has clothed the naked, fed the hungry, and healed the sick—the philosophy of peace, which is converting the sword into the pruning hook, and the spear into the ploughshare."[5] It is a philosophy which, while applying her principles to useful and practical ends, does not pause in the career of investigation and discovery. With relentless purpose, she still pursues Nature through all her

---

[4] Medieval phiosophers.
[5] Samuel Tyler, Discourse on Baconian Philosophy (1844).

departments; who cannot retreat into deeper mysteries without yielding her discovered secrets to this resistless interrogation…. This "philosophy of utility" walks henceforth upon the two equal legs of discovery and application. While perfecting her researches, discovering by stricter analysis the original elements of matter, and unfolding the laws of their combination, she at the same time reduces every new fact to practical use. At the very moment she is discussing the nature of electricity, and testing, if possible, its identity with heat and magnetism, she is also stretching the telegraphic wires over mountain peaks and under the ocean's bed, converting the world into one great whispering gallery—where distant nations over continents and seas exchange thoughts of the passing hour….

It is not our purpose to inquire into the causes of difference between the garrulous and disputatious philosophy of antiquity and the practical and remunerative science of our day…. But we wish you to note the historical line of separation between the two. Until the moment when Sir Francis Bacon expounded the inductive method of inquiry, and exposed the baldness of all a priori researches into nature, there was no comprehensive science in the world. For two thousand years, the great problems of physical and mental science went unresolved. Men stood rooted, like statues, to the earth "their nerves all chained up in alabaster,"[6] or else, bound up in the fetters of a stony logic and balancing in the endless seesaw of the syllogism. But in the 17th century arose the great intellectual Reformer, who, snatching the wand from the hands of the Stagyrite,[7] freed science forever from the enchantments of the wizard.

The date of this new and practical philosophy reads a lesson to those who shamelessly represent scripture and science as irreconcilably at feud. What says history to this? Why, that up to the Christian epoch, and before the revelation of God was either completed or made the inheritance of mankind, philosophy lay in swaddling clothes, rocking and sleeping in her cradle … that during the dark ages, when the Bible was banished into convents and only read there at the end of a rusty chain, philosophy in her slumber raved as one troubled with the nightmare and cannot awake—that at length God, in compassion for man's blindness and misery, sent Wiclif, and Huss, and Jerome,[8] as forerunners of one greater that should come after: and again he sent Copernicus, and Galileo, and Tycho Brahe, as heralds of another style of monarch—that when Luther

---

[6] An allusion to John Milton's *Comus*.

[7] A nickname for Aristotle, who was born in Stagira.

[8] Wiclif or Wycliffe and Huss were early reformers. Jerome translated the Bible into Latin.

entered the pantheon of popery, and shattered the idols of the Church, just one century later another Iconoclast arose who smote the "idols of the tribe," and of "the den," of "the market" and of "the theatre," in the temple of science—and that Tindal's translation of the English Bible preceded by nearly one hundred years the publication of the *Novum Organon*.[9] What does history say more? Why, that up to this hour there is no country unenlightened by the Bible, whose darkness is penetrated by the rays of science—that there is no land in which the suppression or corruption of the scriptures does not prove, in an equal degree, the suppression or corruption of philosophy—and that where genius has been most sanctified by its contact with divine truth, has science found her noblest votaries, and gained her proudest laurels. A recent writer[10] has quaintly enough affirmed that coal is a Protestant formation, since by a singular providential distribution, this mighty agent of civilization and element of political wealth, is possessed almost exclusively by the Christian and Protestant nations of the earth. It might profit some of our dilettanti philosophers gravely to consider what it is that has bound Biblical Christianity and the inductive philosophy and Anglo Saxonism together for the past two hundred years—and whether it is this conjunction of the Bible and Science that has put this race, like ancient Judah, in the leadership of modern nations. At any rate, let this authenticated fact, that the Bible, throughout all history, has been the precursor of genuine philosophy, decree the just doom of him who still persists that they are foes.

These rapid and suggestive touches are sufficient to trace out the historical connection between the Baconian philosophy and Christianity, as agencies intended by God for the elevation of mankind. That there is also a natural affinity between the two, we might safely infer from their constant conjunction. But it will not be difficult to show why this philosophy should be the philosophy of Protestantism; and we enter upon this final track of thought the more readily, inasmuch as it will afford the more abundant illustration, that Revelation, so far from being inimical to science, contributes a powerful incidental influence in its favor.

1. The Theologian and the Inductive Philosopher proceed on similar principle in the construction of their respective systems. The materials of science lie scattered in the utmost disorder through the broad fields of Nature—here a rose and there a star. The business of the philosopher is to collect these, as a printer would his types, and put them together on an

---

[9] Bacon's account of the new science.

[10] Hollis Read, "*The Hand of God in History*," (Hartford: H. E. Robbins, 1852), p. 49.

intelligible page. As he ascends in his generalizations, phenomena the most unlike are grouped in the same class; mere outward analogies are disregarded, and secret affinities are detected, until at length he reaches formulas expressing the great principles upon which nature acts. The key to the cypher once found, nature comes to be read like a great folio; on every leaf a new science, and its various chapters unfolding the history of Providence.

The materials of theology indeed are not gathered precisely in the same way by observation and experiment, but are given immediately by Revelation. Nevertheless, the revelation is not made in a logical and systematic form, but in the most fragmentary and undigested manner. Its doctrines are strong in magnificent profusion though the histories, narratives, poems, epistles, predictions, of the Bible—given sometimes in the form of ethical precepts, and sometimes in the more elaborate form of logical argument. The same patience, and diligence, and caution are required in ranging up and down the Record, as in surveying Nature: the theologian collates his passages as the philosopher collects his facts, and by analogy constructs his divinity as the latter builds up his science....

2. A second feature of resemblance, or point of contact, between the two, is the faith which lies at the foundation of both. The Bible reveals the existence of God, but who can know the Almighty unto perfection?... It demands a testimony which it remits to the most searching scrutiny of impartial and enlightened reason; and then it receives as fact what perhaps may never be compassed as knowledge. But does not faith lie as truly at the foundation of science? The first great injunction of the Inductive Philosophy is faith in well authenticated facts. As reason examines the evidences of a revelation that faith may rest upon a divine testimony, so sense scrutinizes the phenomena of Nature that philosophy may have her facts. These facts, however inexplicable, are received upon their own evidences: and upon this faith, science proceeds to classify them, and finally to eliminate the powers by which they were produced. Thus faith in what is unknown, yet fully attested, is the necessary antecedent of all scientific research and philosophical analysis....

3. A third particular in which the Bible exerts its influence upon philosophy, is by stirring the human intellect, and preserving it from relapsing into apathy. There are obviously two conditions to be fulfilled in all search after knowledge; these must be first the object, and then the organ, of inquiry. As in optics, there must be the material universe, and the open eye; so in philosophy there must be the objective truth and the awakened intellect. If the latter be wanting, there may be truth, but there cannot be knowledge. Now the mind can never stagnate in countries where the Bible lifts up its strong and

solemn voice. It announces truths of the first interest to man. It tells of God, what His glories and perfections are—of the creative power by which He brought all things into being, and of the providential care with which he sustains them. It teaches man what he himself is, partly matter, and partly spirit—explains the mysteries of his earthly lot, what is the source of all his blessings, and the spring of all his sorrows. It speaks of law and accountability, of sin and redemption, of atonement and pardon, of holiness and bliss. It throws a gleam of light into the shadowy land of death, and reveals another state of existence, with its solemn conditions. It enumerates all the relations of human society, and prescribes the duties of each. These topics, moreover, are such as must command the attention of men. There is a congeniality between them and our religious nature, by which they must be received and retained, as the materials both of worship and of thought. From this congruity between our religious consciousness and the spiritual truths taught in the Bible, the latter cannot but arouse the intellect even from its deepest slumbers....

A ray of revelation lights up the edge of some unsearchable mystery, which, like the fringe of gold that the setting sun places on the border of a somber cloud, kindles the imagination to paint the glories hid within its dark ground. Thus incidentally does the Bible lend aid to philosophy, by sharpening the instrument with which all her researches are to be prosecuted.

4. A fourth advantage accrues to philosophy from the complete information afforded on all moral subjects, by which the mind is released to pursue the studies of science. No one can peruse the speculative writings of the ancients without perceiving how these were intermixed with their theological inquiries. What God is...and kindred inquiries were the absorbing themes upon which the speculative genius of antiquity wasted its strength. From what has before been said of man's religious constitution, it will appear, that until they were answered, all other subjects must be kept largely in abeyance. Yet without a special revelation, what data exist from which the solution of these problems may be drawn...? Upon these subjects, however, the Bible pronounces with all the authority of God. A divine testimony reduces conjecture into knowledge, and opinion into faith. The mind is released from the torture of doubt, as well as from the agony of unbelief: with its systems of Theology and morality constructed, it can turn to reap the knowledge which may be gathered from the fields of science....

5. Revelation does not confine itself to these indirect methods of benefiting science. It reveals the uniform laws of God's moral government, and thereby hints to science her true province, that of tracing and expounding the fundamental laws of the physical universe....

If there be one idea, more absolutely a reigning idea, in the scriptures, it is that of *Law*—law written upon man's heart, defining his moral relations—law, whose transgression placed him under the dominion of guilt and death—law, whose demands, inflexible, because just, cannot be realized, but requiring, in the sinner's salvation, all that is involved in the terms atonement and sacrifice. Like the higher generalizations of the inductive philosophy, the Bible extends the empire of law, until its jurisdiction shall embrace angels in their unspotted holiness, and devils in their guilt and despair.

Now this conception of law, embodying the will and operations of one supreme and intelligent being, is the germ of all true science…. As one infinite, designing and governing mind presides over all the phenomena of nature, there must be perfect harmony in all her parts. The philosopher having confidence in the certainty of these connections, and in the energizing power of God, argues boldly from effect to cause….

6. But the Bible contains within itself the highest philosophy. Its subject is man, in the full exercise of all his powers, and exhibited in all the relations which he can sustain…. Is there no philosophy in this? And what finer scope is there for the speculative faculty than to analyze human actions, the compound results of thought and emotion—to detect the processes through which the mind is carried, from the first dawn of light upon it till the volition is consummated in the overt act…?

What philosophy is more comprehensive than that of government and law? Yet the Bible reveals both upon the grandest scale, as God administers them over moral beings in heaven and upon earth. It reveals both, not only in the didactic exposition which we find in statutes and ordinances, especially as summed up in that comprehensive compend known as the Decalogue; but illustrated and enforced by that diffuse commentary running through the whole of sacred history, the narratives and biographies of the inspired volume. We cease then to wonder that the fathers of a true speculative philosophy were not born before the Bible was drawn forth from its concealment. For while this blessed book was given to teach something far better than either philosophy or science; and while…no physical error can be found upon its pages, because its language is discreetly framed to adapt it to the growing discoveries of science, yet even the Bible cannot do its higher office of inculcating religion without at least insinuating philosophy….

We thus discover the relations of true science to revelation. There never could have been a Bacon without the Bible. The world travailed long and anxiously, giving birth to many philosophers; but Francis Bacon was the offspring of the Reformation, doing that for philosophy which Luther had before done for religion. The one brought out the Bible and read it aloud to the nations: the other brought out the older volume of Nature and interpreted its cypher to mankind....

... But error will never cease its struggles to usurp the throne and to sit in the temple of truth until "the Lord shall consume it by the brightness of his coming." The dapper infidelity of our day sits, with a spruce and jaunty air, in the halls of science and in the chairs of philosophy. Too bland and nice ever to distort its features with a sneer, a smile of vanity ever lurking upon its lips, it simply handles its fossils and ignores the Bible. Putting on its wise spectacles, it reads off, from Egyptian monuments and Chinese records, the world's chronology in millions and billions of years, just as calmly as though God had never written a book, in which was set down the age of man.... Would Bacon have done so?... [W]ould he have excluded any verse of scripture, because forsooth this was meant to teach religion and not science? No! the very genius of the inductive philosophy forbids the exclusion of a single pertinent fact from its generalizations, from whatever quarter the fact may come. The philosophy, therefore, which will ignore the Bible, and cancel its testimony, is not only baptized into the spirit of infidelity, but has apostatized from the fundamental articles of the Baconian creed. The union of these two depends upon affinities which cannot be destroyed. If, then, science proclaims a theory seemingly at variance with scripture, the alternative is plainly this: Either the interpretation of scripture is wrong, or else science has made a blunder. If the former, as we have no a priori scheme of interpretation, we are willing to correct our errors by any light which can be turned upon the sacred volume. If the latter, we wait till science shall gather other facts and make a truer induction. By the one or the other method, the two must eventually harmonize in their teachings. But when the theologian employs the facts of science in aiding his interpretations of scripture, he manifests a confidence in the inductive principle, and puts to shame the philosopher who refuses to employ the facts of scripture in generalizing the conclusions of science.

It is with an earnest purpose we labor to establish the harmony of scripture and science. For if they are made antagonists, and science build up its glory upon the ruins of revelation, the issue joined is most appalling. There is no system, either of philosophy or science, which rests upon such various and satisfactory evidences as the Bible. There is no system which has stood for ages as the Bible has done, impregnable against the most furious and preserving assaults. If, then, you shake my faith in it, you destroy belief in every thing. If science turns upon me her discoveries, sweeping away in their ruthless current that system which met all the wants of my nature, and which I had supposed to rest upon immovable foundations, upon what that is firmer and better attested can my faith fall back?... Destroy my faith in the scriptures of God, resting upon higher and broader evidence than every thing else, and you launch me upon a sea of doubt which has neither bottom nor shore. Steering by no chart, guided by no compass, wafted by no breezes, without observation of the stars or sounding of the deep, with no haven in prospect, without cargo to lose or save, with eyes, but nothing to see, and ears, but nothing to hear, without aim and without heart, I drift a wandering wreck, in hopeless Pyrrhonism,[11] till death's vortex swallow me in eternal night. From such a doom reason shrinks back aghast.... Oh, give me not over to the doom of cherishing forever the instinct of faith, with nothing to believe; nourishing powers of reason, with nothing to demonstrate; conscious of an understanding, with nothing to know; and feeling the movements of passion, with nothing to love or to hate.

Such are the appalling consequences of this momentous issue to all who have once been persuaded of the inspiration of the scriptures. Those, indeed, who are content to abide in the solitudes and mists of a dreary deism, may experience no such shock. But all who have gone round about the Bible as the citadel of revealed truth, and have "marked her bulwarks" and "counted her towers," will have nothing left for hope or faith, when philosophy has put this in siege, and science has razed it to the ground. The harmony of science with revelation might be shown in detail, by a particular comparison of the established truths of both. But such a line of proof requires a minuteness of learning which few, outside the Professor's chair, may expect to command. This discourse gives, in two words—Baconianism and the Bible—a portable argument paralyzing the skeptic with the shock of the torpedo. The Baconian philosophy is the mother of that proud science which sheds such glory upon the age in which we live; and this philosophy, as already shown, has historical and logical connections with the Bible, the charter of our religious hopes. We may rest, therefore, in the conviction that as the Bible has conferred the largest benefits upon philosophy, true science will yet repay it with the largest gratitude. Kindling her torch at every light between a glowworm and a star, she will read to us "the silent poem of creation." She will appear, like an ancient priestess, in the sacred temple of religion; and burn the frankincense of all her discoveries upon the altar of inspired truth. She will assemble the elements and powers of Nature in one mighty orchestra, and revelation shall give the key-

---

[11] An extreme skepticism, first formulated in the work of the Greek philosopher Pyrrho.

note of praise, while heaven and earth join in the rehearsal of the grand oratorio.

Document 12

Second Inaugural Address
Abraham Lincoln
1865

In the Temperance Address (Document 10), Lincoln pointed to the harm that might come from pursuing social reform on the assumption that the reformers were morally superior to those they sought to reform. The lack of sympathy and fellow feeling in such an effort defied human nature and contravened the teachings of Christianity. It thus diminished the likelihood of the reform succeeding and created divisions among fellow citizens. The attitude that Lincoln criticized in the Temperance Address was at least in part responsible for the terrible Civil War that erupted almost two decades later. Delivered as that war came to a close, Lincoln's Second Inaugural picks up the theme of the Temperance Address in again calling for reconciliation among American citizens. With numerous references to the Bible, the Second Inaugural moved beyond the rational and natural causes to which Lincoln confined himself in the earlier address, appealing to God's transcendent justice as the source of the charity among Americans necessary to bind the nation's wounds. If we leave judgment, certainly final judgment, to God, then we are left with the admonition to love one another.

Fellow Countrymen:

At this second appearing to take the oath of the presidential office, there is less occasion for an extended address than there was at the first. Then a statement, somewhat in detail, of a course to be pursued, seemed fitting and proper. Now, at the expiration of four years, during which public declarations have been constantly called forth on every point and phase of the great contest which still absorbs the attention, and engrosses the energies of the nation, little that is new could be presented. The progress of our arms, upon which all else chiefly depends, is as well known to the public as to myself; and it is, I trust, reasonably satisfactory and encouraging to all. With high hope for the future, no prediction in regard to it is ventured.

On the occasion corresponding to this four years ago, all thoughts were anxiously directed to an impending civil war. All dreaded it, all sought to avert it. While the inaugural address was being delivered from this place, devoted altogether to saving the Union without war, insurgent agents were in the city seeking to destroy it without war—seeking to dissolve the Union, and divide effects, by negotiation. Both parties deprecated war; but one of them would make war rather than let the nation survive; and the other would accept war rather than let it perish. And the war came.

One eighth of the whole population were colored slaves, not distributed generally over the Union, but localized in the Southern part of it. These slaves constituted a peculiar and powerful interest. All knew that this interest was, somehow, the cause of the war. To strengthen, perpetuate, and extend this interest was the object for which the insurgents would rend the Union, even by war; while the government claimed no right to do more than to restrict the territorial enlargement of it. Neither party expected for the war, the magnitude, or the duration, which it has already attained. Neither anticipated that the cause of the conflict might cease with, or even before, the conflict itself should cease. Each looked for an easier triumph, and a result less fundamental and astounding. Both read the same Bible, and pray to the same God; and each invokes His aid against the other. It may seem strange that any men should dare to ask a just God's assistance in wringing their bread from the sweat of other men's faces;[1] but let us judge not that we be not judged.[2] The prayers of both could not be answered; that of neither has been answered fully. The Almighty has His own purposes. Woe unto the world because of offences! for it must needs be that offences come; but woe to that man by whom the offence cometh![3] If we shall suppose that American Slavery is one of those offences which, in the providence of God, must needs come, but which, having continued through His appointed time, He now wills to remove, and that He gives to both North and South, this terrible war, as the woe due to those by whom the offence came, shall we discern therein any departure from those divine attributes which the believers in a Living God always ascribe to Him? Fondly do we hope, fervently do we pray, that this mighty scourge of war may speedily pass away. Yet, if God wills that it continue, until all the wealth piled by the bond-man's two hundred and fifty years of unrequited toil shall be sunk, and until every drop of blood drawn with the lash, shall be paid by another

---

[1] Genesis 3:19

[2] Matthew 7:1

[3] Matthew 18:7

drawn with the sword, as was said three thousand years ago, so still it must be said "the judgments of the Lord, are true and righteous altogether."[4]

  With malice toward none; with charity for all; with firmness in the right, as God gives us to see the right, let us strive on to finish the work we are in; to bind up the nation's wounds;[5] to care for him who shall have borne the battle, and for his widow, and his orphan[6]—to do all which may achieve and cherish a just and a lasting peace, among ourselves, and with all nations.

---

[4] Psalm 19:9
[5] Psalm 147:3
[6] James 1:27

Document 13

"The Moral Theory of Civil Liberty"
Henry Ward Beecher
July 4, 1869

Henry Ward Beecher (1813–1887), younger brother of Edward Beecher (Document 9), was one of the most popular and influential preachers in nineteenth century America. His church in Brooklyn, New York, then a prosperous middle class community, was well attended and his sermons widely read. On the 93rd anniversary of American independence, Beecher preached on liberty. He argued that human nature prescribed limits to what men should do and that choosing to live within these limits, choosing to live according to the laws of human nature, constituted human liberty. Living in this way was good because it controlled man's lower animal nature and thus freed man's higher spiritual nature. This was God's design, according to Beecher. If men did not choose to follow the law of nature, to govern themselves individually according to it, then they would necessarily be governed by others, even to the point of despotism. Liberty, both individual and civil, required that individuals govern themselves.

In contrast to his older brother's account of holiness, Henry Ward's discussion of the morality of civil liberty is less Biblical. In fact, it is a moral teaching that could be, and had been, articulated on the basis of reason alone. This is in keeping with the fact that Beecher's popularity as a preacher was due in some measure to his turning away from traditional Calvinist notions such as predestination and the utter sinfulness of mankind.

While they promise them liberty, they themselves are the servants of corruption: of whom a man is overcome, of the same is he brought into bondage.

—2 Peter 11:19

This is a true delineation of the fact that animalism leads to despotism, and necessitates it; and the whole chapter, which I read as the opening service of the evening, illustrates that important and fundamental idea.

This day, which is our National Anniversary, will very naturally suggest my subject this evening.

There are two essential conditions of civil liberty: first, self-government, and second, the civil machinery of free national life. And in importance they stand in the order in which I have mentioned them.

Self-government is a better term than *liberty*. We are in the habit of speaking of certain nations as *free people*. There is no such thing as absolute liberty. It is quite inconsistent with the very creative notion which we express. There is no such thing as absolute liberty in one's self; because there is an order of faculty in every man, by the observance of which he can reap happiness, and by the disregard of which he will entail on himself misery. That this is so of the body, we all know. That we are obliged to obey the laws of the ear, of the eye, of the mouth, and of the hand, in order to reap the benefits of these organs, we all know. We can not go backward upon the organization of the body, and have health and comfort. We gain strength and bodily ease and comfort in proportion as we obey law. We are not, therefore, free physically, in regard to the body; and just as little are we free mentally; for there is an order within, which is as real, and the observance of which is as indispensable to comfort and liberty, as the order of the body and its physical organization.

Nor are we absolutely free in our relations to the material world. Physical laws round about us are more potent than walls in a prison are round about the prisoner. Do, obey, and live: disobey, and die. A man is hedged up in his own nature; and he is hedged up just as much in the world in which he was born, and in which he moves. The laws of society—not enacted and voluntary laws, but inevitable civil laws; those laws which existed prior to all human thought about law, and compelled men to think as they did think; the laws which regulate the act of living together in great masses—these laws can not be set at naught, or be disregarded. Society is not a voluntary compact. You might as well say that men are born on compact, as to say that society is the result of agreements among men. The nature of the individual man could never have been developed except by his position in society. Men are necessary to each other. The faculties would grow dumb and dead, if it were not for that help which they get in the expression of themselves by the fact of civil society. This state of things is the design of God; it is the constituted nature of human life; and the laws that regulate it are imperious. So that man is a creature standing in a circle, once, twice, thrice repeated round about him—laws in his own organization, laws in the material world, and laws in the physical world, which demark the bounds beyond which he can not pass—and all his liberty lies in the small space that remains in the center. There is a certain liberty which a man can exercise; but the extent of that liberty is very small. It is choosing among imperative things.

All these restraints would *seem* to be restraints upon the sum of life and individual power; but if you analyze it, if you look at it in the root, it will be found that, while there is no such thing as absolute liberty, these restraints all work primarily against the animal nature. All these laws, whether in a man's own self, in his physical relations, or in his relations to his fellows in civil society, are laws which diminish the liberty, primarily and principally, of the passions and the appetites. And by as much as you diminish the power and dominancy of these elements in man, you give power and liberty to the other parts—to his reason, affections and moral sentiments. So that while a man is restricted at the bottom, he spreads out at the top, and gains again, with amplitude and augmentation, in the higher realms of his being, all that he loses by the restraints and restrictions which are imposed by great cardinal laws upon his lower nature.

He, then, who is self-governed—that is, who accepts his conditions, obeys all these laws, and holds himself willingly subject to them—is free; not in the points in which he is restricted, but in other and equivalent directions, in which a man's life is more to him than his basilar life can be.

All these restraints, therefore, in an intelligent and virtuous society, will be found to fall on the animal propensities, and to set free, by their very limitation, the other part of human nature—its manhood, its divinity.

The more effectually, then, these lower elements are repressed, the more liberty is given to the affections. The degree of liberty attainable by an individual depends upon the restraint which he puts upon the lower nature, and the stimulus which he gives to the higher. The liberty which is attainable by masses of men living together depends on the training that the society which they constitute has had in keeping down the animalism and exalting the true manhood of the citizens in the community. If each man, and all men, have learned self-restraint, then there will be need of but very little restraint on the part of the government; but if self-restraint does not exist in the body of citizens, it must be supplied from without. If men govern the animal that is in them, on which the soul sits astride, like the rider upon his steed, then they are governed. If they will not govern it, it must be governed for them. Government there must be, in some way, if men are going to live together. Society would break up in uproar; it would be like a den of tigers and lions; it would be but a bestial wallow of swine quarreling for their food, and quarreling for their warmth of a winter's night, and quarreling evermore, if there were no government. To live together as men, and in such a way that men can exercise their higher prerogatives, the lower elements of the human organization must be governed. If men would govern these lower elements themselves, there would be no need of bringing in any other instrument of government; but if they will not do it, it must be done by some other agency.

Despotism is the inevitable government of ignorant and savage nature. It is not that the monarch, seeing his power, takes it upon himself to govern the rude in their helplessness; it is this, that the men who represent in themselves only animal qualities are properly governed by absolute government. The animal nature in men must be governed by force, unless they govern it by their own intelligent and free will. Therefore a low and animal condition of national life is properly crowned and dominated by despotism. Under such circumstances it is not a usurpation; it is not a mischief; it is precisely adapted to the work that is to be done. And an indispensable work it is.

Society can not be free, then, except as the reason and the moral sentiments have a sufficient ascendency. You have often heard it said that a free government depends upon the intelligence and virtue of the citizens. This is an empirical fact. It is in accordance with the radical nature of man that it should be so. The first and most important condition of liberty, psychologically stated, is that men should learn how to restrain their lower, basilar, passional natures, and should be willing to restrain them, and so give liberty to their reason, their affections, and their moral sentiments.

The other condition which we mentioned as indispensable to civil liberty is the possession of the machinery of free civil society. There is to be the presence of laws adapted to that state of things, and there is to be a knowledge of those laws. The methods and limitations by which the popular will is ascertained and expressed; the devices which the experience of ages has invented for the reason and the moral sentiments of the masses to adjudicate and decide questions of public policy; the methods by which a free people execute the purposes which they have determined upon—all these are elements indispensable to liberty. Laws, courts, legislatures, all forms of popular assemblies; freedom of speech, and its proper limitations—these are things which, since we possessed them when we were born, we scarcely have analyzed. They have been of slow growth. It took the world a great while to find out what laws were right and proper for a free people. Ages were employed in experimenting and finding out what was the mode by which a free people might discuss, deliberate upon, and decide their own questions of policy. It has been a slow invention, improved and improving from age to age. The whole retinue of apparatus by which a free people acted in public affairs, executed their laws, expressed their will, and maintained their purposes, has been slowly invented and perfected; and it has risen, in these latter years, so near to the finishing touches, that it may now be said that the world knows how to secure to itself that self-government, and that liberty in it, which it has always been sighing for, and has attempted to gain, but has lost, first because it did not know the psychological conditions on which true civil liberty depended, and second, because it did not know what the machinery was by which society should execute its purposes in liberty.

These two elementary conditions—the moral condition of the people, and the apparatus of civil government adapted to freedom—must unite and cooperate, before there can be any permanent civil liberty in any nation....

Document 14

"Herbert Spencer and the Doctrine of Evolution"
E.L. Youmans
1874

Edward L. Youmans (1821–1887), who founded Popular Science Monthly
*in 1872, was a tireless promoter and popularizer of scientific ideas. In this article, he
explains the significance of Herbert Spencer (1820–1903), a British writer who
developed a comprehensive account of man, society and nature based on the idea of
evolution, the gradual development of more complex forms from simpler elements.
As Youmans explains, this was a revolutionary idea, challenging longstanding
Biblical ideas of the creation and God's relation to mankind. Youmans argued that
Spencer's development of the principle of evolution not only predated Darwin's, but
was both more comprehensive and more fundamental.*

*Spencer, who invented the term "survival of the fittest," had broad influence in
the United States. His emphasis on development through time helped make
"progress," a term that, with its cognates, occurred frequently in Youmans's article,
the fundamental principle of political and social thought. As Youmans points out,
applying the concepts of evolution and "survival of the fittest" to human beings leads
to the idea of "divergent varieties of man, some of them higher than others." This
kind of thinking was a direct inspiration for the eugenics movement in the United
States. This movement, in turn, affected popular opinion and law. In 1927, in* Buck
v. Bell, *the Supreme Court ruled that Virginia had the right to sterilize its "feeble
minded" citizens. Justice Holmes, who wrote the opinion (only one justice
dissented), was influenced by Spencer, as was the Chief Justice William Howard
Taft. Holmes remarked in his opinion that "Three generations of imbeciles are
enough."*

A Lecture delivered before the New York Liberal Club

The change that has taken place in the world of thought within our own
time, regarding the doctrine of Evolution, is something quite unprecedented in
the history of progressive ideas. Twenty years ago that doctrine was almost

universally scouted as a groundless and absurd speculation; now, it is admitted as an established principle by many of the ablest men of science, and is almost universally conceded to have a basis of truth, whatever form it may ultimately take. It is, moreover, beginning to exert a powerful influence in the investigation of and mode of considering many subjects; while those who avow their belief in it are no longer pointed at as graceless reprobates or incorrigible fools.

With this general reversal of judgment regarding the doctrine, and from the prominence it has assumed as a matter of public criticism and discussion, there is naturally an increasing interest in the question of its origin and authorship; and also, as we might expect, a good deal of misapprehension about it. The name of Herbert Spencer has been long associated, in the public mind, with the idea of Evolution.... That the system of doctrine put forth by Mr. Spencer would meet with strong opposition was inevitable. Representing the most advanced opinions, and disturbing widely-cherished beliefs at many points, it was natural that it should be strenuously resisted and unsparingly criticized. Nor is this to be regretted, as it is by conflict that truth is elicited....

And, first, let us glance at the general condition of thought in relation to the origination of things when he began its investigation. Character is tested by emergencies, as well in the world of ideas as in the world of action; and it is by his bearing in one of the great crises of our progressive knowledge of Nature that Mr. Spencer is to be measured.

Down to the early part of the present century it had generally been believed that this world, with all that it contains, was suddenly called into existence but a few thousand years ago in much the same condition as we now see it. Throughout Christendom it was held, with the earnestness of religious conviction, that the universe was a Divine manufacture, made out of nothing in a week, and set at once to running in all its present perfection. This doctrine was something more than a mere item of faith; it was a complete theory of the method of origin of natural things, and it gave shape to a whole body of science, philosophy, and common opinion, which was interpreted in accordance with this theory. The problem of *origins* was thus authoritatively solved, and life, mind, man, and all Nature, were studied under the hypothesis of their late and sudden production.

But it was difficult to inquire into the existing order of Nature without tracing it backward. Modern science was long restrained from this procedure by the power of traditional beliefs, but the force of facts and reasoning at length proved too strong for these beliefs, and it was demonstrated that the prevailing notion concerning the recent origin of the world was not true. Overwhelming evidence was found that the universe did not come into existence in the condition in which we now see it, nor in any thing like that condition, but that the present order of things is the outcome of a vast series of changes running back to an indefinite and incalculable antiquity. It was proved that the present forms and distributions of mountains, valleys, continents, and oceans, are but the final terms of a stupendous course of transformations to which the crust of the earth has been subjected. It was also established that life has stretched back for untold millions of years; that multitudes of its forms arose and perished in a determinate succession, while the last appearing are highest in grade, as if by some principle of order and progression.

It is obvious that one of the great epochs of thought had now been reached; for the point of view from which natural things are to be regarded was fundamentally and forever altered. But, as it is impossible to escape at once and completely from the dominion of old ideas, the full import of the position was far from being recognized, and different classes of the thinking world were naturally very differently affected by the new discoveries. To the mass of people who inherit their opinions and rarely inquire into the grounds upon which they rest, the changed view was of no moment; nor had the geological revelations much interest to the literary classes beyond that of bare curiosity about strange and remote speculations. To the theologians, however, the step that had been taken was of grave concern. They were the proprietors of the old view; they claimed for it supernatural authority, and strenuously maintained that its subversion would be the subversion of religion itself.

They maintained, moreover, that the controversy involved the very existence of God. The most familiar conception of Deity was that of a Creator, and creation was held to mean the grand six-day drama of calling the universe into existence; while this transcendent display of power had always been devoutly held as alike the exemplification and the proof of the Divine attributes. How deep and tenacious was the old error is shown by the fact that, although it has been completely exploded, although the immeasurable antiquity of the earth and the progressive order of its life have been demonstrated and admitted by all intelligent people, yet the pulpit still clings to the old conceptions, and the traditional view is that which generally prevails among the multitude.

...The traditional explanation of the origin of the world, and all that belongs to it, being thus discredited, it only remained to seek another explanation: if it has not been done one way, how has it been done? was the inevitable question. One might suppose that the effect of the utter break-down of the old hypothesis would have been to relegate the whole question to the sphere of science, but this was far from being done. The preternatural solution had failed, but its only logical alternative, a natural solution, or the thorough investigation of the subject on principles of causation, was not adopted or urged. The geologists occupied themselves in extending observations and accumulating facts rather than in working out any comprehensive scientific or philosophical principles from the new point of view. The result was a kind of tacit compromise between the contending parties—the theologians conceding the vast antiquity of the earth, and the geologists conceding preternatural intervention in the regular on-working of the scheme; so that, in place of one mighty miracle of creation occurring a few thousand years ago, there was substituted the idea of hundreds of thousands of separate miracles of special creation scattered all along the geological ages, to account for the phenomena of terrestrial life. Two systems of agencies—natural and supernatural—were thus invoked to explain the production of effects. What it now concerns us to note is, that the subject had not yet been brought into the domain of science. One portion of it was still held to be above Nature, and therefore inaccessible to rational inquiry; while that part of the problem which was withheld from science was really the key to the whole situation. Under the new view, the question of the origin of living forms, or of the action of natural agencies in their production, was as completely barred to science as it had formerly been under the literal Mosaic interpretation; and, as questions of origin were thus virtually interdicted, the old traditional opinions regarding the genesis of the present constitution of things remained in full force.

It is in relation to this great crisis in the course of advancing thought that Herbert Spencer is to be regarded. Like many others, he assumed, at the outset, that the study of the whole phenomenal sphere of Nature belongs to science; but he may claim the honor of being the first to discern the full significance of the new intellectual position. It had been proved that a vast course of orderly changes in the past has led up to the present, and is leading on to the future: Mr. Spencer saw that it was of transcendent moment that the laws of these changes be determined. If natural agencies have been at work in vast periods of time to bring about the present condition of things, he perceived that a new set of problems of immense range and importance is open to inquiry, the effect of which must be to work an extensive revolution of ideas. It was apparent to him that the hitherto forbidden question as to how things have originated had at length come to be the supreme question. When the conception that the present order had been called into being at once and in all its completeness was found to be no longer defensible, it was claimed that it makes no difference how it originated—that the existing system is the same whatever may have been its source. Mr. Spencer saw, on the contrary, that the question how things have been caused is fundamental; and that we can have no real understanding of what they are, without first knowing how they came to be what they are. Starting from the point of view made probable by the astronomers, and demonstrated by the geologists, that, in the mighty past, Nature has conformed to one system of laws; and assuming that the existing order, at any time, is to be regarded as growing out of a pre-existing order, Mr. Spencer saw that nothing remained for science but to consider all the contents of Nature from the same point of view. It was, therefore, apparent that life, mind, man, science, art, language, morality, society, government, and institutions, are things that have undergone a gradual and continuous unfolding, and can be explained in no other way than by a theory of growth and derivation. It is not claimed that Mr. Spencer was the first to adopt this mode of inquiry in relation to special subjects, but that he was the first to grasp it as a general method, the first to see that it must give us a new view of human nature, a new science of mind, a new theory of society—all as parts of one coherent body of thought, and that he was, moreover, the first to work out a comprehensive philosophical system from this point of inquiry, or on the basis of the principle of Evolution. In a word, I maintain Spencer's position as a thinker to be this: taking a view of Nature that was not only generally discredited, but was virtually foreclosed to research, he has done more than any other man to make it the starting-point of a new era of knowledge.

For the proof of this I now appeal to his works....

By reading various books upon moral philosophy he had become dissatisfied with the basis of morality which they adopt; and it became clear to him that the question of the proper sphere of government could be dealt with only by tracing ethical principles to their roots. The plan of this work was formed while Mr. Spencer was still a civil-engineer; and it was commenced in 1848, before he abandoned engineering and accepted the position of sub-editor of the *Economist.* It was issued, under the title of *Social Statics,* at the close of 1850.... It will be seen that the conception that there is an adaptation going on between human nature and the social state has become dominant. There is the idea that all social evils result from the want of this adaptation, and are in process of disappearance as the adaptation progresses. There is the notion that all morality consists in conformity to such principles of conduct as allow of the life of each individual being fulfilled, to the uttermost, consistently with the fulfillment of the lives of other individuals; and that the vital activities of the social human being are gradually being molded into such form that they may be realized to the uttermost without mutual hindrance. Social progress is in fact viewed as a natural evolution, in which human beings are molded into fitness for the social state, and society adjusted into fitness for the natures of men, the units and the aggregate perpetually acting and reacting, until equilibrium is reached. There is recognized not only the process of continual direct adaptation of men to their circumstances by the inherited modifications of habit, but there is also recognized the process of the dying out of the unfit and the survival of the fit. And these changes are regarded as parts of a process of general evolution, tacitly affirmed as running through all animate Nature, tending ever to produce a more complete and self-sufficing individuality, and ending in the highest type of man as the most complete individual....

The inquiries thus commenced, together with those respecting the nature of the moral feelings, and those concerning life and development, bodily and mental, into which he had been led, both by *Social Statics* and the "Theory of Population," prepared the way for the *Principles of Psychology*. Some of the fundamental conceptions contained in this remarkable work now began to take shape in his mind. Other ideas connected with the subject began also to form in his mind, an example of which is furnished by the essay on "Manners and Fashion," published in the *Westminster Review* (April, 1854). Various traits of the general doctrine of Evolution are here clearly marked out in their relations to social progress. It is shown that the various forms of restraint exercised over men in society—political, ecclesiastical, and ceremonial—are all divergent unfoldings of one original form, and that the development of social structure, in these as in other directions, takes place by gradual and continuous differentiations, "in conformity with the laws of Evolution of all organized bodies."

...The article "Progress, its Law and Cause"...was written early in 1857.... It is further argued that the new relations in which animals would be placed toward one another would initiate further differences of habit and consequent modifications, and that "there must arise, not simply a tendency toward the differentiations of each race of organisms into several races, but also a tendency to the occasional production of a somewhat higher organism." The case of the divergent varieties of man, some of them higher than others, caused in this same manner, is given in illustration. Throughout the argument there is a tacit implication that, as a consequence of the cause of Evolution, the production of species will go on, not in ascending linear series, but by perpetual divergence and redivergence—branching and again branching. The general conception, however, differs from that of Mr. Darwin in this—that adaptation and re-adaptation to continually changing conditions is the only process recognized. There is no recognition of "spontaneous variations," and the natural selection of those that are favorable ....

In October of the same year, the essay on "Representative Government—What Is It Good For?" appeared in the *Westminster Review*. The law of progress is here applied to the interpretation of state functions, and it is stated that the specialization of offices, "as exhibited in the Evolution of living creatures, and as exhibited in the Evolution of societies," holds throughout; that "the governmental part of the body politic exemplifies this truth equally with its other parts." In January, 1858, the essay on "State Tamperings with Money and Banks" appeared in the same periodical. The general doctrine of the limitations of state functions is there reaffirmed, with further illustration of the mischiefs that arise from traversing the normal laws of life; and it is contended that "the ultimate result of shielding men from the effects of folly is to fill the world with fools"—an indirect way of asserting the beneficial effects of the survival of the fittest ....

We have now passed in rapid review the intellectual work of Mr. Spencer for nearly twenty years, and have shown that, though apparently miscellaneous, it was, in reality, of a highly methodical character. Though treating of many subjects, he was steadily engaged with an extensive problem which was resolved, step by step, through the successive discovery of those processes and principles of Nature which constitute the general law of Evolution. Beginning in 1842 with the vague conception of a social progress, he subjected this idea to systematic scientific analysis, gave it gradually a more definite and comprehensive form, propounded the principles of heredity and adaptation in their social applications, recognized the working of the principle of selection in the case of human beings, and affiliated the conception of social progress upon the more general principle of Evolution governing all animate Nature. Seizing the idea of increasing heterogeneity in organic growth, he gradually extended it in various directions. When the great conception, thus pursued, had grown into a clear, coherent, and well-defined doctrine, he took up the subject of psychology, and, combining the principle of differentiation with that of integration, he placed the interpretation of mental phenomena upon the basis of Evolution. We have seen that two years after the publication of the "Psychology,"[1] or in 1857, Mr. Spencer had arrived at the law of Evolution as a universal principle of Nature, and worked it out both inductively as a process of increasing heterogeneity and deductively from the principles of the instability of the homogeneous and the multiplication of effects. How far

---

[1] The Principles of Psychology, 1855.

Mr. Spencer was here in advance of all other workers in this field will appear, when we consider that the doctrine of Evolution, as it now stands, was thus, in its universality, and in its chief outlines, announced by him two years before the appearance of Mr. Darwin's *Origin of Species.*

A principle of natural changes more universal than any other known, applicable to all orders of phenomena, and so deep as to involve the very origin of things, having thus been established, the final step remained to be taken, which was, to give it the same ruling place in the world of thought and of knowledge that it has in the world of fact and of Nature. A principle running through all spheres of phenomena must have the highest value for determining scientific relations; and a genetic law of natural things must necessarily form the deepest root of the philosophy of natural things. It was in 1858, as Mr. Spencer informs me, while writing the article on the "Nebular Hypothesis," that the doctrine of Evolution presented itself as the basis of a general system under which all orders of concrete phenomena should be generalized. Already the conception had been traced out in its applications to astronomy, geology, biology, psychology, as well as all the various super-organic products of social activity; and it began to appear both possible and necessary that all these various concrete sciences should be dealt with in detail from the Evolution point of view. By such treatment, and by that only, did it appear practicable to bring them into relation so as to form a coherent body of scientific truth—a System of Philosophy....

The facts now presented, I submit, entirely sustain the view with which we set out, in regard to the character of Mr. Spencer's work, and his position in the world of thought. It has been shown that he took up the idea of Progress while it was only a vague speculation, and had not yet become a subject of serious scientific study.... In newness of conception, unity of purpose, subtlety of analyses, comprehensive grasp, thoroughness of method, and sustained force of execution, this series of labors, I believe, may challenge comparison with the highest mental work of any age.

As to the character of the system of thought which Mr. Spencer has elaborated, we have shown that it is such as to form an important epoch in the advance of knowledge. He took up an idea not yet investigated nor entertained by his predecessors or contemporaries, and has made it the corner-stone of a philosophy. If, by philosophy, we understand the deepest explanation of things that is possible to the human mind, the principle of genesis or Evolution certainly answers preeminently to this character; for what explanation can go deeper than that which accounts for the origin, continuance, and disappearance of the changing objects around us? It is the newest solution of the oldest problem; a solution based alike upon the most extended knowledge, and upon a reverent recognition that all human investigation, however extensive, must have its inexorable bounds. The philosophy of Evolution is truly a philosophy of creation, carried as far as the human mind can penetrate. If man is finite, the infinite is beyond him; if finite, he is limited, and his knowledge, and all the philosophy that rests upon knowledge, must be also limited. Philosophy is a system of truth pertaining to the order of Nature, and coextensive with it; and, as the various sciences are but the knowledge of the different parts of Nature, Mr. Spencer bases philosophy upon science, and makes it what may be called a science of the sciences. Resting, moreover, upon a universal law, which governs the course and changes of all phenomena, this philosophy becomes powerful to unify and harmonize the hitherto separate and fragmentary systems of truth; and, as this is the predominant trait of Mr. Spencer's system of thought, he very properly denominates it the *Synthetic Philosophy*[2]....

It is desirable to add a word or two regarding Mr. Darwin's relation to the question. While he has contributed immensely toward the extension and establishment of a theory of organic development, he has never made even an attempt to elucidate the law of Evolution as a general principle of Nature. His works do not treat of this problem at all, and nothing has tended more to the popular confusion of the subject than the notion that "Darwinism" and Evolution are the same thing. Mr. Darwin's fame rests chiefly upon the skill and perseverance with which he has worked out a single principle in its bearing upon the progressive diversity of organic life. The competitions of Nature leading to a struggle for existence, and that consequent winnowing which Mr. Darwin calls "Natural Selection," and Mr. Spencer calls "Survival of the Fittest," were recognized before Mr. Darwin's time: what he did, as I have before explained, was to show how this principle may aid in giving rise to new species from preexisting species. But this principle is secondary and derivative, and its operation may be traced, as Mr. Darwin has traced it, without going back to those primary forces, the resolution of which constitutes the radical problem of Evolution.

---

[2] *A System of Synthetic Philosophy*, published in ten volumes between 1862 and 1893, was Spencer's summative work, comprised of his *First Principles*—that is, an explanation of his theory of the evolution of all natural phenomena—an expanded version of his already-published *Principles of Psychology*, and additional volumes on biology, sociology, and morality.

The principle which Mr. Darwin promulgated is a part of the great theory, and it has a philosophic importance, exactly in proportion to the validity of that larger system of doctrine to which it is tributary as an element. Not only has Mr. Darwin never taken up the question of Evolution from a scientific point of view, but it was not his aim to explain even the evolution of species in terms of ultimate principles, as a part of the universal transformation—that is, in terms of the redistribution of matter and motion; for it is in this way that all proximate principles, including Natural Selection, have to be expressed before the final interpretation is reached. This mode of dealing with the subject, the only thoroughly scientific method of its treatment, belongs to Mr. Spencer alone. As to his following Mr. Darwin, we have already seen that, two years before the *Origin of Species* was published, Mr. Spencer had reached the proof of Evolution as a universal law; had traced its dependence upon the principle of the Conservation of Force; had resolved it into its ultimate dynamical factors; had worked out many of its important features; had made it the basis of a system of Philosophy; and had shown that it furnishes a new starting-point for the scientific interpretation of human affairs.

Document 15

"On Being Born Again"
Dwight Lyman Moody
1877

Dwight L. Moody (1837-1899) was one of the most famous evangelists and
social reformers of the nineteenth century. After experiencing a religious conversion
as a young salesman in Boston, Moody began to volunteer his skills as a public
speaker to his local congregation. Eventually he moved to Chicago, where he started
a Sunday school in a poor neighborhood, providing the attendees with practical as
well as spiritual training. As the parents of the Sunday school students became
interested in what their children were learning, Moody eventually formed a large
urban congregation ministering primarily to the poor and immigrant populations of
the city.

When his church was destroyed in the Chicago Fire of 1871, Moody departed
on an international tour leading revival meetings that drew thousands of listeners in
at a time to hear what he referred to as the "good old Gospel." Yet although he
preached the utter helplessness of man to save his own soul, Moody's ministry was
never primarily one of the spirit, as is evidenced even in this brief message. Being
"born again," Moody argued, had practical consequences for the individual believer,
his or her family, and by extension, the broader society. Not surprisingly, therefore,
he ended his career by returning to the problem of educating poor children,
establishing the Chicago Evangelization Society (today known as the Moody Bible
Institute). The original purpose of the school was to educate a corps of lay people—
men and women—for "practical Christian work," that is, the improvement of
personal behavior through such reforms as temperance, better home hygiene, and
anger management. Such efforts were intended to prove the life-transforming power
of the gospel for individuals and families, and thus its importance for the betterment
of society as a whole. In this sense, Moody is the inheritor of a long tradition of
evangelical pietism in America that linked social transformation to individual
regeneration (see Document 9).

> "Jesus answered and said unto him, 'Verily, verily, I say unto thee, except a man be born again, he can not see the kingdom of God'." — John 3:3

Suppose I put the question to this audience, and ask how many believe in the Word of God. I have no doubt every man and every woman would rise and say, "I believe." There might be an infidel or skeptic here and there, but undoubtedly the great mass would say they believed. Then what are you going to do with this solemn truth, "Except a man be born again, he can not see the kingdom of God," much less inherit it? There are a great many mysteries in the Word of God. There are a great many dark sayings of which we have not yet discovered the depth. But God has put that issue so plainly and simply that he who runs may read if he will. This third chapter of St. John makes the way to Heaven plainer than any other chapter in the Bible; yet there is no truth so much misunderstood, and the church and the world are so troubled about, as this.

Let me just say, before I go any further, what regeneration is not. It is not going to church. How many men think they are converted because they go to church! I come in contact with many men who say they are Christians because they go to church regularly. It is a wrong idea that the devil never frequents any place but billiard-halls, saloons, and theatres; wherever the Word of God is preached, He is there. He is in the audience today. You may go to church all the days of your life, and yet not be converted. Going to church is not being born again. But there is another class who say, "I don't place my hopes in going to church. I have been baptized, and I think I was regenerated when that took place." Where do those persons get their evidence? Certainly not in the Bible. You can not baptize men into regeneration. If you could, I would go up and down the world and baptize every man, woman, and child; and if I could not do it when they were awake, I would do it while they slept. But the Word says, "Except a man be born again"—born in the Spirit, born in righteousness from above—"he can not see the kingdom of God."

There is another class who say, "I was born again when I was confirmed. I was confirmed when I was five years old." But confirmation is not regeneration. A new birth must be the work of God, and not the work of man. Baptism, confirmation, and other ordinances are right in their place, but the moment you build hope on them instead of on new birth, you are being deceived by Satan. Another man says, "That is not what my hope is based upon; I say my prayers regularly." I suppose there was no man prayed more regularly than Paul did before Christ met him; he was a praying man. But saying prayers is one thing, and praying is another. Saying prayers is not conversion. You may pray from education; your mother may have taught you when you were a little boy. I remember that I could not go to sleep when I was a little boy unless I said my prayers, and yet perhaps the very next word I uttered might be an oath. There is just as much virtue in counting beads as in saying prayers, unless the heart has been regenerated and born again.

There is another class who say, "I read the Bible regularly." Well, reading the Bible is very good, and prayer is very good in its place; but you don't see anything in the Scriptures which says, "Except a man read the Bible, he can not see the kingdom of God." There is still another class who say, "I am trying to do the best I can, and I will come out all right." That is not new birth at all; that is not being born of God. Trying to do the best you can is not regeneration. This question of new birth is the most important that ever came before the world, and it ought to be settled in every man's mind. Every one should inquire, Have I been born of the Spirit?—have I passed from death unto life?—or am I building my hopes of Heaven on some form[1]? In the first chapter of Genesis we find God working alone; He went on creating the world all alone. Then we find Christ coming to Calvary alone. His disciples forsook Him, and in redemption He was alone. And when we get to the third chapter of John, we find the work of regeneration is the work of God alone. The Ethiopian can not change his spots; we are born in sin, and the change of heart must come from God.[2] We believe in the good old Gospel.

What man wants is to come to God for this new heart. The moment he gets it he will work for the Lord. He can not help it; it becomes his second nature. Some say, "I would like to have you explain this new birth." Well, I might as well be honest, and own right up that I can not explain it. I have read a great many books and sermons trying to explain the philosophy of it, but they all fail to do it. I don't understand how it is done. I can not understand how God created earth. It staggers me and bewilders me when I think how God created nature out of nothing. But, say the infidels, He did not do it. Then how did He do it? A man came to me in Scotland, and said he could explain it, and I

---

[1] A "form" in this sense refers to any outward ceremony or practice of religious observance (i.e., baptism, communion, even Bible reading or personal prayer). Moody is reminding his readers that such activities in and of themselves are not enough to effect their salvation, but must be accompanied by genuine repentance and the regeneration of the soul.

[2] Moody alludes to Jeremiah 13:23, slightly misquoting: "Can the Ethiopian change his skin, or the leopard his spots? then may ye also do good, that are accustomed to do evil."

asked him how those rocks are made. He said, "They are made from sand." "What makes the sand?" "Oh!" he replied, "rocks." "Then," I asked him, "what made the first sand?" He couldn't tell. Notwithstanding the philosophy of some people, we do believe that God did create the world. We believe in redemption. We believe that Christ came from the Father, and that He grew up and taught men. We believe He went into the sepulcher and burst the bands of death. You may ask me to explain regeneration. I can not do it. But one thing I know—that I have been regenerated. All the infidels and skeptics could not make me believe differently. I feel a different man than I did twenty-one years ago last March, when God gave me a new heart. I have not sworn since that night, and I have no desire to swear. I delight to labor for God, and all the influences of the world can not convince me that I am not a different man.

I heard some time ago about four or five commercial travelers going to hear a minister preach. When they got back to their hotel, they began to discuss the sermon. A good many people just go to church for the purpose of discussing those things, but they should remember that they must be spiritually inclined to understand spiritual things. Those travelers came to the wise conclusion that the minister did not know what he was talking about. An old man heard them say they would not believe anything unless they could reason it out, and he went up to them and said: "While I was coming down in the train this morning I noticed in a field some sheep, some geese, some swine, and cattle eating grass. Can you tell me by what process that grass is turned into hair, feathers, wool, and horns?" "No," they answered, "not exactly." "Well, do you believe it is done?" "Oh yes, we believe that." "But," said the old man, "you said you could not believe anything unless you understood it." "Oh," they answered, "we can not help believing that; we see it." Well I can not help believing that I am regenerated, because I feel it. Christ could not explain it to Nicodemus, but said to him, "The wind bloweth where it listeth, and thou hearest the sound thereof, but canst not tell whence it cometh and whither it goeth."[3] Can you tell all about the currents of the air? He says it is every one that is born of the Spirit. Suppose because I never saw the wind, I say it was all false. I have lived nearly forty years, and I never saw the wind. I never saw a man that ever did see it. I can imagine that little girl down there saying, "That man don't know as much as I do. Didn't the wind blow my hat off the other day? Haven't I felt the effects of wind? Haven't I felt it beating against my face?" And I say you never saw the effects of the wind any more than a child of God felt the Spirit working in his heart. He knows that his eyes have been

---

[3] John 3:8.

opened; that he has been born of the Spirit; that he has got another nature, a heart that goes up to God, after he has been born of the Spirit. It seems to me this is perfectly reasonable.

We have a law that no man shall be elected President unless he was born on American soil. I have never heard any one complain of that law. We have Germans, Scandinavians, foreigners coming here from all parts of the world, and I never heard a man complain of that law. Haven't we got a right to say who shall reign? Had I any right when I was in England, where a Queen reigns, to interfere there? Has not the God of Heaven a right to say how a man shall come into His kingdom, and who shall come? And He says: "Except a man be born again, he can not see the kingdom." How are you going to get in? Going to try to educate men? That is what men are trying to do, but it is not God's way. A man is not much better after he is educated if he hasn't got God in his heart. Other men say, "I will work my way up." That is not God's way, and the only way is God's way—to be born again. Heaven is a prepared place for a prepared people. You take an unregenerated man in Chicago and put him on the crystal pavements of Heaven, and it would be hell! A man that can't bear to spend one Sunday among God's people on earth, with all their imperfections, what is he going to do among those who have made their robes white in the blood of the Lamb? He would say that was hell for him. Take an unregenerated man and put him in the very shadow of the Tree of Life, and he wouldn't want to sit there. A man who is born of the Spirit becomes a citizen of another world. He has been translated into new life, taken out of the power of darkness, and translated into the Kingdom of Light. Haven't you seen all around you men who had become suddenly and entirely changed?

Just draw a picture: Suppose we go down into one of these alleys—and I have been into some pretty dark holes down here in this alley that used to lie back of Madison street, and I have seen some pretty wretched homes. Go to one of those rooms, and you find a wife, with her four or five children. The woman is heartbroken. She is discouraged. When she married that man he swore to protect, love, and care for her, and provide for all her wants. He made good promises and kept them, for a few years, and did love her. But he got led away into one of these drinking saloons. He was a noble-hearted man by nature, and those are just the ones that are led astray. He has now become a confirmed drunkard. His children can tell by his footfall that he comes home drunk. They look upon him as a monster. The wife has many a scar on her body that she has received from that man's arm who swore to love and protect her. Instead of being a kind-hearted husband, he has become a demon. He don't provide for that poor woman. What a struggle there is! And may God have mercy upon the poor drunkard and his family is my prayer constantly! Suppose he is here in that gallery up there, or in the dark back there, and you can't see him. May be he is so ashamed of himself that he has got behind a post. He hears that he may be regenerated; that God will take away the love of strong drink, and snap the fetters that have been binding him, and make him a free man, and he says, "By the grace of God I will ask Him to give me a new heart." And he says, "O God, save me!" Then he goes home. His wife says, "I never saw my husband look so happy for years. What has come over him?" He says, "I have been up there to hear these strangers. I heard Mr. Sankey singing 'Jesus of Nazareth passeth by,' and it touched my heart. The sermon about being born again touched my heart, and, wife, I just prayed right there, and asked God to give me a new heart, and I believe He has done it. Come, wife, pray with me!" And there they kneel down and erect the family altar.

Three months hence you go to that home, and what do you find? All is changed. He is singing "Rock of Ages, cleft for me," or that other hymn his mother once taught him, "There is a fountain filled with blood." His children have their arms upon his neck. That is Heaven upon earth. The Lord God dwells there. That man is passed from death unto life. That is the conversion we are aiming at. The man is made better, and that is what God does when a man has the spirit of Heaven upon him. He regenerates them, re-creates them in His own image. Let us pray that every man here who has the love of strong drink may be converted. Unite in prayer with me now and ask God to save these men that are rushing on to death and ruin.

Document 16

"Philosophy in the United States"
G. Stanley Hall
1879

G. Stanley Hall (1846–1924) was perhaps the most prominent psychologist in America in the later years of the nineteenth century. He founded the American Journal of Psychology *(1887), was the first president of the American Psychological Association (1892), served as president of Clark University for 31 years, taught philosophy, and wrote a good deal about education. In this article, Hall described higher education in America just as it began a period of transition. Until the late nineteenth century, virtually all colleges in the United States were associated with religious denominations and most college presidents were ordained ministers. As Hall noted, undergraduates typically studied ethics under the college president in their final year, which ensured the course reflected religious or denominational views. As the influence of modern science increased, exemplified by the growing acceptance of evolution and historical ways of thinking (see Document 14), clerical control of education came under question and attack. The tone of Hall's article as well as his explicit criticisms showed he was in favor of secularizing education, especially the teaching of philosophy. In addition to conveying the growing strength of secular views, Hall's article also makes clear the influence of German historical thought (Hegel) and the separate and even greater influence, according to Hall, of evolution, which as Document 14 makes clear was a broader set of ideas than those expressed by Darwin. Perhaps as many as 10,000 Americans went to Germany to study in the nineteenth century (Hall was one of them). When these scholars returned to America and took up positions in the new research universities financed with America's new industrial wealth (e.g., the University of Chicago, Cornell University, Johns Hopkins, Stanford University), they became part of a revolutionary change in the way some Americans thought about their society and political life. Hall pointed to an important part of this change in the second to last paragraph of his article. He there noted the degree to which Protestantism, in what Hall claimed was its "most developed forms," had become rationalized and nothing more than morality.*

There are nearly 300 non-Catholic colleges in the United States, most of them chartered by the legislatures of their respective states, and conferring the degree of A.B. upon their students at the end of a four years' course, and A.AM.[1] three years after graduation. In nearly all these institutions certain studies, aesthetical, logical, historical, most commonly ethical, most rarely psychological, are roughly classed as philosophy and taught during the last year almost invariably by the president. The methods of instruction and examination are so varied that it is impossible in the space at our disposal to report in detail upon the nature and value of the work done in these institutions. More than 200 of them are strictly denominational, and the instruction given in philosophy is rudimentary and mediæval. More than 60 which in the annual catalogue claim to be non-sectarian are, if not pervaded with the spirit of some distinct religious party, yet strictly evangelical. Indeed there are less than half a dozen colleges or universities in the United States where metaphysical thought is entirely freed from reference to theological formulae. Many teachers of philosophy have no training in their department save such as has been obtained in theological seminaries, and their pupils are made far more familiar with the points of difference in the theology of Parks, Fairchilds, Hodges and the like, than with Plato, Leibnitz or Kant. Many of these colleges were established by funds contributed during periods of religious awakening, and are now sustained with difficulty as denominational outposts by appeals from the pulpit and sectarian press. The nature of the philosophical instruction is determined by the convictions of constituencies and trustees, while professors are to a great extent without independence or initiative in matters of speculative thought. The philosophical character of some institutions is determined by the conditions attached to bequests. A few are under the personal and perhaps daily supervision of the founders themselves, who engage and discharge the members of their faculties as so many day-labourers, and who are likely to be religious enthusiasts or propagandists.

The traditional college *régime* in the United States was designed to cultivate openness and flexibility of mind by introducing the student hastily to a great variety of studies, so that his own tastes and aptitudes might be consciously developed as guides to ulterior and more technical work. The method of philosophical indoctrination, in striking contrast to this, seeks to prevent the independent personal look at things, and to inoculate the mind

[1] Currently referred to as the B.A. and M.A. degrees.

with insidious orthodoxies which too often close it for ever to speculative interests. The great open questions of psychology and metaphysics are made to dwindle in number and importance as compared with matters of faith and conduct.... It is, in any case, plain that there is very small chance that a well-equipped student of philosophy in any of its departments will secure a position as a teacher of the subject. He may find a career as a writer, editor, or instructor in other branches, or he may bring his mind into some sort of platonising conformity with the milder forms of orthodoxy and teach a philosophy with reservations. That most of the instructors find the limitation of their field of work galling is by no means asserted or implied. Many of them feel no need of a larger and freer intellectual atmosphere. They have never been taught to reason save from dogmatic or scriptural data.... [A]ll these institutions unite in impressing upon their students the lesson that there is an abyss of scepticism and materialism into which, as the greatest of all intellectual disasters, those who cease to believe in the Scriptures as interpreted according to the canons of orthodox criticism, are sure to be plunged.

The spirit and aims of philosophical instruction in very many of the smaller colleges have found an admirable exponent in the Boston Monday lectureship of the Rev. Joseph Cook, whose discourses, now published in several volumes, have had an immense influence upon the semi-theological philosophy of all such centers of learning as we have just characterized.... [In these lectures] with much liberality of interpretation, scriptural doctrines are compared with [summaries of philosophy], all in a conciliatory spirit: but wherever the teachings of science or philosophy are judged to vary from those of Scripture, the supreme authority of the latter is urged with all that intensity of a fervid and magnetic personality which makes dogmatism impressive and often even sublime. The mere brute force of unreasoned individual conviction, which Hegel so wittily characterizes as the animal kingdom of mind, has a peculiar convincing eloquence of its own in religious matters, which, acceptable as it often is to faith, has long been one of the stumbling-blocks in the way of philosophy in America.

Another reason for the backward condition of philosophy in most of these institutions is found in their poverty. A few of them were established by real estate companies to help the sale of land. By the negligence of the more worthy members of trustee-boards, together with mistaken provisions to fill vacancies, others have fallen under the control of ward-politicians, and professorships are retained or declared vacant by a scarcely better than popular suffrage. Still others are under the immediate control of state legislatures, which have it in their power to reduce or even to withhold the annual appropriation. Nearly all of them are poorly endowed, and some are entirely without funds save those accruing from tuition fees; and thus, so numerous are they, so sharp is the competition for patronage, and so quick and sagacious is parental jealousy of any instruction which shall unsettle early and home-bred religious convictions, that it is not surprising that there is little philosophical or even intellectual independence to be found in these institutions....

While thus business conspires with Bethel[2] to bring mental science into general disfavor, the average American college is in no position to lead or even to resist popular opinion and sentiment, supposing it inclined to do so. The shrewd practical money-making man, even in one of the learned professions, can make little use of philosophy; indeed it is liable to weaken his executive powers and make him introspective and theoretical. The popular philistinism which we have heard impressed as a weighty philosophical motto in the exhortation, "Look outward not inward, forward not backward, and keep at work," and which seems no more rational than the superstitious aversion to science in the Middle Ages, has been strangely efficacious against philosophical endeavor here. Hence all branches of mental science have come to be widely regarded as the special appanage[3] of a theological curriculum, where despite the limitations above described a little speculation is a trifle less dangerous than for a practical businessman.

The above, however, we hasten to say, is the darker side of the picture and is truer in general of Western than of Eastern colleges. The most vigorous and original philosophical instruction is almost everywhere given in ethics, though like nearly all other subjects it is taught from textbooks.... The work with textbooks is commonly supplemented by lectures where ethical principles are applied to law, trade, art, conduct, &c., in a more or less hortatory manner. The grounds of moral obligation are commonly deduced from Revelation, supplemented by the intuitions of conscience, which are variously interpreted. The practical questions of daily life are often discussed in the classroom with the professor with great freedom, detail and interest. Current social or political topics are sometimes introduced, and formal debates by students appointed beforehand by the professor, and followed by his comments, may occasionally take the place of regular recitations and lectures.... On the whole the average student completes his course in moral science with the conviction that there is a hard and fast line between certain definite acts and habits which are always

---

[2] The Church.

[3] A grant of land or a title from a King to a subject not provided for by rules of inheritance.

and everywhere wrong, and others which are right; that above all motives, circumstances, insights, the absolute imperative of conscience must determine the content as well as the form of actions. The psychological nature and origin of conscience are questions which have excited very little interest.

... The serious and introspective frame of mind which religious freedom and especially pietism tends to develop; the enterprise and individuality which are characteristic of American life, and which have shown themselves in all sorts of independent speculation; the principle of self-government, which in the absence of historical precedents and tradition inclines men to seek for the first principles of political and ethical science, have combined to invest semi-philosophical themes with great interest even for men of defective education. From the pulpit and even in the adult Sunday-school class or the debating society, in the club-essay and the religious press, metaphysical discussions are often heard or read, and not infrequently awaken the liveliest discussions. Yet, on the other hand, dogmatism and the practical spirit have combined thus far quite too effectually to restrain those who might otherwise have devoted themselves to the vocation of thinking deeply, fearlessly and freely on the ultimate questions of life and conduct. If "philosophers in America are as rare as snakes in Norway," it is because the country is yet too young. The minds of business and working men, whether skeptical or orthodox, have short, plain, and rigid methods of dealing with matters of pure reason or of faith, and are not always tolerant of those who adopt other and more "unsettling" ones. If, however, we may find in Hegel's *Phenomenology* a program of the future, the hard common sense which subdues nature and organizes the objective world into conformity with man's physical needs will, at length, when it has done its work, pause in retrospect, and finally be reflected as conscious self-knowledge which is the beginning of philosophical wisdom. As a nation we are not old enough to develop, and yet too curious and receptive to despair of, a philosophy.

As we pass either from the smaller to the larger or from the Western to the Eastern institutions, we find in general a much better condition of things. The older Edwards,[4] the influence of whose writings is still very great upon the religious philosophy of New England and the Middle States, did much to rationalize Calvinism and to inspire confidence in the verdicts of reason. In his great work on the freedom of the Will, he taught that the essence of right and wrong lies in the nature of acts and motives and not in their cause, that spontaneity and not self-determination is the characteristic of a free act.

---

[4] Jonathan Edwards (1703–1758). See Document 3.

Subjectively, virtue is the love of being in general. Adam's sin was not imputed to his descendants, but its effects were naturally transmitted as the withdrawal of higher spiritual influences. The new birth[5] is not the advent of a new but the new activity of an old principle. The disciples of Edwards[6]—Dr. Dwight, C. G. Finney, E. A. Parks, Horace Bushnell, Moses Stuart, and many others—have modified and widely extended his opinions.

… Outside of schools and colleges, philosophical interests have taken on the whole a wide range. Trendelenburg, Schleiermacher, Krause, Schelling, Fichte, Herbart and Lotze[7] have all found more or less careful students and even disciples among men of partial leisure in the various professions, who have spent the last year or two of student life in Germany. Above all these, however, stand first the influence of Hegel, which since 1867 has been represented by the quarterly *Journal of Speculative Philosophy*, edited by Wm. T. Harris of St. Louis, and secondly that of Herbert Spencer and other English evolutionists, which has been greatly extended by the *Popular Science Monthly*, edited by Dr. E. L. Youmans of New York. Mr. Harris …. as superintendent of the public schools of his city … has had but little time for original contributions to his *Journal*, but all English students who wish to understand Hegel's *Logic*, particularly the third part, should not fail to read Mr. Harris's compendious articles as part of the necessary propaedeutic.[8] He has gathered about him a circle of young men who have been led by his influence to interest themselves in German speculations, and whose contributions are found in nearly every number of the Journal.

… [Harris] has from the first carefully studied the bearings of philosophical speculation upon methods of education, and the high character of the schools under his care and the wide interest felt among teachers in his annual reports, bear witness to the discretion with which abstract principles have been utilized as practical suggestions. German pedagogical methods have also been introduced to the notice of teachers in the pages of the *Journal* ….

The appearance of such a journal in America, and above all in a great center of western trade, supported by enthusiastic self-trained thinkers who had the hardihood to attempt to translate into Anglo-Saxon the ponderous nomenclature of the absolute idealism of the *Wissenschaftslehre*[9] and the

---

[5] The experience of being born again. See Moody, document 15.

[6] Jonathan Edwards. See Document 4.

[7] German philosophers.

[8] Preparatory study.

[9] *Wissenschaftslehre*, theory of knowledge or science, was the title of a work by Fichte.

Hegelian *Logic*, has been often spoken of as surprising and even anomalous. The explanation, however, may not be far to seek. There is perhaps no spot in America where during the last quarter of a century illustrations of the powers of the human mind over nature have been so numerous and so impressive as in St. Louis. In a city so young and so large, the geographical and commercial center between west, east, and south, the inference that in a more than poetic sense thought is creative and man is the maker of the world, is not merely congenial, but to a certain degree spontaneous and irresistible. Again there is such a pleasing sense of liberty in the perpetual recurrence of dialectic alternatives, and yet of security, inspired by the regularity with which the beats and clicks of the triadic engine[10] are heard, and above all there is such a largeness and scope in the formula of Hegel, as if the Universe itself might be "done" once for all by reading a few thousand pages, that it is no wonder his sun should rise upon the new as it sets in the old world. Where every thing is an open question it is pleasing to feel that "all progress is advancement in the consciousness of freedom."[11] But this is not all. No one can spend a week among the philosophical coteries of St. Louis without feeling—still more perhaps than by reading the *Journal*—that these causes, aided by the influences of reaction from a severely practical and business life, have awakened the faculty of philosophy to a most hopeful and inquiring receptivity. There seems scarcely a doubt that, should Mr. Harris decide to open his journal to psychological as well as to metaphysical discussions, and in preference to the aesthetical selections which have been so often weary and unprofitable, it would soon become not only self-supporting but remunerative.

...In Germany it is said that Hegelianism has been an excellent *Vorfrucht*[12] to prepare the philosophical soil for the theories of evolution. It limbers and exercises without fevering the mind, making a safe and easy transition from the orthodox to the scientific standpoint. Even its adversaries often admit that as a mental discipline at a certain stage of philosophical culture it is unsurpassed. However this may be, it is certain that the theories of Herbert Spencer, G. H. Lewes and other English evolutionists, which have exerted such an immense influence in the United States during the last decade, are not indebted to Hegelianism, but are represented almost entirely by scientific men not

---

[10] The three phases of Hegel's dialectic: thesis, antithesis, synthesis.

[11] A quotation or paraphrase from Hegel's *Philosophy of History*.

[12] This German word means a previous crop, as in a crop rotation system which uses certain crops to put nutrients into the soil. In other words, the study of Hegel is preparation for understanding evolution.

especially interested in the history of speculation. If the worst side of the American college is the philosophical, its best is the scientific department. The value and thoroughness of the work done here is probably too little appreciated abroad. While in some of the smaller colleges it is poor enough, in many others the professors have had a thorough European training and lack only leisure and library and laboratory opportunities for valuable and original work. With comparatively few exceptions, all the most competent teachers of natural or physical science either tacitly accept or openly advocate the fundamental principles of evolution. Even the most orthodox institutions are often no exceptions to this rule. One of the largest of these long and vainly sought for a professor of zoology who would consent to pledge himself beforehand to say nothing in favor of Darwinism. In eight or nine out of more than thirty of those institutions which the writer has visited, instructors in this department are allowed to teach the principles of Huxley and Haeckel,[13] if they wish, unmolested. It must be said, however, that very often the adoption of the formulae of the development theory is so premature as seriously to interfere with the patient mastery of scientific details, or, through the students' impatience with other methods, to lower the standard of work and attainment in other departments. In a country of such remarkably rapid development as our own, where the ploughboy is never allowed to forget that he may become a millionaire or even President if he wills it earnestly enough, the catchwords of evolution often excite an enthusiasm which is inversely as the power to comprehend its scope and importance. Many of the more semi-popular aspects of Herbert Spencer's philosophy have been admirably presented by Mr. John Fiske in courses of lectures in Harvard University, in Boston, New York, and in several of the Western cities. In the periodical, especially the religious, press criticisms almost without number have been published. Professor Bowne of the new Boston University has elaborated his strictures of Herbert Spencer into a small volume which is one of the most subtle and forcible criticisms of the *First Principles* and the *Psychology*[14] that have ever proceeded from an essentially evangelical standpoint.[15]

...Perhaps the most general characteristic of American intellectual life is its heterogeneity. Not only has each religious sect or denomination its own revered and authoritative founders or reformers, its own newspapers and literature, and often its own set of duties and associations, beyond the limit of

---

[13] Two popularizers of Darwin.

[14] Hall refers to two works of Spencer, *First Principles* and *The Principles of Psychology*.

[15] Borden Parker Bowne (1847–1910), *The Philosophy of Herbert Spencer*.

which the thoughts and interests of its more uneducated members rarely pass, but also many semi-philosophical sects have a more or less numerous representation....

The influence of German modes of thought in America is very great and is probably increasing: Du Bois Reymond[16] observed in a public address some years ago that no two countries could learn so much from each other. Scores of American students may be found in nearly all the larger German universities. Most of even the smaller colleges have one or two professors who have spent from one to three or four years in study in that country, whose very language is a philosophical discipline. The market for German books in the United States is in several departments of learning larger than in Germany itself, though this is partly, of course, to be accounted for by the number of German residents. The Hegelianism of St. Louis was not only first imported but has always been to some extent supported by native Germans.

...Protestantism in America has its well-developed grammar of dissent, and has been in the past an invaluable philosophical discipline. The American, perhaps, even more than the English, Sunday might almost be called a philosophical institution. A day of rest, of family life and introspection, it not only gives seriousness and poise to character and brings the saving fore-, after-, and over-thought into the midst of a hurrying objective and material life, to which its wider sympathies and interests and new activities are a wholesome alternative, but it teaches self-control, self-knowledge, self-respect, as the highest results of every intellectual motive and aspiration. In its most developed forms, especially among the Unitarians, Protestantism has more or less completely rationalized not only the dogmas of theology but their scriptural data, and now inculcates mainly the practical lessons of personal morality and the duty of discriminative intellectual, political and esthetical activity.

Finally we shall venture to call patriotism a philosophical sentiment in America. It is very deeply rooted and persistent even in those who take the most gloomy view of the present aspect of our political life, who insist that the Constitution needs careful and radical revision, and who are not disposed to overrate the magnitude of events in our national history thus far. It is philanthropic, full of faith in human nature and in the future. And if, according

---

[16] Either Emil or Paul du Bois Reymond, two German brothers, the first a mathematician, the second a physician and physiologist.

to a leading canon of the new psychology,[17] the active part of our nature is the essential element in cognition and all possible truth is practical, then may we not rationally hope that even those materialisms of faith and of business which we now deplore, are yet laying the foundations for a maturity of philosophical insight deep enough at some time to intellectualize and thus harmonize all the diverse strands in our national life?

---

[17] Hall refers to the philosophy of pragmatism and the psychology associated with William James (1842–1910).

Document 17

"Religious Education and Contemporary Social Conditions"
Jane Addams
1911

By 1911, Jane Addams (1860-1935) had been running Hull House, one of America's leading social settlements, for twenty years. Addams' own religious views are somewhat enigmatic: although she was baptized and received membership in a Presbyterian congregation as an adult, she wrote rarely about Christianity as such, more often about "religion" in the generic sense. It is clear, however, that Addams considered religion—understood as the attempt to connect the individual human soul to some spiritual element in the universe external to it—to have the potential to elevate humanity above the cares and strife of the material realm. She argued that religious instruction, to be effective, must be connected to the practicalities of life, particularly life in modern, industrialized, urban areas with their attendant social problems. The church had failed (and socialism triumphed—see Document 22), she observed, at precisely the point where it was most needed: in bringing light and hope to the poor, the sick, the uneducated multitudes who comprised the laboring class in early twentieth century America. Oppressed at every turn, and unsupported by the church, such people were labeled as degenerates and made the targets of enthusiasts for eugenic experiments in social control (see Document 14). Addams, however, rejects such measures and calls for the church—for religious educators, in particular—to increase their efforts to save such people, not only spiritually, but in physical and practical ways that will allow them to live with dignity as contributing members of society. In making this argument, Addams responded not only to the problems created by industrialization, but also to those created by the influential ideas of evolution and materialism (Documents 14 and 16).

...The religious educator is...handicapped by the fact that much of the final curricula which he uses is left over from the days when education was carefully designed for men who had withdrawn from the world, and that of necessity, it does not avail with the youth who is fretting with impatience to throw himself into the stream of life and to become a part of its fast flowing current.

This divergence between the unreality of religious education and the demands of stirring religious experiences never became more apparent than it did in England and America during the last decade of the past century. The religious educator lost hundreds of young men and women who by training and temperament should have gone into the ministry or the missionary field, simply because his statements appeared to them as magnificent pieces of self-assertion totally unrelated to the world.

This failure to make religious teaching appear valid was due to many causes; the times were ripe for such divergence, and there are several reasons why life at this moment should have seemed more real outside of that which we call the religious world, than it did within it. In the first place, modern economists had taught that man was abjectly dependent upon the material world about him, and had demonstrated as never before the iron clamp which industry imposes upon life; they had moreover gravely asserted that man's very freedom, morality and progress may be overwhelmed by the material conditions which surround him.

Secondly, the situation was further complicated by the fact that at this very same time the doctrine of evolution, having made clear man's intimate connection with the entire external world, was establishing itself in ethics and social philosophy. Students of the social order in the spirit of the scientist became content merely to collect data and to arrange it in orderly sequence. The social field still contains hundreds of them devotedly considering the reactions of economic forces upon human life, who have for the most part disregarded all theological considerations as they have long since lightly renounced the theological explanations of a final cause.

Thirdly, during these decades hundreds of young people were drawn into the congested quarters of the modern city by sheer humanitarianism, by the impulse at least to know the worst. In their reaction against materialism they would warm their affections and renew their beliefs in those places where humanity appeared most pitiable and infirm, somewhat in the spirit of Carlyle[1] who impatiently bade his contemporaries to worship and admire the hero if they could no longer worship and admire the saint. It is as if various types of young people ardently desiring reality above all else had said to the religious

---

[1] Thomas Carlyle (1795–1881), a Scottish writer, argued in *On Heroes, Hero-Worship, and the Heroic in History* (London, 1841), that great men make history.

teachers, "we wish to know truth for ourselves, we care not how logical your theological tenets may be unless we can make them valid."

It was therefore inevitable that these lines of development should shift the center of the difficulties in religious education to the most crowded industrial districts where materialism holds undisputed sway.

The Failure of the Church

And yet, it was during these same decades that the churches, as if appalled by the industrial situation, failed to hold their own in these very districts. The church apparently felt no lure in the hideously uncouth factories in which men sometimes worked twelve hours a day for seven days in the week until they were utterly brutalized by fatigue; nor in the insanitary tenements so crowded that the mere decencies of life were often impossible; nor in the raw towns of newly arrived immigrants where the standard of life was pushed below that of their European poverty unmitigated by either natural beauty or social resources.

And yet it was into these very regions that the young people whom the church lost were most often attracted, and it was no unworthy lure which drew them into the thick of that industrial misery into which the church had not only failed to precede them, but for so long a time had failed to follow them.

Did the religious educator at the present moment but enter into this industrial inferno he would find many ardent young people, possibly not his own pupils, but those who would gladly unite with him in asserting the reality of spiritual forces, could he but share their experiences, and reach conclusions by a method they could comprehend. Among these young people he would find those who might have brought enthusiasm and ability to his own profession had it but seemed to them valid and dealing with realities. His experience would indeed be similar to that of Dante when he hesitated to enter the Inferno dreading above all else his loneliness there, although when he boldly proceeded step by step he found it peopled with old friends and comrades, speaking the beautiful language of Florence and cherishing the same great hopes as his own.[2]

---

[2] This is a strikingly creative interpretation of Dante's hesitation to enter the Inferno. Addams cites a fear Dante himself does not directly express, and in attributing "hopes" to the damned she would seem to ignore Dante's understanding of hell—although it is true that Dante's guide, Virgil, hints at the possible redemption of those who through no fault of their own never learned about Christ. See, for example, *Inferno*, Canto IV, lines 15 – 60.

This adventurous educator would find traces of a new religious expression, although with marked scientific and humanitarian aspects as befitting its period. Even as the humanism which grew out of the Renaissance was a reaction against grotesque Ecclesiasticism he would discover in the beginning of this humanitarianism a reaction against Materialism arising in the very midst of it.

He would find the economists groping their way from the 19th century darkness which considered the nation as an agglomeration of selfish men each moved by self-interest, forgetful of the women and children, to a conception of a state maintained to develop and nurture the highest type of human life, and testing its success by the care afforded to the most defenseless women and children within its borders. One of these economists whom we used to call 'hard headed' has actually made out a program to protect wage-earners from what he calls the five great misfortunes to which they are exposed: industrial accidents, preventable illness, premature death, unemployment, and neglected old age.

... The religious educator venturing into the industrial inferno would be much startled by the discovery of the anomaly that the most enthusiastic believers in economic determinism are at the present moment giving us the most inspiring demonstration of religious enthusiasm: that the socialist party is drawing to itself thousands of ardent young people simply because it holds up an ideal and demands sacrifices on its behalf. It is as if the socialists had picked up the banner inscribed with the promises of a future life, which had slipped from the hands of the ecclesiastic, as if they had changed the promise of salvation from individual to social, had substituted the word earth for heaven and had then raised the banner aloft once more. To the crowd of young people who follow this banner is happening that which always happens to those who are held together in a mutual purpose; certain readjustments take place as they realize that their own future is dependent upon the consummation of their ideal, and as they demand that the whole world unite in a common effort for its realization. There are thirty millions of these socialists in the world with a definite political program in every civilized nation. The religious teacher may well long to claim this enthusiastic host for his own, and to turn these myriad idealists into a living church.

The religious educator as he proceeded would also find those humbler investigators of social conditions living either singly or in groups in the thick of untoward industrial conditions. At moments these find their own carefully collected data gathered into statistical tables and monographs almost as discouraging and overwhelming in its bulk as in the dreary conditions it discloses. They are beginning to mutter darkly concerning degeneracy and to assert that evolutionary processes are not always upward or ethnogenic, as they prefer to say.

… Such investigators feel that their efforts should be supplemented by the religious teachers through a vigorous appeal to the public conscience and to the higher affections. They claim that as social development is an essentially continuing process, it is the business of morality to share its growth, not only to modify its harshness and brutality, but to actually direct it; and they also are thus again brought close to the religious purpose.

Would not these beginnings of a new religious expression among the economists, the investigators, and the humanitarians point to a moment in which the religious teacher might avail himself of a great opportunity? Could he but make the old formulas express the scruples, the painful sense of difference between rich and poor which haunt these dwellers in industrial quarters day by day; could he but transmute the comradeship of mutual suffering into a religious communion he would find them ready to walk in the old paths.

After all, the business of religion is not only to comfort and conserve, but to prophecy and fortify men for coming social changes. He who in a moment of transition boldly formulates his hidden scruples, does so not only for himself but for many others, and finds himself surrounded by a multitude of followers…. Again and again during its history, the church has been obliged to leave the temples and the schools in order to cast in its lots with the poor, and to minister without ceremony or ritual, directly to the needs of the sinner and the outcast.

A Religious Mission

Is it not possible that such a moment has come now, that the religious teacher must go forth into the midst of modern materialism if only effectually to insist upon the eternal antithesis between the material and the spiritual, and to prove that religious enthusiasm is all-enduring when founded upon the realities of life?

A noted English publicist once told me that twenty-five years ago at every public meeting in the industrial quarters of London, whatever the subject of discussion, some working men always arose and in fiery terms agitated the disestablishment of the English Church, but that during the last decade such a speech was seldom heard owing entirely to the efforts of certain High-Church clergymen who had gone to live throughout the industrial districts of London, and had thus identified themselves with all the leading movements of social reform until the working men had become convinced that the church wanted the thing that they wanted, and that they and the clergymen were working towards a common goal.

Thus to convince thousands of young people of the validity and reality of religion, the church must go out to meet them—both willing to take their point of view, and to understand social methods. Could the religious teacher unite in the deed with the social reformers, could he formulate for many others a course of action which would relieve their consciences in regard to social maladjustments, he would discover that he had become part of a new fellowship, while at the same time his teaching was attaining a new sense of reality.

No one in considering this subject could for a moment ignore the great social awakening at present going forward in the churches. The federal organization of thirty-four Protestant Denominations with its social department;[3] the YMCA with its well-directed social work in a dozen departments; the church committees to improve the conditions of labor, and the departments of sociology in all the theological seminaries would all indicate a new emphasis which the church is placing upon social welfare. Perhaps after all the difference is not so profound. A story is told of a country clergyman who was not a great scholar, but who had much experience with church choirs. A parishioner in all seriousness asked him one day what was the difference between the cherubim and the seraphim; the poor clergyman hesitated a moment, and somewhat confusedly replied that he believed that there had once between a difference, but that now all was amicably adjusted.

Could the differences between progressive churchmen and the social reformer be amicably adjusted, I venture to predict that we should find ourselves united in a new religious fellowship and living in the sense of a religious revival.

---

[3] The Federal Council of Churches, founded in Philadelphia in 1908, was an ecumenical association of Protestant denominations in the US and a precursor of the National Council of Churches, founded in 1950.

Document 18

"The Bible at the Center of the Modern University"

A.C. Dixon

1920[1]

A. C. Dixon (1854–1925) was a well-known Baptist minister, writer and evangelist. Along with R. A. Torrey, he was one of the original Fundamentalists, that is, an organizer and editor of The Fundamentals: A Testimony to the Truth *(published between 1910 and 1915), a collection of essays from which the fundamentalist movement took its name. This address does not discuss all of the fundamentals (defined in 1910 as the inerrancy of the Bible; the virgin birth of Christ; his death to atone for man's sinfulness; his resurrection; and the authenticity of Biblical miracles). It focuses on just two, the Bible and man's salvation through Christ's death. It also touches on other issues important to the fundamentalists: the wayward character of a merely ethical Christianity; urbanization; the changing roles and status of women; and secularization, especially the secularization of education (see Document 16). Perhaps its dominant theme is the identification of Christianity and the United States as the defenders of justice in the modern world, particularly as this concerns the defense of the weak from the power of the strong. Abraham Lincoln is its hero, second only to Christ. Darwin and Friedrich Nietzsche are the enemy, encouraging the belief that might makes right.*

The first verse of Genesis, "In the beginning God created the heaven and the earth," reads like a perfect creation. There is no hint of fiery nebulosity. "The heaven" and "the earth" have clearly defined meanings in the Pentateuch. The inspired comment upon it in Isaiah 45:18 informs us that God "formed the earth and made it: he established it: he created it *not waste*; he formed it to be inhabited." "The heaven" remained perfect, but "the earth," by some power not revealed, was wrecked. Mr. Anstey, author of "The Romance of

---

[1] *Baptist Fundamentals, Being Addresses Delivered at the Pre-Convention Conference, Buffalo, New York, June 21 and 22, 1920* (The Judson Press, Philadelphia, 1920), 119–140.

Chronology,"[2] insists that the Hebrew word rendered "was" in the Authorized Version must be translated "became." "The earth *became* without form and void, and darkness was upon the face of the deep." Other authorities admit that it may be thus translated. The first three verses give us an epitome of the whole Bible:

1. Construction: God's perfect creations.
2. Destruction: The wreck of God's perfect creations.
3. Reconstruction: Restoration of order out of chaos....

Mature Product First

"God said, Let the earth bring forth grass, the herb yielding seed, and the fruit tree yielding fruit after its kind." It is plain that the mature product comes first. The herb yields the seed; not the seed the herb. The tree yields the fruit; not the fruit the tree.

"And God said, Let the waters bring forth abundantly the moving creature that hath life, and let the fowl fly above the earth." As in the vegetable, so in the animal kingdom, the mature product comes first, not the life germ producing the living creature, but the living creature that has the life germ. Not the egg that produces the fowl, but the fowl that produces the egg. This is economy of miracle. If the germ of animal or egg of fowl comes first, then there must be a series of many miracles to produce the mature product without the fostering care of motherhood. But if the mature product comes first, reproduction takes place by natural law. No further miracle is needed. We will not pause to view this in relation to present-day science. Of that later. What appears now is that the Genesis record places the mature product first, whatever its relation to modern "science."

A Perfect Civilization

It is also evident that in the moral and social world the perfect comes first. In the second chapter of Genesis is the highest type of civilization this world has ever seen. There is a perfect man and a perfect woman. And there can be no perfect society unless there be perfect individuals.

---

[2] Martin Anstey, *The Romance of Bible Chronology: an Exposition of the Meanings, and a Demonstration of the Truth, of every Chronological Statement Contained in the Hebrew Text of the Old Testament*, 2 vols., (London: Marshall Brothers, 1913).

There is for this perfect man and perfect woman perfect environment. "God planted a garden eastward in Eden, and there he put the man whom he had formed." They are in the midst of fertility, beauty, and plenty....

There is perfect love in the marriage of one man and one woman. "Therefore shall a man leave his father and his mother, and shall cleave unto his wife: and they shall be one flesh." It is not said that the woman shall leave all and cleave to her husband. It is taken for granted that she will do that. But the husband leaves all for her. She has preeminence in the realm of love, and even a suffragette ought to be satisfied with that.

Has any civilization on earth given woman a higher position than that? Verily not.

There is perfect life. In the material, mental, moral, and spiritual realm all things are good. There is no disease or death. Perfect life of body and soul prevails. A civilization of perfect character, perfect environment, perfect employment, perfect rest, perfect law, perfect love, and perfect life has never been surpassed in the history of the world.

The Wreck of God's Perfect Order

But there comes a change. A powerful personality, who may have had something to do with wrecking the perfect earth at first, comes on the scene. Speaking to those who had been listening to God's Word, he first calls in question the fact of revelation. "Yea, hath God said?" "Are you sure that God has spoken at all? Does God speak directly to his creatures? Is there such a thing as revelation from God?" Satan puts an interrogation point after the fact of revelation; and the fact that he continues to do so is clear proof that the personality who operated in Eden is at work in the world today....

...Then he goes a step farther and offers knowledge as a substitute for revelation. "God doth know that in the day ye eat thereof, then your eyes shall be open, and ye shall be as gods, KNOWING."... A desire to know the evil as well as the good has wrecked the character of many a young man in a few weeks after he has come from the pure atmosphere of a Christian home in the country to the great city with its monstrous mixture of good and evil.

Some of our educational institutions do not hesitate to offer to students in lecture and textbook the evil as well as the good. At the commencement of a theological seminary, I heard the baccalaureate speaker say that seminaries ought to keep on their faculties at least one heretical professor, so that the students may learn the other side. That is, one professor at least should be permitted to play the part of Satan by calling in question or denying the revelation from God, so that the students may know the evil as the good. Another proof that the personality in Eden still lives, and has to do with the preparation of baccalaureate addresses....

Two Civilizations

In 1620 there landed on Plymouth Rock a little company of men and women who were chased from their homes in England by the violent spirit of this unholy alliance [of church and state]. In the hold of the "Mayflower" they wrote a compact which had in it two phrases, "for the common good," and "just and equal laws," which have been mighty factors in fostering the spirit of democracy and the love of justice among the American people.

When I was in Old Boston, England, I went to the Guild Hall where are the prison cells in which John Bradford, William Brewster, and others were incarcerated. I requested the janitor to shut me in one of the cells, that I might sit in the dark on the hard stone seat and meditate upon the "Mayflower" and what the little vessel with its Puritan passengers meant to the world. My mind flew across the Atlantic to the museum at Plymouth in which are John Alden's well-worn Bible and the cradle in which little Peregrine White, the baby born on the "Mayflower," was rocked. Nearby is the pot in which the pilgrims cooked their common dinners, and beside it, the long flint-lock gun of Miles Standish, the only soldier in the company. Here are the four pillars of the American commonwealth, the Bible, the home, the pot, and the gun. As I sat in the narrow cell, I saw the "Mayflower" still sailing across the ocean of time with all the nations on earth trying to get on board. And then I saw her multiplied a hundredfold crossing the Atlantic with three hundred thousand soldiers every month,[3] still carrying the open Bible, the Christian home, the pot, and the gun, that all the nations of the earth may now enjoy the liberty which the Pilgrim Fathers braved the perils of the ocean to secure.

Then I saw another ship landing at Jamestown, Va., with a civilization on board which approved of human slavery without thought of "just and equal laws" or "the common good." The "Plymouth Rock" and "Jamestown" civilizations were...like the confluence of the Rhone and the Arve, mud and crystal in conflict; and the mud at length prevailed. The spirit of slavery mastered New England. In the Old South Church, Boston, is still preserved the gallery under the belfry in which the slaves sat during the Sunday services. But

---

[3] Dixon refers to the American soldiers who sailed across the Atlantic to fight in World War I.

finally the Plymouth Rock civilization was victorious, and since 1865 there have been no slaves under the American flag. Today "Old Glory" has the new glory of having delivered little Cuba from her strong oppressor and of having joined with Great Britain and her allies in defending the weak against the aggression of the strong. The same spirit has led to the victory of prohibition over the oppressive powers of the drink traffic in America, and now seeks to drive this enslaver of man from the face of the earth.

Genesis of "Evolution"

Let us trace this modern conflict between the weak and their oppressors back to its source. The Greek philosophers, between 700 and 300 B.C., were, with one exception, evolutionists. Thales, of Miletus, taught that water was the primordial germ. Heraclitus believed that fire originated all things, and Pythagoras, the mathematician, was confident that number somehow brought life and form into existence. Plato, the greatest of all Greek philosophers, did not agree with his compeers. He believed that man began equal with the gods, and the beasts were degenerated men, contending that the monkey came down from man and not man up from the monkey. And Plato had the weight of evidence on his side even without a revelation, for any one with eyes in his head can see that there is more tendency in men to become monkeys than in monkeys to become men.

Darwin and Malthus

Charles Darwin, in his university course, caught the vision of the Greek philosophers and, rejecting the theory of Plato, became an ardent advocate of the hypothesis that everything was evolved from beneath; that life originated with germinal, embryonic beginnings; that in nature there is perpetual war, which is called "the struggle for existence," the strong and fit destroying the weak and unfit, and thus causing everything to move upward.... Darwin confesses in his autobiography that he received this suggestion from the Rev. Thomas Robert Malthus, an Anglican clergyman, who died in 1834.... Malthus taught that man increases with geometrical ratio, while food supply increases with only arithmetical ratio. Therefore wars and pestilences are necessary, that the surplus population may be killed off, in order that the remainder may survive.

A little clear thinking makes it clear that Malthus was wrong. Man does not increase with geometrical ratio, while food does increase "some thirty, some sixty, and some an hundredfold."[4] But Darwin was deceived by the plausible reasoning of Malthus, and made this mistake one of the foundation-stones of his scientific system. It is a libel upon a benevolent God, who has provided enough for man and beast without demanding that the strong shall kill the weak…. [T]here is no struggle for existence even among carnivorous animals, a benevolent God having provided a kinder method of preventing their dangerous increase.

Of course, we are all evolutionist in the sense of Mark 4: 28, "First the blade, then the ear, after that the full corn in the ear." Everybody knows that the embryo or germ in plant and animal develops by growth into the mature product.

But evolutionary processes have no history. The growth of embryo or germ into mature product, as we see it, simply suggests to the imagination a similar process which, it is claimed by evolutionists, took place in the abysmal past. No one has ever observed it and its history, therefore, cannot be written. If, however, life began on earth with immature embryonic beginnings and evolved through countless ages into the mature product, it must have done so in obedience to the same laws which govern the development of the immature embryo as we see it develop today, and must be subject to the same limitations. Bear this in mind, for it is a fact of great importance.

Now, though I confess a repugnance to the idea that an ape or an orang-outang was my ancestor, I have been willing to accept the humiliating fact, if proved; but… there are insurmountable difficulties in the way of my permitting eminence to decide this matter for me.

Facts Against Evolution

1. Immature, embryonic life is never reproductive….

2. Immature, embryonic life is unimprovable….

3. Embryos and germs are easily destroyed….

4. There are two things lacking which are essential to the evolutionary theory: *spontaneous generation and transmutation of species*…. No scientist of any repute claims that life has really originated from lifeless matter. Naturalistic evolution which ignores God has no explanation of the origin of life. And

---

[4] Matthew 13:8.

theistic evolution which admits that God must have created matter and introduced life can give no good reason why a God who introduces one kind of life into suitable environment, should not introduce another kind of life under similar fitting conditions.

The claim that one species of living things in plants or animals develops into another species has no facts in nature to support it. "After its kind," as in the first chapter of Genesis, is universal law. When one species unites with another, the result is a hybrid which is sterile, so that stubborn mule stands in the path of [the] evolutionist and will not let him pass on his way of error.

5. Evolution, whether naturalistic, theistic, atheistic, or Christian, is pagan in origin and spirit. The Bible, which is the text-book of Christianity, teaches that God created the mature product first and left this mature product to reproduce itself by natural law....

[W]hen we observe that the effect of the theory in others is to drag them down from the spiritual to the natural, from the realm of music, poetry, painting, and religion to the realm of the worm as it works in the dirt and dark, we are driven to the conclusion that there is something in this pagan theory which drags us down into the mud, and robs us of the clearer vision and purer atmosphere of the higher spiritual realms.

6. Evolution with its "struggle for existence" and "survival of the fittest," which gives the strong and fit the scientific right to destroy the weak and unfit, is responsible for the oppression and destruction of the weak and unfit by the strong and fit. It has fostered autocratic class distinctions and is no friend to the democracy which stands for the protection of the weak against the oppression of the strong. The greatest war in history, which has drenched the world with blood and covered it with human bones, can be traced to this source. If the strong and fit have the scientific right to destroy the weak and unfit, that human progress may be promoted, then might is right, and Germany should not be criticized for acting upon this principle.

The "Superman"

Nietzsche, the neurotic German philosopher, hypnotized the German mind with his pagan brute philosophy. "The 'weak and the botched,'" said he, "shall perish; first principle of humanity. And they ought to be helped to perish. What is more harmful than any vice? Practical sympathy with the botched and weak—Christianity."[5] "If what I publish be true," he wrote to an invalid woman, "a feeble woman like you would have no right to exist."

"Christianity," he said again, "is the greatest of all conceivable corruptions, the one immortal blemish of mankind."[6] And he hated it because of its sympathy with the weak and botched. He glorified his ideal of the German "blond beast" and gave to the world a "superman," one-third brute, one-third devil, and one-third philosopher. Under the spell of his daring brutality, Germany adopted the motto, "Corsica has conquered Galilee."[7] Nietzsche's philosophy of beastliness has its roots in the evolutionary assumption that the strong and fit, in the struggle for existence, have the scientific right to destroy the weak and unfit. Under the spell of Nietzsche's "superman" there came into the brain of the Kaiser the vision of a supernation, a national brute, devil and philosopher, with the scientific right to destroy all weaker nations and erect his throne upon their ruins. One Sunday morning, four months after the war began, I spoke something like this from the Metropolitan Tabernacle pulpit in London; and, after the service a gentleman with military bearing appeared in the vestry and said: "I am a German, brought into London on a captured ship; and why I have not been interned I do not know; but I have an intimation that I shall be interned next week, and before I go I would like to give you a piece of my mind. You have said that this terrible war was due to Darwinian evolution, and I believe it. I hope I am a Christian. I love Jesus Christ and believe the Bible, but my wife and daughter have had their faith wrecked by Nietzsche and his pagan gang. But what I want to say to you is that we Germans got Darwinism from England. We took it from you and worked it out to its legitimate consequences. So, when you mention it again, speak softly, for you are really getting back what you sent." I could not deny it. Back of this war and responsibility for it is Darwin's pagan teaching that the strong and fit have the scientific right to destroy the weak and unfit.

---

[5] Friedrich Nietzsche, *The Anti-Christ* (1888).

[6] Nietzsche, The Anti-Christ.

[7] "Corsica" is Napoleon; "Galilee" is Christ. Napoleon stands for the doctrine of force, Christ for the doctrine of justice and charity for all. The phrase is attributed to a professor J. A. Cramb. It was a frequently used expression among evangelical and conservative Christians at the time Dixon wrote.

England and France

This suggests the fact that France gave to Germany her first lessons in the destructive higher criticism of the Bible. It was Jean Astruc,[8] a learned, dissolute French physician, of Marseilles, who first suggested that Genesis had two authors. Doctor Eichhorn,[9] of Germany, took Astruc's suggestion as a clue and announced that he had discovered many authors. Thus began a movement which has done more to discredit the Bible than any other movement of modern times. The scientists of Germany took Darwinism from England with its struggle for existence, giving the strong and fit the scientific right to destroy the weak and unfit, and gave to the politicians the infernal dictum that might is right, while the German theologians took from Jean Astruc his composite-authorship-of-Genesis theory and worked it out to the discrediting of the Bible as a revelation from God.... While victory on the side of liberty and humanity has checked, if not destroyed, German militarism, it remains for those who believe and love the Bible to mobilize and fight the battle for the truth which has given to the world its passion for liberty and humanity.

Darwin and Lincoln

It is an interesting fact that Charles Darwin and Abraham Lincoln were born on the same day, February 12, 1809, and in the lives of these two men continue the battle between mud and crystal. Darwin, born into an environment of wealth, through the teachings of Greek philosophers and of Malthus became the champion of the strong and fit against the weak and unfit. Abraham Lincoln, born into an environment of poverty and struggle, became the champion of the weak against the strong. He believed that the weakest and worst have the right of existence with fair treatment, and that the strong and fit, instead of destroying and weak and unfit, should be their protectors and benefactors. When he saw a negro woman in a New Orleans slave-market auctioned off to a rich slave-owner, he said, "If I ever get a chance to strike that thing, I will hit it hard." And he did hit it hard, when he led the movement which resulted in the abolition of slavery under the American flag.

Let us turn again to Genesis and trace the crystal river of faith in the coming Messiah in conflict with the mud of unbelief. In the curse upon the serpent there is a promise that the seed of the woman (not man) shall bruise

---

[8] Astruc (1684–1766) published his analysis of Genesis anonymously in 1753.
[9] Johann Gottfried Eichhorn (1752–1827), *Introduction to the Old Testament* (3 vols., 1780–1783).

his head. Of course, we know who the serpent is: "that old serpent, which is the devil and Satan" (Rev. 20:2). But do not think of Satan as Doré[10] painted him, with horns, hoofs, bats' wings, and forked tail. Such a monster could tempt no one, except to run and get out of his way. Paul declares that Satan in this age is transformed as a messenger of light.[11] His mission is to give light, historic light, scientific light, all kinds of light, if by any means he may satisfy the world with light without Him who is the light of the world. Satan would have our colleges, universities, seminaries, and churches blazing centers of light without Him who is the light of the world. Satan would have our colleges, universities, seminaries, and churches blazing centers of light without the Light, Christ Jesus, as atoning Saviour. And Satan wishes his ministers to be ministers of righteousness. His favorite is the ethical minister who preaches a high standard of morality and humanity, urging people to be good and to do good without salvation through the atoning blood of Christ.

One of the great needs of the Christian Church today is a university with the Bible at its center as the standard of all truth, religious, moral, historic, and scientific, and the Lord Jesus Christ preeminent in the realm of knowledge as in all other realms. The Bible, "the Impregnable Rock of Scripture," as Gladstone[12] called it, is the only book in which its religion, ethics, history, and science, are always and everywhere up to date. You have doubtless heard of the "scientific morgue" in Paris, a rather gruesome place, where dead scientific theories are laid out for inspection. Most of them died under twenty-five years of age. Almost every theory I studied in college is in the scientific morgue. But the Bible is not there and never will be. Its statements have frequently been denied by the high authorities, but time has always proved that the Bible is right....

[*Dixon mentions three examples in which modern historians questioned Biblical accounts but were later themselves disproved.*]

And now the facts of science against the fancies of all scientific romancers, ancient and modern, are confirming the teachings of Moses and the dim vision of Plato that man began perfect and was wrecked by sin.

---

[10] Paul Gustave Louis Christophe Doré (1832–1883) was a French artist and illustrator. He illustrated an English language Bible published in 1866, as well as other books with religious themes.

[11] 2 Corinthians 11:13–15.

[12] William Gladstone (1809–1898), British statesman, four times Prime Minister, was known for his religious concerns.

In some universities the theological schools are clustered about the halls of history, philosophy, and science. It is time that the order should be reversed. Let the Bible school with teachers who believe in the infallible Book and give Christ preeminence in all realms, be at the center with the halls of history, philosophy, and science clustered about it. Let the Sun, and not the earthly, be the center of God's solar system of truth.

Paradise Restored

In Genesis 6:14 we are told that God commanded Noah to make an ark, and "pitch it within and without with pitch." And the Hebrew scholar is almost startled to find, as he reads Leviticus, that the Hebrew word translated "pitch" in this verse is rendered "atonement" all through Leviticus. It was the pitch which made the ark seaworthy, keeping out the waters of judgment and keeping in Noah and his family. So the atoning blood of Christ it is, which keeps out the waters of judgment and keeps in the subjects of grace. And all through the Bible we can trace the Messianic idea which grows fuller and fuller until it finds complete fulfillment in the "Lamb as it had been slain standing in the midst of the throne."[13] "The Lamb as it had been slain standing" suggests life from the dead, and standing in the midst of the throne suggests royalty. It is the risen, living Christ with the marks of the cross upon him who gives us paradise restored. The perfect civilization in Eden with its perfect environment, perfect employment, perfect rest, perfect law, perfect love, and perfect life, has been restored.

> All hail the power of Jesus' name;
> Let angels prostrate fall;
> Bring forth the royal diadem
> (Ye men of the schools, colleges, and seminaries, and universities)
> AND CROWN HIM LORD OF ALL!

---

[13] Revelation 5:6.

Document 19

"Shall the Fundamentalists Win?"

Harry Emerson Fosdick

1922

Like A. C. Dixon, Harry Emerson Fosdick (1878–1969) was a well-known Baptist minister and writer, but a self-described liberal rather than a fundamentalist. In this sermon, widely noted in its time, Fosdick offered liberal accounts of several of the fundamentals. To the list of their tenets provided in Document 18, he added an expectation many fundamentalists discussed: that Jesus Christ would soon reappear on earth. This view, known more technically as dispensational pre-millennialism, held that human history consisted of different ages, culminating in the return of Christ, after which the millennium (the thousand year reign of Christ) would begin. Immediately preceding Christ's return, conditions on earth would worsen. (Compare this view with the view of the millennium in Document 9.) Fosdick and others were critical of this view because it implied that there was no point in addressing the various social and political problems Christians saw around them. The pre-millennialists, Fosdick said, "sit still and do nothing and expect the world to grow worse and worse until he comes." Not only that, but in anticipation of the coming troubles, fundamentalists tend to want to separate themselves from the sinful world, preserving the virtues or "holiness" that they think God requires of them.

This separatist tendency forms part of the fundamentalist attitude that receives most of Fosdick's attention. Above all, Fosdick criticized the fundamentalists as intolerant. Fosdick's own view, the core of his liberalism, was that revelation was progressive, a point he made several times. The Bible is "the record of the progressive unfolding of the character of God;" and "development is God's way of working out his will." This was a theology well suited to the progressive, reformist politics of the day. In noting that some Christians find it hard to reconcile their traditional beliefs with the new science because they believed that "all truth comes from the one God," Fosdick commented on one of the key doctrines of the Protestant synthesis (see Document 11). In highlighting dispensational pre-millennialism, he commented on an element of conservative or fundamentalist Christianity that remains influential.

"Shall the Fundamentalists Win?"[1] This morning we are to think of the Fundamentalist controversy which threatens to divide the American churches, as though already they were not sufficiently split and riven. A scene, suggestive for our thought, is depicted in the fifth chapter of the book of the Acts, where the Jewish leaders have before them Peter and other of the apostles because they have been preaching Jesus as the Messiah. Moreover, the Jewish leaders propose to slay them, when in opposition Gamaliel speaks: "Refrain from these men, and let them alone: for if this counsel or this work be of men, it will come to nought: but if it be of God, ye cannot overthrow it; lest haply ye be found even to fight against God."[2]

One could easily let his imagination play over this scene and could wonder how history would have come out if Gamaliel's wise tolerance could have controlled the situation. For though the Jewish leaders seemed superficially to concur in Gamaliel's judgment, they nevertheless kept up their bitter antagonism and shut the Christians from the synagogue. We know now that they were mistaken. Christianity, starting within Judaism, was not an innovation to be dreaded; it was the finest flowering out that Judaism ever had. When the Master looked back across his heritage and said, "I am not come to destroy, but to fulfill,"[3] he perfectly described the situation. The Christian ideas of God, the Christian principles of life, the Christian hopes for the future, were all rooted in the Old Testament and grew up out of it, and the Master himself, who called the Jewish temple his Father's house, rejoiced in the glorious heritage of his people's prophets. Only he did believe in a living God. He did not think that God was dead, having finished his words and works with Malachi. Jesus had not simply a historic, but a contemporary God, speaking now, working now, leading his people now from partial into fuller truth. Jesus believed in the progressiveness of revelation, and these Jewish leaders did not understand that. Was this new gospel a real development which they might welcome, or was it an enemy to be cast out? And they called it an enemy and excluded it. One does wonder what might have happened had Gamaliel's wise tolerance been in control.

We, however, face today a situation too similar and too urgent and too much in need of Gamaliel's attitude to spend any time making guesses at supposititious history. Already all of us must have heard about the people who

---

[1] Harry Emerson Fosdick, "Shall the Fundamentalists Win?" *Christian Work* 102 (June 10, 1922): 716–722.

[2] Gamaliel was one of the Jewish leaders. This episode is recounted in Acts 5:34–40.

[3] Matthew 5:17.

call themselves the Fundamentalists. Their apparent intention is to drive out of the evangelical churches men and women of liberal opinions. I speak of them the more freely because there are no two denominations more affected by them than the Baptist and the Presbyterian. We should not identify the Fundamentalists with the conservatives. All Fundamentalists are conservatives, but not all conservatives are Fundamentalists. The best conservatives can often give lessons to the liberals in true liberality of spirit, but the Fundamentalist program is essentially illiberal and intolerant. The Fundamentalists see, and they see truly, that in this last generation there have been strange new movements in Christian thought. A great mass of new knowledge has come into man's possession: new knowledge about the physical universe, its origin, its forces, its laws; new knowledge about human history and in particular about the ways in which the ancient peoples used to think in matters of religion and the methods by which they phrased and explained their spiritual experiences; and new knowledge, also, about other religions and the strangely similar ways in which men's faiths and religious practices have developed everywhere.

Now, there are multitudes of reverent Christians who have been unable to keep this new knowledge in one compartment of their minds and the Christian faith in another. They have been sure that all truth comes from the one God and is his revelation. Not, therefore, from irreverence or caprice or destructive zeal, but for the sake of intellectual and spiritual integrity, that they might really love the Lord their God not only with all their heart and soul and strength, but with all their mind, they have been trying to see this new knowledge in terms of the Christian faith and to see the Christian faith in terms of this new knowledge. Doubtless they have made many mistakes. Doubtless there have been among them reckless radicals gifted with intellectual ingenuity but lacking spiritual depth. Yet the enterprise itself seems to them indispensable to the Christian church. The new knowledge and the old faith cannot be left antagonistic or even disparate, as though a man on Saturday could use one set of regulative ideas for his life and on Sunday could change gear to another altogether. We must be able to think our modern life clear through in Christian terms, and to do that we also must be able to think our Christian life clear through in modern terms.

There is nothing new about the situation. It has happened again and again in history, as, for example, when the stationary earth suddenly began to move, and the universe that had been centered in this planet was centered in the sun around which the planets whirled. Whenever such a situation has arisen, there has been only one way out: the new knowledge and the old faith had to be blended in a new combination. Now the people in this generation who are trying to do this are the liberals, and the Fundamentalists are out on a campaign to shut against them the doors of the Christian fellowship. Shall they be allowed to succeed?

It is interesting to note where the Fundamentalists are driving in their stakes to mark out the deadline of doctrine around the church, across which no one is to pass except on terms of agreement. They insist that we must all believe in the historicity of certain special miracles, preeminently the virgin birth of our Lord; that we must believe in a special theory of inspiration—that the original documents of the scripture, which of course we no longer possess, were inerrantly dictated to men a good deal as a man might dictate to a stenographer; that we must believe in a special theory of the atonement—that the blood of our Lord, shed in a substitutionary death, placates an alienated Deity and makes possible welcome for the returning sinner; and that we must believe in the second coming of our Lord upon the clouds of heaven to set up a millennium here, as the only way in which God can bring history to a worthy denouement. Such are some of the stakes which are being driven, to mark a deadline of doctrine around the church.

If a man is a genuine liberal, his primary protest is not against holding these opinions, although he may well protest against their being considered the fundamentals of Christianity. This is a free country and anybody has a right to hold these opinions, or any others, if he is sincerely convinced of them. The question is: has anybody a right to deny the Christian name to those who differ with him on such points and to shut against them the doors of the Christian fellowship? The Fundamentalists say that this must be done. In this country and on the foreign field they are trying to do it. They have actually endeavored to put on the statute books of a whole state binding laws against teaching modern biology.[4] If they had their way, within the church, they would set up in Protestantism a doctrinal tribunal more rigid than the Pope's. In such an hour, delicate and dangerous, when feelings are bound to run high, I plead this morning the cause of magnanimity and liberality and tolerance of spirit. I would, if I could reach their ears, say to the Fundamentalists about the liberals what Gamaliel said to the Jews, "Refrain from these men, and let them alone: for if this counsel or this work be of men, it will come to nought: but if it be of God ye cannot overthrow it; lest haply ye be found even to fight against God."[5]

---

[4] Such efforts were made in several states. The legislature of Tennessee passed such a law. It became the basis for the Scopes Trial, in which John Scopes, a high school teacher, was tried and convicted for teaching evolution in 1925.
[5] Acts 5:38.

That we may be entirely candid and concrete and may not lose ourselves in any fog of generalities, let us this morning take two or three of these Fundamentalist items and see with reference to them what the situation is in the Christian churches. Too often we preachers have failed to talk frankly enough about the differences of opinion that exist among evangelical Christians, although everybody knows that they are there. Let us face this morning some of the differences of opinion with which somehow we must deal.

We may well begin with the vexed and mooted question of the virgin birth of our Lord. I know people in the Christian churches—ministers, missionaries, laymen, devoted lovers of the Lord and servants of the Gospel—who, alike as they are in their personal devotion to the Master, hold quite different points of view about a matter like the virgin birth. Here, for example, is one point of view: that the virgin birth is to be accepted as historical fact; it actually happened; there was no other way for a personality like the Master to come into this world except by a special biological miracle. That is one point of view, and many are the gracious and beautiful souls who hold it. But, side by side with them in the evangelical churches is a group of equally loyal and reverent people who would say that the virgin birth is not to be accepted as an historic fact. To believe in virgin birth as an explanation of great personality is one of the familiar ways in which the ancient world was accustomed to account for unusual superiority.

Many people suppose that only once in history do we run across a record of supernatural birth. Upon the contrary, stories of miraculous generation are among the commonest traditions of antiquity. Especially is this true about the founders of great religions. According to the records of their faiths, Buddha and Zoroaster[6] and Lao-Tzu[7] and Mahavira[8] were all supernaturally born. Moses, Confucius and Mohammed are the only great founders of religions in history to whom miraculous birth is not attributed. That is to say, when a personality arose so high that men adored him, the ancient world attributed his superiority to some special divine influence in his generation, and they commonly phrased their faith in terms of miraculous birth. So Pythagoras[9] was called virgin born, and Plato, and Augustus Caesar, and many more.

---

[6] The founder of Zoroastrianism, a religion from the ancient near east.
[7] The founder of Taoism, an ancient Chinese religious and philosophical movement.
[8] A sacred figure in Jainism.
[9] An ancient Greek philosopher and mathematician.

Knowing this, there are within the evangelical churches large groups of people whose opinion about our Lord's coming would run as follows: those first disciples adored Jesus—as we do; when they thought about his coming they were sure that he came specially from God—as we are; this adoration and conviction they associated with God's special influence and intention in his birth—as we do; but they phrased it in terms of a biological miracle that our modem minds cannot use. So far from thinking that they have given up anything vital in the New Testament's attitude toward Jesus, these Christians remember that the two men who contributed most to the church's thought of the divine meaning of the Christ were Paul and John, who never even distantly allude to the virgin birth.

Here in the Christian churches are these two groups of people, and the question that the Fundamentalists raise is this: shall one of them throw the other out? Has intolerance any contribution to make to this situation? Will it persuade anybody of anything? Is not the Christian church large enough to hold within her hospitable fellowship people who differ on points like this, and agree to differ until the fuller truth be manifested? The Fundamentalists say not. They say that the liberals must go. Well, if the Fundamentalists should succeed, then out of the Christian church would go some of the best Christian life and consecration of this generation—multitudes of men and women, devout and reverent Christians, who need the church and whom the church needs.

Consider another matter on which there is a sincere difference of opinion among evangelical Christians: the inspiration of the Bible. One point of view is that the original documents of the scripture were inerrantly dictated by God to men. Whether we deal with the story of creation or the list of the dukes of Edom or the narratives of Solomon's reign or the Sermon on the Mount or the thirteenth chapter of First Corinthians, they all came in the same way and they all came as no other book ever came. They were inerrantly dictated; everything there—scientific opinions, medical theories, historical judgments, as well as spiritual insight—is infallible. That is one idea of the Bible's inspiration. But side by side with those who hold it, lovers of the Book as much as they, are multitudes of people who never think about the Bible so. Indeed, that static and mechanical theory of inspiration seems to them a positive peril to the spiritual life. The Koran similarly has been regarded by Mohammedans as having been infallibly written in heaven before it came to earth. But the Koran enshrines the theological and ethical ideas of Arabia at the time when it was written. God an Oriental monarch, fatalistic submission to his will as man's chief duty, the use of force on unbelievers, polygamy, slavery—they are all in the Koran. When it was written, the Koran was ahead of the day but, petrified by an artificial idea of inspiration, it has become a millstone about the neck of Mohammedanism. When one turns from the Koran to the Bible, he finds this interesting situation. All of these ideas, which we dislike in the Koran, are somewhere in the Bible. Conceptions from which we now send missionaries to convert Mohammedans are to be found in the Bible. There one can find God thought of as an Oriental monarch; there too are patriarchal polygamy, and slave systems, and the use of force on unbelievers.

Only in the Bible these elements are not final; they are always being superseded; revelation is progressive. The thought of God moves out from Oriental kingship to compassionate fatherhood; treatment of unbelievers moves out from the use of force to the appeals of love; polygamy gives way to monogamy; slavery, never explicitly condemned before the New Testament closes, is nevertheless being undermined by ideas that in the end, like dynamite, will blast its foundations to pieces. Repeatedly one runs on verses like this: "it was said to them of old time … but I say unto you;"[10] "God, having of old time spoken unto the fathers in the prophets by divers portions and in divers manners, hath at the end of these days spoken unto us in his Son;"[11] "The times of ignorance therefore God overlooked; but now he commandeth men that they should all everywhere repent;"[12] and over the doorway of the New Testament into the Christian world stand the words of Jesus: "When he, the Spirit of truth, is come, he will guide you into all truth."[13] That is to say, finality in the Koran is behind; finality in the Bible is ahead. We have not reached it. We cannot yet compass all of it. God is leading us out toward it. There are multitudes of Christians, then, who think, and rejoice as they think, of the Bible as the record of the progressive unfolding of the character of God to his people from early primitive days until the great unveiling in Christ; to them the Book is more inspired and more inspiring than ever it was before. To go back to a mechanical and static theory of inspiration would mean to them the loss of some of the most vital elements in their spiritual experience and in their appreciation of the Book.

Here in the Christian church today are these two groups, and the question the Fundamentalists have raised is this: shall one of them drive the other out? Do we think the cause of Jesus Christ will be furthered by that? If he should

---

[10] Matthew 5:27–28.
[11] Hebrew 1:1–2.
[12] Acts 17:30.
[13] John 16:13.

walk through the ranks of this congregation this morning, can we imagine him claiming as his own those who hold one idea of inspiration, and sending from him into outer darkness those who hold another? You cannot fit the Lord Christ into that Fundamentalist mold. The church would better judge his judgment. For in the Middle West the Fundamentalists have had their way in some communities, and a Christian minister tells us the consequence. He says that the educated people are looking for their religion outside the churches.

Consider another matter upon which there is a serious and sincere difference of opinion between evangelical Christians: the second coming of our Lord. The second coming was the early Christian phrasing of hope. No one in the ancient world had ever thought, as we do, of development, progress, gradual change, as God's way of working out his will in human life and institutions. They thought of human history as a series of ages succeeding one another with abrupt suddenness. The Greco-Roman world gave the names of metals to the ages—gold, silver, bronze, iron. The Hebrews had their ages too—the original Paradise in which man began, the cursed world in which man now lives, the blessed Messianic Kingdom some day suddenly to appear on the clouds of heaven. It was the Hebrew way of expressing hope for the victory of God and righteousness. When the Christians came they took over that phrasing of expectancy and the New Testament is aglow with it. The preaching of the apostles thrills with the glad announcement, "Christ is coming!"

In the evangelical churches today there are differing views of this matter. One view is that Christ is literally coming, externally on the clouds of heaven, to set up his kingdom here. I never heard that teaching in my youth at all. It has always had a new resurrection when desperate circumstances came and man's only hope seemed to lie in divine intervention. It is not strange, then, that during these chaotic, catastrophic years there has been a fresh rebirth of this old phrasing of expectancy. "Christ is coming!" seems to many Christians the central message of the gospel. In the strength of it some of them are doing great service for the world. But, unhappily, many so overemphasize it that they outdo anything the ancient Hebrews or the ancient Christians ever did. They sit still and do nothing and expect the world to grow worse and worse until he comes.

Side by side with these to whom the second coming is a literal expectation, another group exists in the evangelical churches. They, too, say, "Christ is coming!" They say it with all their hearts; but they are not thinking of an external arrival on the clouds. They have assimilated as part of the divine revelation the exhilarating insight which these recent generations have given to us, that development is God's way of working out his will. They see that the most desirable elements in human life have come through the method of development. Man's music has developed from the rhythmic noise of beaten sticks until we have in melody and harmony possibilities once undreamed. Man's painting has developed from the crude outlines of the cavemen until in line and color we have achieved unforeseen results and possess latent beauties yet unfolded. Man's architecture has developed from the crude huts of primitive men until our cathedrals and business buildings reveal alike an incalculable advance and an unimaginable future. Development does seem to be the way in which God works. And these Christians, when they say that Christ is coming, mean that, slowly it may be, but surely, his will and principles will be worked out by God's grace in human life and institutions, until "he shall see of the travail of his soul, and shall be satisfied."[14]

These two groups exist in the Christian churches, and the question raised by the Fundamentalists is: shall one of them drive the other out? Will that get us anywhere? Multitudes of young men and women at this season of the year are graduating from our schools of learning, thousands of them Christians who may make us older ones ashamed by the sincerity of their devotion to God's will on earth. They are not thinking in ancient terms that leave ideas of progress out. They cannot think in those terms. There could be no greater tragedy than that the Fundamentalists should shut the door of the Christian fellowship against such.

I do not believe for one moment that the Fundamentalists are going to succeed. Nobody's intolerance can contribute anything to the solution of the situation we have described. If, then, the Fundamentalists have no solution of the problem, where may we expect to find it? In two concluding comments let us consider our reply to that inquiry.

The first element that is necessary is a spirit of tolerance and Christian liberty. When will the world learn that intolerance solves no problems? This is not a lesson which the Fundamentalists alone need to learn; the liberals also need to learn it. Speaking, as I do, from the viewpoint of liberal opinions, let me say that if some young, fresh mind here this morning is holding new ideas, has fought his way through, it may be by intellectual and spiritual struggle, to novel positions, and is tempted to be intolerant about old opinions, offensively to condescend to those who hold them and to be harsh in judgment on them, he may well remember that people who held those old opinions have given the world some of the noblest character and the most rememberable service that it

14 Isaiah 53:11.

ever has been blessed with, and that we of the younger generation will prove our case best, not by controversial intolerance, but by producing, with our new opinions, something of the depth and strength, nobility and beauty of character that in other times were associated with other thoughts. It was a wise liberal, the most adventurous man of his day—Paul the apostle—who said, "Knowledge puffs up, but love builds up."[15]

Nevertheless, it is true that just now the Fundamentalists are giving us one of the worst exhibitions of bitter intolerance that the churches of this country have ever seen. As one watches them and listens to them, he remembers the remark of General Armstrong of Hampton Institute: "Cantankerousness is worse than heterodoxy."[16] There are many opinions in the field of modern controversy concerning which I am not sure whether they are right or wrong, but there is one thing I am sure of: courtesy and kindliness and tolerance and humility and fairness are right. Opinions may be mistaken; love never is.

...My friends, nothing in all the world is so much worth thinking of as God, Christ, the Bible, sin and salvation, the divine purposes for humankind, life everlasting. But you cannot challenge the dedicated thinking of this generation to these sublime themes upon any such terms as are laid down by an intolerant church.

The second element which is needed, if we are to reach a happy solution of this problem, is a clear insight into the main issues of modern Christianity and a sense of penitent shame that the Christian church should be quarreling over little matters when the world is dying of great needs. If, during the war, when the nations were wrestling upon the very brink of hell and at times all seemed lost, you chanced to hear two men in an altercation about some minor matter of sectarian denominationalism, could you restrain your indignation?...

Consider all the multitudes of men who so need God, and then think of Christian churches making of themselves a cockpit of controversy when there is not a single thing at stake in the controversy on which depends the salvation of human souls. That is the trouble with this whole business. So much of it does not matter! And there is one thing that does matter—more than anything else in all the world—that men in their personal lives and in their social relationships should know Jesus Christ.

Just a week ago I received a letter from a friend in Asia Minor. He says that they are killing the Armenians yet; that the Turkish deportations still are going

---

[15] 1 Corinthians 8:1.

[16] Samuel C. Armstrong was a Civil War officer who led Black troops. After the war, he started and lead the Hampton Institute, a school for freemen.

on; that lately they crowded Christian men, women and children into a conventicle of worship and burned them together in the house where they had prayed to their Father and to ours. During the war, when it was good propaganda to stir up our bitter hatred against the enemy, we heard of such atrocities, but not now! Two weeks ago Great Britain, shocked and stirred by what is going on in Armenia, did ask the government of the United States to join her in investigating the atrocities and trying to help. Our government said that it was not any of our business at all. The present world situation smells to heaven! And now in the presence of colossal problems, which must be solved in Christ's name and for Christ's sake, the Fundamentalists propose to drive out from the Christian churches all the consecrated souls who do not agree with their theory of inspiration. What immeasurable folly!

Well, they are not going to do it; certainly not in this vicinity. I do not even know in this congregation whether anybody has been tempted to be a Fundamentalist. Never in this church have I caught one accent of intolerance. God keep us always so and ever increasing areas of the Christian fellowship: intellectually hospitable, open-minded, liberty-loving, fair, tolerant, not with the tolerance of indifference as though we did not care about the faith, but because always our major emphasis is upon the weightier matters of the law.

Document 20

"The Bible," *Christianity and Liberalism*
J. Gresham Machen
1923

J. Gresham Machen (1881–1937) was the last of a long line of Presbyterian theologians at Princeton who thought of themselves as upholding the traditional teachings of the denomination. In chapter four of Christianity and Liberalism *(printed here almost in its entirety), Machen asserted that the Bible as both God's revelation and as inerrant was essential to Christianity. He contrasted this view with the view of religious liberals (e.g. Harry Emerson Fosdick, see document 19), who he argued placed human experience at the center of religion. In noting that nature was part of God's revelation, Machen echoes a traditional view, which we have encountered in detail in Palmer, "Baconianism and the Bible"(see document 11). Writing several decades after Palmer, however, in a world of increased secularism and scientific influence (see documents 14 and 16), Machen felt the need to argue for the authority of the Bible, an authority Palmer could take for granted. The writings of Machen, Fosdick, and Dixon included in this collection were part of the modernist-fundamentalist controversy of the first decades of the twentieth century. In large measure, that controversy still defines America's religious world and influences our politics.*

Chapter 4: "The Bible"

Modern liberalism, it has been observed so far, has lost sight of the two great presuppositions of the Christian message—the living God, and the fact of sin. The liberal doctrine of God and the liberal doctrine of man are both diametrically opposite to the Christian view. But the divergence concerns not only the presuppositions of the message, but also the message itself.

The Christian message has come to us through the Bible. What shall we think about this Book in which the message is contained?

According to the Christian view, the Bible contains an account of a revelation from God to man, which is found nowhere else. It is true, the Bible also contains a confirmation and a wonderful enrichment of the revelations which are given also by the things that God has made and by the conscience of man. "The heavens declare the glory of God; and the firmament showeth his handywork"[1]—these words are a confirmation of the revelation of God in nature; "all have sinned and fall short of the glory of God"[2]—these words are a confirmation of what is attested by the conscience. But in addition to such reaffirmations of what might conceivably be learned elsewhere—as a matter of fact, because of men's blindness, even so much is learned elsewhere only in comparatively obscure fashion—the Bible also contains an account of a revelation which is absolutely new. That new revelation concerns the way by which sinful man can come into communion with the living God.

The way was opened, according to the Bible, by an act of God, when, almost nineteen hundred years ago, outside the walls of Jerusalem, the eternal Son was offered as a sacrifice for the sins of men. To that one great event the whole Old Testament looks forward, and in that one event the whole of the New Testament finds its center and core. Salvation then, according to the Bible, is not something that was discovered, but something that happened. Hence appears the uniqueness of the Bible. All the ideas of Christianity might be discovered in some other religion, yet there would be in that other religion no Christianity. For Christianity depends, not upon a complex of ideas, but upon the narration of an event. Without that event, the world, in the Christian view, is altogether dark, and humanity is lost under the guilt of sin. There can be no salvation by the discovery of eternal truth, for eternal truth brings naught but despair, because of sin. But a new face has been put upon life by the blessed thing that God did when He offered up His only begotten Son.

An objection is sometimes offered against this view of the contents of the Bible. Must we, it is said, depend upon what happened so long ago? Does salvation wait upon the examination of musty records? Is the trained student of Palestinian history the modern priest without whose gracious intervention no one can see God? Can we not find, instead, a salvation that is independent of history, a salvation that depends only on what is with us here and now?

The objection is not devoid of weight. But it ignores one of the primary evidences for the truth of the gospel record. That evidence is found in Christian experience. Salvation does depend upon what happened long ago, but the event of long ago has effects that continue until today. We are told in the New Testament that Jesus offered Himself as a sacrifice for the sins of those who should believe on Him. That is a record of a past event. But we can

---

[1] Psalm 9:1
[2] Romans 3:23

make trial of it today, and making trial of it we find it to be true. We are told in the New Testament that on a certain morning long ago Jesus rose from the dead. That again is a record of a past event. But again we can make trial of it, and making trial of it we discover that Jesus is truly a living Savior today.

But at this point a fatal error lies in wait. It is one of the root errors of modern liberalism. Christian experience, we have just said, is useful as confirming the gospel message. But because it is necessary, many men have jumped to the conclusion that it is all that is necessary. Having a present experience of Christ in the heart, may we not, it is said, hold that experience no matter what history may tell us as to the events of the first Easter morning? May we not make ourselves altogether independent of the results of Biblical criticism? No matter what sort of man history may tell us Jesus of Nazareth actually was, no matter what history may say about the real meaning of His death or about the story of His alleged resurrection, may we not continue to experience the presence of Christ in our souls?

The trouble is that the experience thus maintained is not Christian experience. Religious experience it may be, but Christian experience it certainly is not. For Christian experience depends absolutely upon an event. The Christian says to himself: "I have meditated upon the problem of becoming right with God, I have tried to produce a righteousness that will stand in His sight; but when I heard the gospel message I learned that what I had weakly striven to accomplish had been accomplished by the Lord Jesus Christ when He died for me on the Cross and completed His redeeming work by the glorious resurrection. If the thing has not yet been done, if I merely have an idea of its accomplishment, then I am of all men most miserable, for I am still in my sins. My Christian life, then, depends altogether upon the truth of the New Testament record."

Christian experience is rightly used when it confirms the documentary evidence. But it can never possibly provide a substitute for the documentary evidence. We know that the gospel story is true partly because of the early date of the documents in which it appears, the evidence as to their authorship, the internal evidence of their truth, the impossibility of explaining them as being based upon deception or upon myth. This evidence is gloriously confirmed by present experience, which adds to the documentary evidence that wonderful directness and immediacy of conviction which delivers us from fear. Christian experience is rightly used when it helps to convince us that the events narrated in the New Testament actually did occur; but it can never enable us to be Christians whether the events occurred or not. It is a fair flower, and should be prized as a gift of God. But cut it from its root in the blessed Book, and it soon withers away and dies.

Thus the revelation of which an account is contained in the Bible embraces not only a reaffirmation of eternal truths—itself necessary because the truths have been obscured by the blinding effect of sin—but also a revelation which sets forth the meaning of an act of God.

The contents of the Bible, then, are unique. But another fact about the Bible is also important. The Bible might contain an account of a true revelation from God, and yet the account be full of error. Before the full authority of the Bible can be established, therefore, it is necessary to add to the Christian doctrine of revelation the Christian doctrine of inspiration. The latter doctrine means that the Bible not only is an account of important things, but that the account itself is true, the writers having been so preserved from error, despite a full maintenance of their habits of thought and expression, that the resulting Book is the "infallible rule of faith and practice."[3]

This doctrine of "plenary inspiration"[4] has been made the subject of persistent misrepresentation....

As a matter of fact, the doctrine of plenary inspiration does not deny the individuality of the Biblical writers; it does not ignore their use of ordinary means for acquiring information; it does not involve any lack of interest in the historical situations which gave rise to the Biblical books. What it does deny is the presence of error in the Bible. It supposes that the Holy Spirit so informed the minds of the Biblical writers that they were kept from falling into the errors that mar all other books. The Bible might contain an account of a genuine revelation of God, and yet not contain a true account. But according to the doctrine of inspiration, the account is as a matter of fact a true account; the Bible is an "infallible rule of faith and practice."

Certainly that is a stupendous claim, and it is no wonder that it has been attacked. But the trouble is that the attack is not always fair. If the liberal preacher objected to the doctrine of plenary inspiration on the ground that as a matter of fact there are errors in the Bible, he might be right and he might be

---

[3] This is probably a reference to Machen's predecessor at Princeton, A. A. Hodge (1823–1886). Chapter three of Hodge's *Outlines of Theology* (1860) is "The Rule of Faith and Practice," which argues that "the scriptures of the Old and New Testaments, having been given by inspiration of god, are the all-sufficient and only rule of faith and practice, and judge of controversies." Hodge spends much of the chapter criticizing the "Romish" or Roman Catholic approach to the Bible.

[4] Machen defines this term in the next paragraph.

wrong, but at any rate the discussion would be conducted on the proper ground. But too often the preacher desires to avoid the delicate question of errors in the Bible—a question which might give offence to the rank and file— and prefers to speak merely against "mechanical" theories of inspiration, the theory of "dictation," the "superstitious use of the Bible as a talisman," or the like. It all sounds to the plain man as though it were very harmless. Does not the liberal preacher say that the Bible is "divine"—indeed that it is the more divine because it is the more human? What could be more edifying than that? But of course such appearances are deceptive. A Bible that is full of error is certainly divine in the modern pantheizing sense of "divine," according to which God is just another name for the course of the world with all its imperfections and all its sin. But the God whom the Christian worships is a God of truth.

It must be admitted that there are many Christians who do not accept the doctrine of plenary inspiration. That doctrine is denied not only by liberal opponents of Christianity, but also by many true Christian men. There are many Christian men in the modern Church who find in the origin of Christianity no mere product of evolution but a real entrance of the creative power of God, who depend for their salvation, not at all upon their own efforts to lead the Christ life, but upon the atoning blood of Christ—there are many men in the modern Church who thus accept the central message of the Bible and yet believe that the message has come to us merely on the authority of trustworthy witnesses unaided in their literary work by any supernatural guidance of the Spirit of God. There are many who believe that the Bible is right at the central point, in its account of the redeeming work of Christ, and yet believe that it contains many errors. Such men are not really liberals, but Christians; because they have accepted as true the message upon which Christianity depends. A great gulf separates them from those who reject the supernatural act of God with which Christianity stands or falls.

It is another question, however, whether the mediating view of the Bible which is thus maintained is logically tenable, the trouble being that our Lord Himself seems to have held the high view of the Bible which is here being rejected. Certainly it is another question—and a question which the present writer would answer with an emphatic negative—whether the panic about the Bible,[5] which gives rise to such concessions, is at all justified by the facts. If the

---

[5] Machen referred here to what some saw as attacks on the authority of the Bible because of the claims of modern science and the results of the "higher criticism" that subjected the Bible to philological and historical analysis (see Documents 14, 16, 18).

Christian make full use of his Christian privileges, he finds the seat of authority in the whole Bible, which he regards as no mere word of man but as the very Word of God.

Very different is the view of modern liberalism. The modern liberal rejects not only the doctrine of plenary inspiration, but even such respect for the Bible as would be proper over against any ordinarily trustworthy book. But what is substituted for the Christian view of the Bible? What is the liberal view as to the seat of authority in religion?

The impression is sometimes produced that the modern liberal substitutes for the authority of the Bible the authority of Christ. He cannot accept, he says, what he regards as the perverse moral teaching of the Old Testament or the sophistical arguments of Paul. But he regards himself as being the true Christian because, rejecting the rest of the Bible, he depends upon Jesus alone.

This impression, however, is utterly false. The modern liberal does not really hold to the authority of Jesus. Even if he did so, indeed, he would still be impoverishing greatly his knowledge of God and of the way of salvation. The words of Jesus, spoken during His earthly ministry, could hardly contain all that we need to know about God and about the way of salvation; for the meaning of Jesus' redeeming work could hardly be fully set forth before that work was done. It could be set forth indeed by way of prophecy, and as a matter of fact it was so set forth by Jesus even in the days of His flesh. But the full explanation could naturally be given only after the work was done. And such was actually the divine method. It is doing despite,[6] not only to the Spirit of God, but also to Jesus Himself, to regard the teaching of the Holy Spirit, given through the apostles, as at all inferior in authority to the teaching of Jesus.

As a matter of fact, however, the modern liberal does not hold fast even to the authority of Jesus. Certainly he does not accept the words of Jesus as they are recorded in the Gospels. For among the recorded words of Jesus are to be found just those things which are most abhorrent to the modern liberal Church, and in His recorded words Jesus also points forward to the fuller revelation which was afterwards to be given through His apostles. Evidently, therefore, those words of Jesus which are to be regarded as authoritative by modern liberalism must first be selected from the mass of the recorded words by a critical process. The critical process is certainly very difficult, and the suspicion often arises that the critic is retaining as genuine words of the historical Jesus only those words which conform to his own preconceived

---

[6] Giving insult or treating contemptuously

ideas. But even after the sifting process has been completed, the liberal scholar is still unable to accept as authoritative all the sayings of Jesus; he must finally admit that even the "historical" Jesus as reconstructed by modern historians said some things that are untrue.

So much is usually admitted. But, it is maintained, although not everything that Jesus said is true, His central "life-purpose" is still to be regarded as regulative for the Church. But what then was the life-purpose of Jesus? According to the shortest, and if modern criticism be accepted the earliest of the Gospels, the Son of Man "came not to be ministered unto, but to minister, and to give his life a ransom for many" (Mark 10:45). Here the vicarious death is put as the "life-purpose" of Jesus. Such an utterance must of course be pushed aside by the modern liberal Church. The truth is that the life-purpose of Jesus discovered by modern liberalism is not the life purpose of the real Jesus, but merely represents those elements in the teaching of Jesus—isolated and misinterpreted—which happen to agree with the modern program. It is not Jesus, then, who is the real authority, but the modern principle by which the selection within Jesus' recorded teaching has been made. Certain isolated ethical principles of the Sermon on the Mount are accepted, not at all because they are teachings of Jesus, but because they agree with modern ideas.

It is not true at all, then, that modern liberalism is based upon the authority of Jesus. It is obliged to reject a vast deal that is absolutely essential in Jesus' example and teaching—notably His consciousness of being the heavenly Messiah. The real authority, for liberalism, can only be "the Christian consciousness" or "Christian experience." But how shall the findings of the Christian consciousness be established? Surely not by a majority vote of the organized Church. Such a method would obviously do away with all liberty of conscience. The only authority, then, can be individual experience; truth can only be that which "helps" the individual man. Such an authority is obviously no authority at all; for individual experience is endlessly diverse, and when once truth is regarded only as that which works at any particular time, it ceases to be truth. The result is an abysmal skepticism.

The Christian man, on the other hand, finds in the Bible the very Word of God. Let it not be said that dependence upon a book is a dead or an artificial thing. The Reformation of the sixteenth century was founded upon the authority of the Bible, yet it set the world aflame. Dependence upon a word of man would be slavish, but dependence upon God's word is life. Dark and gloomy would be the world, if we were left to our own devices and had no blessed Word of God. The Bible, to the Christian is not a burdensome law, but the very Magna Charta of Christian liberty.

It is no wonder, then, that liberalism is totally different from Christianity, for the foundation is different. Christianity is founded upon the Bible. It bases upon the Bible both its thinking and its life. Liberalism on the other hand is founded upon the shifting emotions of sinful men.

Document 21

Address to the National Conference of Catholic Charities

Franklin D. Roosevelt

1933

Franklin Roosevelt won election in 1932 with a coalition that included Catholics. In this speech, he addressed a major Catholic organization a year after the election. In his talk, Roosevelt used the term "social justice," a term that Pope Pius XI had used frequently in his encyclical "Quadragesimo Anno," "On Reconstruction of the Social Order," issued a few years before, in 1931. For example, the Pope had written "it is contrary to social justice when, for the sake of personal gain and without regard for the common good, wages and salaries are excessively lowered or raised." Roosevelt's use of the term "social justice" was just one of the ways in which he assimilated Catholic teaching and charitable work to the efforts of his own "New Deal," arguing that both were doing God's work on earth. Roosevelt noted, however, two ways in which private charity was superior to public welfare: it is more personal; and operates in an awareness that spiritual rather than material values are most important, making religion "essential to permanent progress."

Cardinal Hayes, Your Excellency, ladies and gentlemen: [1]

Coming down through the crowd this evening, my old friend, Monsignor Keegan, paid me the nicest compliment I have had since the fourth of March because he said, "Remember, way back before the fourth of March, when you said you would come to this dinner in October? And now you have come."

In the midst of problems of material things, in the machine age of invention, of finance, of international suspicion and renewed armaments, every

---

[1] Franklin D. Roosevelt: "Address to the National Conference of Catholic Charities," October 4, 1933. Online by Gerhard Peters and John T. Woolley, *The American Presidency Project.* http://www.presidency.ucsb.edu/ws/?pid=14522.

one of us must gain satisfaction and strength in the knowledge that social justice is becoming an ever-growing factor and influence in almost every part of the world today. With every passing year I become more confident that humanity is moving forward to the practical application of the teachings of Christianity as they affect the individual lives of men and women everywhere.

It is fitting that this annual National Conference of Catholic Charities should celebrate also, at the same time, the centennial of the Society of St. Vincent de Paul.[2] I like to remember the day a hundred years ago, the taunt of atheists, the taunt of the enemies of the Christian religion in the Paris of 1833, when they demanded of the churches, "Show us your works." Yes, I like to remember it because of the acceptance of that challenge, and the decision to show that Christianity was not dead, and that the deeds of Christians were in accordance with their faith. This one Society, this past year, in their task of visitation and relief of the poor in their own homes and in hospitals and institutions, aided more than one hundred and fifty thousand families within the borders of our country; and, with other great organizations of men and women connected with all the churches in all the land, it is working with similar unselfishness for the alleviation of human suffering and the righting of human wrong. When I think of this I am confirmed in my deep belief that God is marching on.

Monsignor Keegan has mentioned the fact that seven months ago this very day, standing at the portals of the capitol at Washington, about to assume the responsibilities of the Presidency, I told the people of America that we were going to face facts, no matter how hard and how difficult those facts might be, and that it was my firm belief that the only thing we had to fear was fear itself.

I believed then—and I know now—that our people would support definite action that sought the goal of giving every man his due. Leadership, I have tried to give, but the great and the outstanding fact, my friends, has been the response—the wholehearted response—of America. As we have recaptured and rekindled our pioneering spirit, we have insisted that it shall always be a spirit of justice, a spirit of teamwork, a spirit of sacrifice, and, above all, a spirit of neighborliness.

We have sought to adjust the processes of industrial and agricultural life, and in so doing we have sought to view the picture as a whole. Revival of industry, redemption of agriculture, reconstruction of banking, development of public works, the lifting of crushing debt—all these in every part of the

---

[2] St. Vincent de Paul (1581–1660) was a Catholic priest famous for his work with the poor.

Nation call for a willingness to sacrifice individual gains, to work together for the public welfare and for the success of a broad national program of recovery. We have to have courage and discipline and vision to blaze the new trails in life; but underlying all our efforts is the conviction that men cannot live unto themselves alone. A democracy, the right kind of democracy, is bound together by the ties of neighborliness.

That tie, my friends, has been the guiding spirit of your work for the sick, for the children in need, and for the aged and friendless. And you who have participated in the actual day-to-day work of practical and useful charity understand well that no program of recovery can suddenly restore all our people to self-support. This is the time when you and I know that though we have proceeded a portion of the way, the longer, harder part still lies ahead; we must redouble our efforts to care for those who must still depend upon relief, to prevent the disintegration of home life, and to stand by the victims of the depression until it is definitely past.

The Federal Government has inaugurated new measures of relief on a vast scale, but the Federal Government cannot, and does not intend to, take over the whole job. Many times we have insisted that every community and every State must first do its share.

Out of this picture we are developing a new science of social treatment and rehabilitation—working it out through an unselfish partnership, a partnership between great church and private social service agencies and the agencies of Government itself. From the point of view of fixing responsibilities, the prevention of overlapping, the prevention of waste, and the coordination of effort, we are, all of us, making enormous strides with every passing day. But back of that cooperative leadership that is showing itself so splendidly in every part of the country, there are two other vital reasons for the maintenance of the efforts of the churches and other non-governmental groups in every part of the land.

The first of these is that much as you and I strive for the broad principles of social justice, the actual application of these principles is of necessity an individual thing—a thing that touches individual lives and individual families. No governmental organization in all history has been able to keep the human touch to the same extent as church and private effort. Government can do a great many things better than private associations or citizens, but in the last analysis, success in this kind of personal work in which you are engaged depends upon personal contact between neighbor and neighbor.

The other reason lies in the fact that the people of the United States still recognize, and, I believe, recognize with a firmer faith than ever before, that spiritual values count in the long run more than material values. Those people in other lands, and I say this advisedly, those in other lands who have sought by edict or by law to eliminate the right of mankind to believe in God and to practice that belief, have, in every known case, discovered sooner or later that they are tilting in vain against an inherent, essential, undying quality, indeed necessity, of the human race—a quality and a necessity which in every century have proved an essential to permanent progress—and I speak of religion.

Clear thinking and earnest effort and sincere faith will result in thoroughgoing support throughout the whole Nation of efforts such as yours. The spirit of our people has not been blunted; it has not been daunted. It has come through the trials of these days unafraid. We have ventured and we have won; we shall venture further and we shall win again. Yes, the traditions of a great people have been enriched. In our measures of recovery and of relief we have preserved all that is best in our history and we are building thereon a new structure—strong and firm and permanent.

I can never express in words what the loyalty and trust of the Nation have meant to me. Not for a moment have I doubted that we would climb out of the valley of gloom.[3] Always I have been certain that we would conquer, because the spirit of America springs from faith—faith in the beloved institutions of our land, and a true and abiding faith in the divine guidance of God.

---

[3] Psalm 23:4: "Yea, though I walk through the valley of the shadow of death, I will fear no evil: for thou art with me; thy rod and thy staff they comfort me."

Document 22

"Can a Christian Be a Communist?"
Martin Luther King, Jr.
1962

A Christian cannot be a communist, King argues, because communism as a philosophical system denies the existence of anything beyond the material realm and, as a related principle, denies the existence of universal moral truth. Worst of all, it denies the essential quality of humanity: the freedom of the individual soul. For King, therefore, communism was a dangerous system, for it denied the only reasonable basis upon which men could relate to one another with any kind of dignity. Yet although a Christian cannot be a communist, King declares that communism "is the only serious rival of Christianity" in the modern world because it does two things well and rightly that the majority of American Christians either fail to do, or do badly. Indeed, he says "It may well be that the success of communism is due to the failure of Christians to live up to the basic principles of Christianity."

The first lesson to be learned from communism, King argues, is that Christians must take seriously the cries of the oppressed and assert themselves in the name of justice wherever it is lacking. The second lesson is that Christians must be as fiercely committed to spreading the Gospel message of freedom and brotherhood as communists are to spreading their own doctrines. To succeed in either of these areas, King observed, Christians must live their faith not only on Sundays but on weekdays, working not simply to secure material goods but to serve others in their professions, help the hungry and ill-housed poor, and defend human freedom. The sermon ends with a hopeful vision: if American Christians will meet the challenge of communism with a faith-based zeal for justice, they will "make this old world a new world"—a promise reminiscent of Winthrop's claims of nearly four hundred years earlier (Document 1).

The following text is taken from an audio recording of the service. Any typographical errors are from the original source and therefore have not been changed.

[*Gap in tape*] elicit your undivided attention as I attempt to discuss with you one of the vital issues of our day. It is a rather controversial subject, and yet I think it is the responsibility of the preacher to keep his congregation informed on the major issues of the day, to bring the kind of tenets of our gospel to bear on these various issues. Now, this will not be the traditional sermon with a text, and you may feel when it's over that it's more of an academic lecture than a moving sermon. But I think it is important for me to discuss the question of communism with you, and so I am using as a subject from which to preach, "Can a Christian Be a Communist?"

Now, there are at least three reasons why I feel obligated as a Christian minister to talk to you about communism. The first reason grows out of the fact that communism is having widespread influence in the contemporary world. Like a mighty tidal wave, it has moved through China, Russia, Eastern Europe, and now has rolled within ninety miles of the borders of our nation. More than a billion of the peoples of the world believe in communism. And many of these people have accepted it as a new religion, and they are willing to surrender their total being to this system. A force so potent cannot be ignored.

A second reason that I feel compelled to talk about communism this morning is that it is the only serious rival of Christianity. The other historic and great religions of the world such as Judaism, Mohammedanism, Buddhism, and Hinduism may stand as alternatives to Christianity. But for the most formidable competitor that Christianity faces in the world today, we must look to communism. No one conversant with the hard facts of modern life can deny the truth that communism is Christianity's most serious rival.

The third reason that I feel compelled to talk about communism this morning is that it is unfair and certainly unscientific to condemn a system of thought without knowing what that system of thought says and without knowing why it is wrong and why it is evil. So, for these reasons, I choose to talk about this troubling issue.

Now, let us begin by answering the question which our sermon topic raises: Can a Christian be a communist? I answer that question with an emphatic "no." These two philosophies are diametrically opposed. The basic philosophy of Christianity is unalterably opposed to the basic philosophy of communism, and all of the dialectics of the logician cannot make them lie down together. They are contrary philosophies.

How, then, is communism irreconcilable with Christianity? In the first place, it leaves out God and Jesus Christ. Communism is avowedly secularistic and materialist. The great philosopher of communism, Karl Marx, based his total philosophy on what he called dialectical materialism. There was a philosopher by the name of Hegel who had used what he called the dialectical system to analyze concepts, and Karl Marx was willing to take Hegel's dialectic. And then he studied another man by the name of Feuerbach, a German philosopher. This man was a materialist. And so he took the materialism of this man and added it to the dialectic that he got from Hegel, and this is why his system is called dialectic materialism.

Now, what is materialism? It says in substance that the whole of reality can be explained in terms of matter in motion. In other words, it says that the basic stuff of reality is the material stuff. Materialism says, in substance, that idealism is wrong when it talks about the ultimate reality of mind and spirit and all of that. Karl Marx was a materialist, and he believed that the whole of human history moved on, driven by economic forces. This was his idea. There was no place in that system for God, and so from that moment on, communism became an atheistic system. And to this very day it is atheistic. It denies the existence of God. And if one goes to Russia, even today, he will find many of the churches fill on Sunday morning, but we know that in spite of that, the Russian government has had a campaign against religion, and against God and belief in God, ever since the revolution in 1917.

So that no Christian can be a communist because communism leaves out God. It regards religion psychologically as wishful thinking, regards religion intellectually as the product of fear and ignorance. And it regards religion historically as an instrument serving the ends of exploiters. This is what communism teaches about religion. And so, in a real sense, we disagree with this because we believe that history is moved not by economic forces but by spiritual forces. [*Congregation:*] (*Amen, Yeah*) We believe that there is a God (*Pray on*) in this universe (*Yes sir, Yes*), a God who loves his children, and a God who works through history for the salvation of man. (*Pray on*) Consequently, we can't accept communism at that point.

A second reason that we can't accept communism is that its methods are opposed to Christianity. (*Pray on*) Since for the communist there is no divine government or no absolute moral order, there are no fixed, immutable principles. So force, violence, murder, and lying are all justifiable means to bring about the millennial end. Lenin, the man who was something of the technician of communism, putting the philosophy of Karl Marx into practical action, said on one occasion, "We must be ready to employ trickery, deceit, and lawbreaking, withholding and concealing truth." That the followers of Lenin have been willing to act upon these instructions is a matter of history. For communism the end justifies the means.

There again we can't go along with this. We believe that there are certain moral principles in this universe that are eternal and absolute. We believe that there are some things right and there are some things wrong. It's wrong to lie. It always has been wrong, and it always will be wrong. It's wrong to hate. (*Yes sir*) It always has been wrong, and it always will be wrong. It's wrong to throw away the precious lives that God has given us in riotous living. It was wrong in 1800 B.C., and it's wrong in 1962 A.D. It's wrong in Russia. It's wrong in China. It's wrong in India. It's wrong in New York. It's wrong in Atlanta. (*Yeah*) We believe that there are some things right, eternally and absolutely so, and there are some things wrong. Then we don't believe that the end justifies the means if those means happen to be bad. For we know that the end represents the means in process and the ideal in the making. The end is preexistent in the means. And so destructive means cannot bring about constructive ends. Immoral methods cannot achieve moral goals. And so we disagree with the ethical relativism of communism.

In the third place, we have to disagree with communism because the end of communism is the state. I should qualify this by saying that the state in communist theory is a temporary reality, an interim reality, which is to be eliminated when the classless society emerges. (*Yeah, yeah*) Karl Marx talks of that day when there will be a classless society. The ruling class, or rather the workers, what he called the proletariat, will through the revolution take power from the ruling class, which were the producers or the capitalists. And finally they will come to power, and through their power, they will establish a classless society. He says that while you are on the way to this classless society the state is the end. Man becomes only a means to that end. And if any man's so-called rights or liberties stand in the way of that end, they are simply swept aside. And so in the communistic system, you do not have freedom of the press. You do not have freedom of speech. You do not have freedom of assembly. All of these things are under the scrutiny of the state, which is manipulated through the party. And whatever the Party says, that must be done. All of the freedoms that are dear to us are denied. Man has to be a servant, a dutiful and submissive servant of the state. The state is omnipotent and supreme, and so if one lived in Russia today, he couldn't just get up and make a speech against the Communist Party. (*Right*) If one lived in Russia today, he could not write a book saying certain things without the condemnation of the Party, he may be searched and even killed. (*Yeah*) You remember the great book that Pasternak wrote, and you remember the problems that he faced because there were within that book some things that they didn't like in Russia. It had some criticisms of the system.

We know that the most creative moments in history are those moments when individuals are left free to think. The thing that makes man <u>man</u> is his freedom. This is why I could never agree with communism as a philosophical system, because it deprives man of freedom. And if a man is not free, he is not fully man. If a man does not have the capacity to deliberate, to decide, and to respond, as Paul Tillich would say, he is not a man, for a man is man because he is free. And, therefore, communism is on the wrong road because it denies freedom.

And so for these three reasons, I am convinced that no Christian can be a communist. These two systems are opposed to each other. These two systems are contradictory. We must try to understand communism. We must love communists. But never can we accept communism and be true Christians.

Yet, we must realize that there is something in communism which challenges us all. It was the late Archbishop of Canterbury, William Temple, that referred to communism as a Christian heresy. I want you to follow me as I go through this other aspect of the message. By this he meant that communism had laid hold on certain truths which are essential parts of the Christian view of things but that it had bound up with them concepts and practices which no Christian can ever accept or profess. In other words, although communism can never be accepted by a Christian, it emphasizes many essential truths that must forever challenge us as Christians. Indeed, it may be that communism is a necessary corrective for a Christianity that has been all too passive and a democracy that has been all too inert.

Communism should challenge us to be more concerned about social justice. However much is wrong with communism, we must admit that it arose as a protest against the hardships of the underprivileged. *The Communist Manifesto*, which was published in 1847 by Marx and Engels, emphasizes throughout how the middle class has exploited the lower class. Communism in society is a classless society. Along with this goes a strong attempt to eliminate racial prejudice. Communism seeks to transcend the superficialities of race and color (*Yeah*), and you are able to join the Communist Party whatever the color of your skin or the quality of your blood, the quality of blood in your veins. (*Yeah, Right on*)

No one can deny that we need to be concerned about social justice. (*Yeah*) Karl Marx arouses our conscience at this point. Karl Marx was born a Jew in a rabbinic family. Somewhere along the way as a child, he must have heard his parents reading the words of Amos: "Let justice roll down like waters and righteousness like a mighty stream."[1] Then, when he was six years old, his parents became Christians, and somewhere along the way he must have heard them reading over the New Testament: "Ye do it unto the least of these, ye do it unto me."[2] So with this passionate concern for social justice, Christians are bound to be in accord. Such concern is implicit in the Christian doctrine of the Fatherhood of God and the brotherhood of man. Christians are always to begin with a bias in favor of a movement which protests against unfair treatment of the poor, but surely Christianity itself is such a protest. *The Communist Manifesto* might express a concern for the poor and the oppressed, but it expresses no greater concern than the manifesto of Jesus, which opens with the words, "The spirit of the Lord is upon me, because He hath anointed me to preach the gospel to the poor; He has sent me to heal the brokenhearted, to preach deliverance to the captive, recovering the sight of the blind; to set at liberty them that are bruised, to proclaim the acceptable year of the Lord."[3] And so a passionate concern for social justice must be a concern of the Christian religion.

We must admit that we, as Christians, have often lagged behind at this point. Slavery could not have existed in the United States for almost 250 years if the church had really taken a stand against it. Segregation could not exist today in the United States if the church took a stand against it. (*Well*) Mr. Meredith would be in the University of Mississippi right now (*Say it*) if the church of Mississippi had taken a stand against segregation. (*Preach brother*) The tragic fact is that, in spite of Mr. Barnett's defiance of the Supreme Court of the land and the moral law of the universe, we haven't heard a single word from the churches of Mississippi.[4] (*All right*) This morning, if we stand at eleven o'clock to sing "In Christ There Is No East or West" (*Yeah*), we stand in the most segregated hour of America. (*Yes it does*)

Oh, we have a high blood pressure of creeds and an anemia of deeds, and this is the tragedy facing us today. We must admit that the church has often

---

[1] Amos 5:24.

[2] Matt 25:40.

[3] Luke 4:18-19.

[4] On the day after this sermon was delivered, James Meredith would finally be enrolled at the University of Mississippi. Governor Ross Barnett, who had publicly vowed to keep the University of Mississippi segregated, had reluctantly agreed in secret meetings with the Kennedy administration to have Meredith escorted to campus by Mississippi Highway Police. Meredith would be protected from hostile classmates by US Marshals and Army troops until he graduated in August 1963.

lagged behind, that the church has too often been an institution seeming to crystallize the patterns of the status quo. Oh, we've identified the name of Christ with so many evil things. I heard Mr. Barnett saying the other day that he had to do what he was doing because of the righteousness that had been handed down from God through Jesus Christ. I said to myself, "Isn't it tragic that we will take the name of Christ, identify it with so many evils of history. Oh, how we've lost Christ." You remember the words of Shakespeare's *Othello*. As he stood there before the villain Iago, cried out, "Who steals my purse steals trash; 'tis something, nothing, 'twas mine, 'tis his, has been the slave of thousands. But he who filches from me my good name robs me of that which might enrich him but makes me poor indeed." (*Yes*) This is what we've done to Christ. (*Yes*) We robbed him of his good name. (*Yeah*) And we've identified that name with segregation. We've identified that name with exploitation and with oppression and with so many of the evils of history.

This is why Karl Marx one day looked out, and this is why others following him have looked out and decided to say, "Religion is the opiate of the people." It has too often been the opiate of the people. Too often the churches talk about a future good over yonder and not concerned about the present evil over here. Oh, I tell you this morning, and I believe in immortality. (*Yes sir*) I believe in it firmly and absolutely. But I'm tired of people telling me about the hereafter and they don't tell me about the here. (*Yeah*) You can't say hereafter (*Yeah*) without saying here. It's all right to talk about silver slippers in a symbolic sense over in heaven, but give me some shoes to wear down here. (*Preach it brother*) It's all right to talk about long white robes over yonder, but give me some clothes to wear down here. It's all right to talk about streets flowing with milk and honey, but I want to see men in decent homes right here in the world. (*Amen*) It's all right to talk about all of these things in terms of a new Jerusalem, but I want to see a new Atlanta, a new New York, a new America, and a new world right here. (*Amen*)

This is what we've got to see—that the church has a social gospel that it must be true to. We must certainly work with individuals and seek to change the soul, that's very important. But we've got to deal with these social conditions that corrupt the soul, and any religion that professes to be concerned about the souls of men and not concerned about the city government that damns the soul (*Yeah*), the economic conditions that corrupt the soul, the slum conditions, the social evils that cripple the soul, is a dry, dead, do-nothing religion (*Amen*) in need of new blood. It is already spiritually dead, and the only thing I'm uncertain about it is the day that it will be dead. (*All right*) We've got to see that we are challenged to have a greater social consciousness in this church. We must be concerned about the gulf between superfluous wealth and abject, deadening poverty. One does not have to be a communist to be concerned about this. I would say to you this morning that one-tenth of one percent of the population of this nation controls almost fifty percent of the wealth, and I don't mind saying that there's something wrong with that.

I don't mind saying this morning that too often in capitalism we've taken necessities from the many to pave luxuries to the few. *I* will never be content, I will never rest until all of God's children can have the basic necessities of life. (*Amen, amen, amen*) Oh, they tell me, and I think it's true, that Atlanta has the finest homes for Negroes of any city in the United States. (*Yeah*) That's true. Never forget that all these fine homes you see represent less than five percent of the Negro population of Atlanta. I'm not concerned about five percent of the Negroes living all right. (*Well*) I want to see *all* of God's children (*Yeah*) with a decent home and three square meals a day and *able* to educate their children. (*Amen*) God wants this for everybody. (*Yes Jesus*) And I will never be content as long as somebody over here can make five hundred thousand dollars a year, and I've met black men and women down in Mississippi who make less than five hundred dollars a year. (*Amen, Brother, Keep it going*) Something wrong with that. (*Jesus*) And I see hungry boys and girls in this nation and other nations and think about the fact that we spend more than a million dollars a day storing surplus food. (*Yes*) And I say to myself, "I know where we can store that food free of charge—in the wrinkled stomachs of the millions of people in our nation and in this world who go to bed hungry at night." (*Hungry at night*) And God has left enough and to spare in this world for all of his children to have the basic necessities of life. (*Yes*)

There is another thing Marx reveals: the danger of the profit motive as the sole basis for an economic system. We must heed this challenge. I'm afraid that there are too many people in America concerned about making a living rather than making a life. (*Yes, Yes*) I'm afraid this morning there are too many medical doctors concerned about making a big salary and getting a big home and a fine car than there are about healing the sick bodies of men. (*Yes*) I'm afraid that there are too many school teachers in America more concerned about the check that comes at the first of the month than introducing their students to the great, inexhaustible treasuries of knowledge and loving them and watching them grow. I'm afraid that there are too many preachers in the pulpit (*Yes*) more concerned (*Yes*) about their anniversaries (*Yes*) than they are about saving the souls of man. (*Yeah*) I'm afraid, my friends (*Yes, Go on*), that we are prone to judge the success of our profession by the size of the wheel base (*Yes*) of our automobiles (*That's right*) rather than the size of our service to humanity. (*All right*) Something is telling us today (*That's true*) that there is something more than making a lot of money. (*Yeah*) We must make money to live, but we must always remember that money is just an ingredient in the objective which we seek in life. (*Yes*) And if we don't see that, we'll make money-making an end rather than a means. (*Amen*) Jesus said, "I know you need it. I know you need money. I know you have need of clothes. I know you need a car to ride in. I know you need a home to live in and to sleep in. I know that you have need of all these things. (*Yeah*) But seek ye first the kingdom of God. (*Yes*) Seek ye first righteousness (*Righteousness*), and all of these (*Yes*) things will be added unto you." (*Add them Lord*) And this is what we must do. (*Yes*)

Let me rush on now toward my conclusion and say this. We are challenged to dedicate and devote our lives to the cause of Christ as the communists do to communism. We cannot accept their creed, but we must admire their dream (*Yeah*) and their readiness to sacrifice themselves to the very utmost and even to lay down their lives for a cause that they believe in, a cause that they believe is going to make the world a better place. One watches that zeal, and one has to say, "Why is it that Christians don't have this zeal? (*Amen*) Why is it that we don't have this zeal for Christ? Why is that we don't have this sense of purpose, this sense of dedication for his kingdom?" Oh, these problems that we face in America and the world wouldn't be here today if we were as dedicated to Christianity as we ought to be. And it may well be that communism is in this world today because Christians haven't been Christian enough and democracies haven't been democratic enough. (*Well*) It may well be that the success of communism is due to the failure of Christians to live up to the basic principles of Christianity. (*Yeah*) [*Words inaudible*] communists will take their system, and they will go out, and they will dedicate themselves to the path of winning others to communism. (*Well, Well*) They'll go out in cell groups and work day and night trying to convert somebody to communism. We'll go day in and day out, year in and year out and never speak to anybody about Jesus Christ. (*Well*) We've got to bring some lost boy or girl, some lost man or woman, into the church and into the kingdom.

If I would ask each of you here this morning to raise your hand if you've spoken to somebody about Christ, and about the church, and about the kingdom, and tried to bring them in (*Yeah*), I would be ashamed to see (*Yeah*) the small number of hands that would go up if you were really being true. Then they get together, communists, and study Marx and Lenin and Stalin and all of the thinkers of communism. They study at night and in the day. They know their creed. (*Yeah*) And yet we can't get Christians to read the Bible. (*Well, Yeah*) They won't come to Sunday School. (*Yeah*) They won't come to Baptist Training Union. (*Amen*) And *I* submit to you that every person sitting in church this morning is biblically and is religiously illiterate. (*Yeah*) If I'd ask somebody here this morning, where is the Book of Exodus? You'd say it's in the New Testament. If I'd ask you, where the Book of Revelation? You may say it's the first book in the Bible, in the Old Testament. Our children come up religiously illiterate. (*Yeah*) Adults go through life religiously and biblically illiterate. We don't study about it. We don't have this zeal. We don't have this concern. Oh, there is a voice saying to us this morning (*Yes it is, Yes it is*), "You shall be my witnesses." (*Yes*) That means that if we are to be witnesses for Christ we've got to talk about it. (*Yeah*) We've got to be willing to convert others. (*Yes it is*)

The word "witness" in the New Testament has three meanings. You start out in the Gospels, the Book of Acts. The word "witness" means just verbal affirmation, talking about the life and the death and the resurrection of Jesus Christ. We've got to talk about this [*gospel?*] (*Yes, we do*) You know talking can help someone, don't let anybody fool you. Hitler used to say that even if you tell a lie, tell a big one, and if you tell it long and loud enough, you'll convince everybody that it is true, even yourself. And he took that method and convinced the German people that the Jews were the cause of all of their misfortunes (*Well*) and led that great nation with all of its great minds to the killing of six million Jews. (*Well*) Now, if a man could tell a *lie* and turn a nation upside-down toward an evil end, it seems that we could tell the truth about Jesus Christ and turn this world right side-up. (*Yeah*) Let's talk about it some.

Then, the word "witness" goes on, and it says that not only that, when you get to the Pauline epistles, it means living a triumphant life. It's not enough to talk about it, you've got to live about it. (*Yeah*) Too many people have religion on Sunday, but it doesn't apply to Monday. If they'll do it every Sunday, they'll be all right on Monday, just a little song they've acquired. But if one is to be a witness for Jesus Christ, he must live this thing. (*Yes Lord*) He must not only preach a sermon (*Well*) with words, but he must preach it with his life (*Amen*) so that his very walking down the street is the embodiment of the principles of Jesus Christ. (*Yeah*)

And then finally open the Book of Revelation. The word "witness" means being willing to die for the cause of Jesus Christ. (*Yes Lord*) This morning, my friends, we must believe that there is something so dear, something so precious, something so eternal, that we'll die for it. (*That's right*) And lf you haven't discovered something that you will die for, you aren't fit to live. (*That's right*) You may be thirty, as I've said so often, at that moment some great principle stands before you, some great truth, some great decision, and you fail to take a stand because you are afraid that (*Well, Well*) something will happen to you or that you will be lulled and you want to live a few more years. (*Yeah*) Well, you might go on and live until eighty, but I submit to you that you were just as dead at thirty as you are at eighty and the cessation of breathing in your life is merely the belated announcement of an earlier death of the spirit. (*Yeah*)

You died when you failed to stand up for something. (*Yes sir*) You died when you failed to give yourself to some great principle. (*Yes, yes*) You *died* when you refused to stand up against segregation. (*Tell it preacher*) You died (*Preach*) when you refused to stand up against some great evil of society. (*Yes*) Somebody's calling us this morning (*Yes*), saying "Go preach my gospel. (*Yes*) You shall be witnesses unto me in Samaria (*Yes*), Judea, and unto every part of the earth, carry this gospel (*Pray on*) into the villages, to the hedges and the highways (*Yes*), and tell them about Jesus."[5]

And if we will do this, we will make this old world a new world. (*New world, Yes*) We won't have to worry (*Right on*) about communism. (*Nope*) We won't have to be stacking up on nuclear weapons, for that can't defeat communism. (*Yes*) It can never be defeated with ammunition. It can never be defeated with missiles. (*Amen*) The only way that we can defeat communism is to get a better idea, and we have it in our democracy. (*Yeah*) We have it in our Christianity. And if we will live by it (*Yeah*), we won't have to worry about communism. And men the world over will join hands as brothers, and they will walk this earth knowing that we are all God's children. (*Yeah*) Once again, we will be able to sing, not only in Ebenezer on Sunday morning. (*Well*) We will hear the very angels in heaven stop silent and the eternity stand still. (*Yes, Yes*) And we will hear Peter cry out (*Yes*), "The kingdom of this world has become the kingdom of our Lord and Christ. And He shall reign forever and ever.[6] Hallelujah (*Yeah*), hallelujah!" (*Oh, yes*)

This is our faith, and this is our hope. We open the doors of the church now. Someone here this morning needs Christ. Someone here needs to follow Him. Who this morning will accept Him? We have a challenge, we have a faith. We don't need communism. We have it within our religion and within our faith, if we would only live it, if we would only be true to Jesus Christ. This is it. Who this morning will accept Him, as we come to the invitational hymn, hymn number 229, "Jesus Is Calling." You here this morning, wherever you are, Jesus

---

[5] King is quoting the Great Commission, Matthew 28:16-20.
[6] Revelation 11:15.

is calling. [*Music*] Are you here this morning? We bid you come. Who this morning will come make a decision to Christ? Come and unite with this church. Who will this morning? [*words inaudible*] [*Congregation sings*]

Document 23

"A Christian Manifesto"
Francis Schaeffer
1982

A student of J. Gresham Machen (Document 20), Schaeffer (1912–1984) was among the most forceful voices in late twentieth century American Christianity to speak against the social and political repercussions of the materialist and evolutionary view of human nature (see Documents 14, 16). This view—in which man and man alone is the apex and standard of all things—was characteristic of the modern philosophy of Humanism (sometimes referred to as Secular Humanism, to differentiate it from the Christian Humanism of the Renaissance). In this sermon, delivered on several occasions in the 1980s, and in his earlier book of the same title, Schaeffer tackled the problem of such humanist philosophy directly by attempting to instigate a religious revival that would take seriously the traditional Christian proposition that all things—temporal as well as spiritual, and political as well as moral or religious—are the gifts of a Creator God, and thus, subject to His sovereignty.

It was this theistic understanding of the nature of the world—insurgent at the time of the Reformation, and again during the American founding—that provided the only solid foundation for human flourishing, Schaeffer argued. Yet Americans had allowed scientific materialism—and its philosophical variant of "humanism"—to supplant their traditional theistic understanding of the nature of reality, and in doing so, untethered themselves from the sense of ultimate accountability. Without it, Schaeffer argued that the nation's inherited political principles of liberty and consent were devolving into licentiousness and arbitrary majoritarianism. Schaeffer urged American Christians to remember that they were part of a heritage of cultural revolution and transformation stretching back to the Reformation and to prepare themselves for actions of civil disobedience in the name of Christ if necessary. While Schaeffer's rhetoric is more aggressive than that of many of the others in this collection, his message is in keeping with the tradition of American exceptionalism and millennialism we see in Documents 1, 7, and 9. It is also worth comparing this sermon to Ronald Reagan's address to the National Association of Evangelicals (Document 24).

[There has been] a change in our society, a change in our country, a change in the Western world from a Judeo-Christian consensus to a Humanistic one. That is, instead of the final reality that exists being the infinite creator God... now largely, all else is seen as only material or energy which has existed forever in some form, shaped into its present complex form only by pure chance.

... The word Humanism should be carefully defined.... Humanism means that the man is the measure of all things.... If this other final reality of material or energy shaped by pure chance is the final reality, it gives no meaning to life. It gives no value system. It gives no basis for law, and therefore, in this case, man must be the measure of all things.... If, indeed, the final reality is silent about these values, man must generate them from himself.

So, Humanism is the absolute certain result, if we choose this other final reality and say that is what it is. You must realize that when we speak of man being the measure of all things under the Humanist label, the first thing is that man has only knowledge from himself. That he, being finite, limited, very faulty in his observation in many things, yet nevertheless, has no possible source of knowledge except what man, beginning from himself, can find out by his own observation. Specifically, in this view, there is no place for any knowledge from God.

But it is not only that man must start from himself in the area of knowledge and learning, but any value system must come arbitrarily from man himself by arbitrary choice. More frightening still, in our country, at our own moment of history, is the fact that any basis of law then becomes arbitrary— merely certain people making decisions as to what is for the good of society at the given moment.

Now this is the real reason for the breakdown in morals in our country. It's the real reason for the breakdown in values in our country, and it is the reason that our Supreme Court now functions so thoroughly upon the fact of arbitrary law. They have no basis for law that is fixed, therefore, like the young person who decides to live hedonistically upon their own chosen arbitrary values, society is now doing the same thing legally. Certain few people come together and decide what they arbitrarily believe is for the good of society at the given moment, and that becomes law.

... It should be noticed that this new dominant world view is a view which is exactly opposite from that of the founding fathers who founded this country. Now, not all the founding fathers were individually, personally, Christians.

That certainly is true. But, nevertheless, they founded the country on the base that there is a God who is the Creator... who gave the inalienable rights.

We must understand something very thoroughly. If society—if the state gives the rights, it can take them away—they're not inalienable. If the states give the rights, they can change them and manipulate them. But this was not the view of the founding fathers of this country. They believed (although not all of them were individual Christians) that there was a Creator and that this Creator gave the inalienable rights: it is this upon which our country was founded and which has given us the freedoms which we still have—even the freedoms which are being used now to destroy the freedoms.

The reason that these freedoms were there is because they believed there was somebody who gave the inalienable rights, which indeed, therefore, limited the power of the state and the government specifically by these inalienable rights. But if we have the view that the final reality is material or energy which has existed forever in some form, we must understand that this view never, never, never would have given the rights which we now know and which, unhappily, I say to you (those of you who are Christians) that too often you take all too much for granted. You forget that the freedoms which we have had in northern Europe after the Reformation (and the United States is an extension of that, as would be Australia or Canada, New Zealand, and so on) are absolutely unique in the world.

Occasionally, some of you who have gone to universities have been taught that these freedoms are rooted in the Greek city-states. That is not true. All you have to do is read Plato's Republic and you understand that the Greek city-states never had any concept of the freedoms that we have. Go back into history. The freedoms which we have (the form/freedom balance of government) are unique in history and they are also unique in the world at this day.

...We are now losing those freedoms and we can expect to continue to lose them if this other world view continues to take increased force and power in our county. We can be sure of this....

A good illustration is in the public schools. This view is taught in our public schools exclusively—by law. There is no other view that can be taught.... There is only one view of reality that can be taught, and that is that the final reality is only material or energy shaped by pure chance.

It is the same with the television programs. Public television gives us many things that many of us like culturally, but is also completely committed to a propaganda position that the last reality is only material/energy shaped by pure chance....

The abortion ruling is a very clear one. The abortion ruling, of course, is also a natural result of this other world view because with this other world view, human life—your individual life—has no intrinsic value. You are a wart upon the face of an absolutely impersonal universe. Your aspirations have no fulfillment in the "what-isness" of what is. Your aspirations damn you.... The universe cannot fulfill anything that you say when you say, "It is beautiful"; "I love"; "It is right"; "It is wrong." These words are meaningless words against the backdrop of this other world view....

In this case, human life has no distinct value whatsoever, and we find this Supreme Court in one ruling overthrew the abortion laws of all 50 states, and they made this form of killing human life (because that's what it is) the law. The law declared that this form of killing human life was to be accepted, and for many people, because they had no set ethic, when the Supreme Court said that it was legal... it [became] ethical.

The courts of this country have forced this view and its results on the total population. What we find is that as the courts have done this, without any longer that which the founding fathers comprehended of law... that there is a law of God which gives foundation. It becomes quite natural then, that they would also cut themselves loose from a strict constructionism concerning the Constitution.

Everything is relative. So as you cut yourself loose from the Law of God, in any concept whatsoever, you also soon are cutting yourself loose from a strict constructionism and each ruling is to be seen as an arbitrary choice by a group of people as to what they may honestly think is for the sociological good of the community, of the country, for the given moment.

Now, along with that is the fact that the courts are increasingly making law and thus we find that the legislatures' powers are increasingly diminished in relationship to the power of the courts. Now the pro-abortion people have been very wise about this in the last, say, 10 years, and Christians very silly. ...because the courts are not subject to the people's thinking, nor their will, either by election nor by a re-election. Consequently, the courts have been the vehicle used to bring this whole view and to force it on our total population. It has not been largely the legislatures. It has been rather, the courts.

The result is a relativistic value system. A lack of a final meaning to life— that's first. Why does human life have any value at all, if that is all that reality is? Not only are you going to die individually, but the whole human race is going to die, someday. It may not take the falling of the atom bombs, but someday the world will grow too hot, too cold.... Someday all you people not only will be individually dead, but the whole conscious life on this world will be dead, and nobody will see the birds fly. And there's no meaning to life.

... It was this view that opened the door to all that followed in Germany prior to Hitler. It's an interesting fact here that the only Supreme Court in the Western World that has ruled against easy abortion is the West German Court. The reason they did it is because they knew ... that this view of human life in the medical profession and the legal profession combined, before Hitler came on the scene, is what opened the way for everything that happened in Hitler's Germany. And so, the German Supreme Court has voted against easy abortion because they know very well where it leads.

... Abortion itself would be worth spending much of our lifetimes to fight against, because it is the killing of human life, but it's only a symptom of the total. What we are facing is Humanism: Man, the measure of all things— viewing final reality being only material or energy shaped by chance; therefore, human life having no intrinsic value; therefore, the keeping of any individual life or any groups of human life, being purely an arbitrary choice by society at the given moment....

I have a question to ask you, and that is: Where have the Bible-believing Christians been in the last 40 years?... This country is almost lost because the Bible-believing Christians, in the last 40 years, who have said that they know that the final reality is this infinite-personal God who is the Creator and all the rest, have done nothing about it as the consensus has changed. There has been a vast silence!

Christians of this country have simply been silent.... It's not only the Christian leaders. Where have the Christian lawyers been? Why haven't they been challenging this change in the view of what the First Amendment means, which I'll deal with in a second. Where have the Christian doctors been— speaking out against the rise of the abortion clinics and all the other things? Where have the Christian businessmen been—to put their lives and their work on the line concerning these things which they would say as Christians are central to them? Where have the Christian educators been—as we have lost our educational system? Where have we been? Where have each of you been? What's happened in the last 40 years ... ?

Now I want to say something with great force, right here. What I have been talking about, whether you know it or not, is true spirituality. This is true spirituality. Spirituality, after you are a Christian and have accepted Christ as your Savior, means that Christ is the Lord of ALL your life—not just your religious life, and if you make a dichotomy in these things, you are denying your Lord His proper place.... All of life is spiritual and all of life is equally spiritual. That includes (as our forefathers did) standing for these things of freedom and standing for these things of human life and all these other matters that are so crucial, if indeed, this living God does exist as we know that He does exist.

We have forgotten our heritage. A lot of the evangelical complex like to talk about the old revivals and they tell us we ought to have another revival. We need another revival—you and I need revival. We need another revival in our hearts. But they have forgotten something.... That is the factor that every single revival that has ever been a real revival, whether it was the great awakening before the American Revolution; whether it was the great revivals of Scandinavia; whether it was Wesley and Whitefield; wherever you have found a great revival, it's always had three parts. First, it has called for the individual to accept Christ as Savior, and thankfully, in all of these that I have named, thousands have been saved. Then, it has called upon the Christians to bow their hearts to God and really let the Holy Spirit have His place in fullness in their life. But there has always been, in every revival, a third element. It has always brought social change!

...It was the Great Awakening, that great revival prior to the founding of the United States, that opened the way and prepared for the founding of the United States. Every one of the great revivals had tremendous social implications. What I am saying is, that I am afraid that we have forgotten our heritage....

...When the government negates the law of God, it abrogates its authority. God has given certain offices to restrain chaos in this fallen world, but it does not mean that these offices are autonomous, and when a government commands that which is contrary to the Law of God, it abrogates its authority....

...At a certain point, it is not only the privilege but it is the duty of the Christian to disobey the government. Now that's what the founding fathers did when they founded this country. That's what the early Church did. That's what Peter said. You heard it from the Scripture: "Should we obey man?...rather than God?" That's what the early Christians did.

...The people of the Reformation, the founding fathers of this country, faced and acted in the realization that if there is no place for disobeying the government, that government has been put in the place of the living God. In such a case, the government has been made a false god. If there is no place for disobeying a human government, that government has been made GOD. Caesar, under some name, thinking of the early Church, has been put upon the final throne. The Bible's answer is NO! Caesar is not to be put in the place of

God and we as Christians, in the name of the Lordship of Christ, and all of life, must so think and act on the appropriate level. It should always be on the appropriate level. We have lots of room to move yet with our court cases, with the people we elect—all the things that we can do in this country. If, unhappily, we come to that place, the appropriate level must also include a disobedience to the state.

If you are not doing that, you haven't thought it through. Jesus is not really on the throne. God is not central. You have made a false god central. Christ must be the final Lord and not society and not Caesar.

Document 24

Remarks at the Annual Convention of the National Association of Evangelicals

Ronald Reagan

1983

Although they were less important for his victory than was thought in its immediate aftermath, conservative evangelical Christians were a part of the coalition that elected Ronald Reagan in 1980. In a manner similar to FDR's appeal to Catholic voters in 1933 (Document 21), Reagan addressed an organization of conservative evangelicals to highlight the policy goals of his administration, such as support for prayer in school and limiting abortion, most likely to resonate with the interests of the movement.

The speech generated a lot of negative commentary because of its reference to the Soviet Union as the "evil empire" and "the focus of evil in the modern world." These remarks and the explicitly religious language of the speech were unusual for a presidential speech at that time but not in the larger context of American history (see Documents 12, 21). Even two decades before, President Kennedy in his inaugural address had stated his "belief that the rights of man come not from the generosity of the state but from the hand of God," a view that Reagan reiterated in this speech by quoting a famous remark of Thomas Jefferson's; and in 1962, citing Lenin as Reagan would, Martin Luther King had already argued that communists held that any action was moral as long as it promoted world revolution (see Document 22). Here, Reagan framed both his anti-communist foreign policy and his domestic "social" agenda as efforts to combat the rise of secularism, an issue his audience, as the heirs of Dixon and Machen (Documents 18 and 20) saw as critically important.

Reverend Clergy all, Senator Hawkins, distinguished members of the Florida congressional delegation, and all of you: I can't tell you how you have warmed my heart with your welcome. I'm delighted to be here today.

Those of you in the National Association of Evangelicals are known for your spiritual and humanitarian work. And I would be especially remiss if I didn't discharge right now one personal debt of gratitude. Thank you for your prayers. Nancy and I have felt their presence many times in many ways. And believe me, for us they've made all the difference.

The other day in the East Room of the White House at a meeting there, someone asked me whether I was aware of all the people out there who were praying for the President. And I had to say, "Yes, I am. I've felt it. I believe in intercessionary prayer."[1] But I couldn't help but say to that questioner after he'd asked the question that if sometimes when he was praying he got a busy signal, it was just me in there ahead of him. I think I understand how Abraham Lincoln felt when he said, "I have been driven many times to my knees by the overwhelming conviction that I had nowhere else to go"[2] ....

I tell you there are a great many God-fearing, dedicated, noble men and women in public life, present company included. And yes, we need your help to keep us ever-mindful of the ideas and the principles that brought us into the public arena in the first place. The basis of those ideals and principles is a commitment to freedom and personal liberty that itself is grounded in the much deeper realization that freedom prospers only where the blessings of God are avidly sought and humbly accepted.

The American experiment in democracy rests on this insight. Its discovery was the great triumph of our Founding Fathers, voiced by William Penn when he said: "If we will not be governed by God, we must be governed by tyrants."[3] Explaining the inalienable rights of men, Jefferson said, "The God who gave us life, gave us liberty at the same time."[4] And it was George Washington who said that, "of all the dispositions and habits which lead to political prosperity, religion and morality are indispensable supports."[5]

And finally, that shrewdest of all observers of American democracy, Alexis de Tocqueville, put it eloquently after he had gone on a search for the secret of America's greatness and genius—and he said: "Not until I went into the churches of America and heard her pulpits aflame with righteousness did I

---

[1] Usually called "intercessory," these are prayers said for the benefit of others.

[2] This remark was attributed to Lincoln after his death.

[3] From a letter Penn wrote to Peter the Great.

[4] "The god who gave us life gave us liberty at the same time: the hand of force may destroy, but cannot disjoin them," Jefferson, *A Summary View of the Rights of British America,* 1774.

[5] From the "Farewell Address," September 19, 1796 (see Document 5).

understand the greatness and the genius of America. America is good. And if America ever ceases to be good, America will cease to be great."[6]

Well, I'm pleased to be here today with you who are keeping America great by keeping her good. Only through your work and prayers and those of millions of others can we hope to survive this perilous century and keep alive this experiment in liberty, this last, best hope of man.[7]

I want you to know that this administration is motivated by a political philosophy that sees the greatness of America in you, her people, and in your families, churches, neighborhoods, communities: the institutions that foster and nourish values like concern for others and respect for the rule of law under God.

Now, I don't have to tell you that this puts us in opposition to, or at least out of step with, a prevailing attitude of many who have turned to a modern-day secularism, discarding the tried and time-tested values upon which our very civilization is based. No matter how well intentioned, their value system is radically different from that of most Americans. And while they proclaim that they're freeing us from superstitions of the past, they've taken upon themselves the job of superintending us by government rule and regulation. Sometimes their voices are louder than ours, but they are not yet a majority.

An example of that vocal superiority is evident in a controversy now going on in Washington. And since I'm involved I've been waiting to hear from the parents of young America. How far are they willing to go in giving to government their prerogatives as parents?

Let me state the case as briefly and simply as I can. An organization of citizens, sincerely motivated, deeply concerned about the increase in illegitimate births and abortions involving girls well below the age of consent, some time ago established a nationwide network of clinics to offer help to these girls and, hopefully, alleviate this situation. Now, again, let me say, I do not fault their intent. However, in their well-intentioned effort, these clinics

---

[6] Various politicians, including Presidents Eisenhower and Clinton, have used this quotation or a version of it. No one has been able to locate it in Tocqueville's writings. See John J. Pitney, Jr., "The Toqueville Fraud," *The Weekly Standard* (November 13, 1995) http://www.freerepublic.com/focus/chat/2545306/posts .

[7] Reagan alludes to Lincoln's characterization of American democracy in his Second Annual Message to Congress (December 1862), delivered near the conclusion of two years of civil war. After urging Congress to adopt a plan he believed would hasten the war's successful conclusion—compensated emancipation of the slaves—Lincoln warned that "we cannot escape history…. We shall nobly save, or meanly lose, the last best hope of earth."

decided to provide advice and birth control drugs and devices to underage girls without the knowledge of their parents.

For some years now, the federal government has helped with funds to subsidize these clinics. In providing for this, the Congress decreed that every effort would be made to maximize parental participation. Nevertheless, the drugs and devices are prescribed without getting parental consent or giving notification after they've done so. Girls termed "sexually active"—and that has replaced the word "promiscuous"—are given this help in order to prevent illegitimate birth or abortion.

Well, we have ordered clinics receiving federal funds to notify the parents such help has been given. One of the nation's leading newspapers has created the term "squeal rule" in editorializing against us for doing this, and we're being criticized for violating the privacy of young people. A judge has recently granted an injunction against an enforcement of our rule. I've watched TV panel shows discuss this issue, seen columnists pontificating on our error, but no one seems to mention morality as playing a part in the subject of sex.

Is all of Judeo-Christian tradition wrong? Are we to believe that something so sacred can be looked upon as a purely physical thing with no potential for emotional and psychological harm? And isn't it the parents' right to give counsel and advice to keep their children from making mistakes that may affect their entire lives? Many of us in government would like to know what parents think about this intrusion in their family by government. We're going to fight in the courts. The right of parents and the rights of family take precedence over those of Washington-based bureaucrats and social engineers.

But the fight against parental notification is really only one example of many attempts to water down traditional values and even abrogate the original terms of American democracy. Freedom prospers when religion is vibrant and the rule of law under God is acknowledged. When our Founding Fathers passed the First Amendment, they sought to protect churches from government interference. They never intended to construct a wall of hostility between government and the concept of religious belief itself.[8]

The evidence of this permeates our history and our government. The Declaration of Independence mentions the Supreme Being no less than four times. "In God We Trust" is engraved on our coinage. The Supreme Court opens its proceedings with a religious invocation. And the members of Congress open their sessions with a prayer. I just happen to believe the schoolchildren of the United States are entitled to the same privileges as Supreme Court justices and congressmen.

Last year, I sent the Congress a constitutional amendment to restore prayer to public schools. Already this session, there's growing bipartisan support for the amendment, and I am calling on the Congress to act speedily to pass it and to let our children pray.

Perhaps some of you read recently about the Lubbock school case, where a judge actually ruled that it was unconstitutional for a school district to give equal treatment to religious and nonreligious student groups, even when the group meetings were being held during the students' own time.[9] The First Amendment never intended to require government to discriminate against religious speech.

Senators Denton and Hatfield have proposed legislation in the Congress on the whole question of prohibiting discrimination against religious forms of student speech. Such legislation could go far to restore freedom of religious speech for public school students. And I hope the Congress considers these bills quickly. And with your help, I think it's possible we could also get the constitutional amendment through the Congress this year.

---

[8] Reagan alludes to an oft-quoted clause in Jefferson's letter to the Danbury Baptist Association (1802), which in 1947 the Supreme Court took to be the proper interpretation of the First Amendment. Jefferson wrote: "Believing with you that religion is a matter which lies solely between man and his God, that he owes account to none other for his faith or his worship, that the legislative powers of government reach actions only, and not opinions, I contemplate with sovereign reverence that act of the whole American people which declared that their legislature should 'make no law respecting an establishment of religion, or prohibiting the free exercise thereof,' thus building a wall of separation between church and State."

[9] In *Lubbock Civil Liberties Union v. Lubbock School District* (1982), the Fifth Circuit Court of Appeals ruled that a school district's allowance for student-led religious meetings on school grounds was unconstitutional. The Supreme Court declined to review the decision.

More than a decade ago, a Supreme Court decision literally wiped off the books of fifty states statutes protecting the rights of unborn children.[10] Abortion on demand now takes the lives of up to one and a half million unborn children a year. Human life legislation ending this tragedy will someday pass the Congress, and you and I must never rest until it does. Unless and until it can be proven that the unborn child is not a living entity, then its right to life, liberty, and the pursuit of happiness must be protected.

You may remember that when abortion on demand began, many, and indeed, I'm sure many of you, warned that the practice would lead to a decline in respect for human life, that the philosophical premises used to justify abortion on demand would ultimately be used to justify other attacks on the sacredness of human life—infanticide or mercy killing. Tragically enough, those warnings proved all too true. Only last year a court permitted the death by starvation of a handicapped infant.[11]

I have directed the Health and Human Services Department to make clear to every health care facility in the United States that the Rehabilitation Act of 1973 protects all handicapped persons against discrimination based on handicaps, including infants. And we have taken the further step of requiring that each and every recipient of federal funds who provides health care services to infants must post and keep posted in a conspicuous place a notice stating that "discriminatory failure to feed and care for handicapped infants in this facility is prohibited by federal law." It also lists a twenty-four-hour, toll-free number so that nurses and others may report violations in time to save the infant's life.

In addition, recent legislation introduced in the Congress by Representative Henry Hyde of Illinois not only increases restrictions on publicly financed abortions, it also addresses this whole problem of infanticide. I urge the Congress to begin hearings and to adopt legislation that will protect the right of life to all children, including the disabled or handicapped.

Now, I'm sure that you must get discouraged at times, but you've done better than you know, perhaps. There's a great spiritual awakening in America,

---

[10] With *Roe v. Wade* (1973), the Supreme Court ruled unconstitutional a Texas state law that banned abortions except to save the life of the mother.

[11] The Indiana State Supreme Court ruled in 1982 that parents of a child born with both Downs Syndrome and a defective esophagus could (as their physician advised) deny the child surgery that would have allowed him to be fed. The child died of starvation six days after his birth.

a renewal of the traditional values that have been the bedrock of America's goodness and greatness.

One recent survey by a Washington-based research council concluded that Americans were far more religious than the people of other nations; 95 percent of those surveyed expressed a belief in God and a huge majority believed the Ten Commandments had real meaning in their lives. And another study has found that an overwhelming majority of Americans disapprove of adultery, teenage sex, pornography, abortion, and hard drugs. And this same study showed a deep reverence for the importance of family ties and religious belief.

I think the items that we've discussed here today must be a key part of the nation's political agenda. For the first time the Congress is openly and seriously debating and dealing with the prayer and abortion issues and that's enormous progress right there. I repeat: America is in the midst of a spiritual awakening and a moral renewal. And with your Biblical keynote, I say today, "Yes, let justice roll on like a river, righteousness like a never-failing stream."[12]

Now, obviously, much of this new political and social consensus I've talked about is based on a positive view of American history, one that takes pride in our country's accomplishments and record. But we must never forget that no government schemes are going to perfect man. We know that living in this world means dealing with what philosophers would call the phenomenology of evil or, as theologians would put it, the doctrine of sin.

There is sin and evil in the world, and we're enjoined by Scripture and the Lord Jesus to oppose it with all our might. Our nation, too, has a legacy of evil with which it must deal. The glory of this land has been its capacity for transcending the moral evils of our past. For example, the long struggle of minority citizens for equal rights, once a source of disunity and civil war, is now a point of pride for all Americans. We must never go back. There is no room for racism, anti-Semitism, or other forms of ethnic and racial hatred in this country.

I know that you've been horrified, as have I, by the resurgence of some hate groups preaching bigotry and prejudice. Use the mighty voice of your pulpits and the powerful standing of your churches to denounce and isolate these hate groups in our midst. The commandment given us is clear and simple: "Thou shalt love thy neighbor as thyself."[13]

---

[12] Amos 5:24. Martin Luther King frequently quoted this verse.
[13] Mark 12:31; Matthew 22:39; Luke 10:27.

But whatever sad episodes exist in our past, any objective observer must hold a positive view of American history, a history that has been the story of hopes fulfilled and dreams made into reality. Especially in this century, America has kept alight the torch of freedom, but not just for ourselves but for millions of others around the world.

And this brings me to my final point today. During my first press conference as president, in answer to a direct question, I pointed out that, as good Marxist-Leninists, the Soviet leaders have openly and publicly declared that the only morality they recognize is that which will further their cause, which is world revolution. I think I should point out I was only quoting Lenin, their guiding spirit, who said in 1920 that they repudiate all morality that proceeds from supernatural ideas—that's their name for religion—or ideas that are outside class conceptions. Morality is entirely subordinate to the interests of class war. And everything is moral that is necessary for the annihilation of the old, exploiting social order and for uniting the proletariat.

Well, I think the refusal of many influential people to accept this elementary fact of Soviet doctrine illustrates a historical reluctance to see totalitarian powers for what they are. We saw this phenomenon in the 1930s. We see it too often today.

This doesn't mean we should isolate ourselves and refuse to seek an understanding with them. I intend to do everything I can to persuade them of our peaceful intent, to remind them that it was the West that refused to use its nuclear monopoly in the forties and fifties for territorial gain and which now proposes a 50 percent cut in strategic ballistic missiles and the elimination of an entire class of land-based, intermediate-range nuclear missiles.

At the same time, however, they must be made to understand we will never compromise our principles and standards. We will never give away our freedom. We will never abandon our belief in God. And we will never stop searching for a genuine peace....

A number of years ago, I heard a young father, a very prominent young man in the entertainment world, addressing a tremendous gathering in California. It was during the time of the cold war, and communism and our own way of life were very much on people's minds. And he was speaking to that subject. And suddenly, though, I heard him saying, "I love my little girls more than anything." And I said to myself, "Oh, no, don't. You can't—don't say that." But I had underestimated him. He went on: "I would rather see my little girls die now; still believing in God, than have them grow up under communism and one day die no longer believing in God."

There were thousands of young people in that audience. They came to their feet with shouts of joy. They had instantly recognized the profound truth in what he had said, with regard to the physical and the soul and what was truly important.

Yes, let us pray for the salvation of all of those who live in that totalitarian darkness. Pray they will discover the joy of knowing God. But until they do, let us be aware that while they preach the supremacy of the State, declare its omnipotence over individual man, and predict its eventual domination of all peoples on the earth, they are the focus of evil in the modern world.... [I]f history teaches anything, it teaches that simpleminded appeasement or wishful thinking about our adversaries is folly. It means the betrayal of our past, the squandering of our freedom.

So, I urge you to speak out against those who would place the United States in a position of military and moral inferiority.... I urge you to beware the temptation of pride—the temptation of blithely declaring yourselves above it all and labeling both sides equally at fault, to ignore the facts of history and the aggressive impulses of an evil empire, to simply call the arms race a giant misunderstanding and thereby remove yourself from the struggle between right and wrong and good and evil. I ask you to resist the attempts of those who would have you withhold your support for our efforts, this administration's efforts, to keep America strong and free, while we negotiate real and verifiable reductions in the world's nuclear arsenals and one day, with God's help, their total elimination.

While America's military strength is important, let me add here that I've always maintained that the struggle now going on for the world will never be decided by bombs or rockets, by armies or military might. The real crisis we face today is a spiritual one; at root, it is a test of moral will and faith.

Whittaker Chambers, the man whose own religious conversion made him a witness to one of the terrible traumas of our time, the Hiss-Chambers case,[14] wrote that the crisis of the Western world exists to the degree in which the West is indifferent to God, the degree to which it collaborates in communism's

---

[14] A major dividing line between left and right in the United States during the Cold War and after, the Hiss-Chambers case arose because Whittaker Chambers, who had been a member of the communist party and a Soviet spy, following a conversion to Christianity identified Alger Hiss, a high ranking U.S. government official, as a communist and eventually accused him of spying for the Soviet Union. Hiss was eventually convicted of perjury in connection with testimony he gave in response to Chambers's charges. Subsequent research in Soviet archives has vindicated Chambers.

attempt to make man stand alone without God. And then he said, for Marxism-Leninism is actually the second-oldest faith, first proclaimed in the Garden of Eden with the words of temptation, "Ye shall be as gods."

The Western world can answer this challenge, he wrote, "but only provided that its faith in God and the freedom He enjoins is as great as communism's faith in Man." I believe we shall rise to the challenge. I believe that communism is another sad, bizarre chapter in human history whose last pages even now are being written. I believe this because the source of our strength in the quest for human freedom is not material, but spiritual. And because it knows no limitation, it must terrify and ultimately triumph over those who would enslave their fellow man. For in the words of Isaiah: "He giveth power to the faint; and to them that have no might He increaseth strength. But they that wait upon the Lord shall renew their strength; they shall mount up with wings as eagles; they shall run, and not be weary."[15]

Yes, change your world. One of our Founding Fathers, Thomas Paine, said, "We have it within our power to begin the world over again."[16] We can do it, doing together what no one church could do by itself.

God bless you and thank you very much.

---

[15] Isaiah 40: 29, 31.

[16] This remark occurs in the Appendix to *Common Sense* (1776), in which Paine advocated American independence.

Document 25

Address at Cairo University
Barack Obama
2009

As President Obama noted in his Address, he spoke in Cairo, Egypt at a time of tension between the United States and the Islamic world. He identified six areas of tension, from violent extremism to economic development, including women's rights and religious freedom. Throughout, the President sought to establish common ground with his Muslim audience by appealing to such principles as humanity, human nature, and progress, and the hopes and dreams that all people have in common, such as the aspirations "to live in peace and security, to get an education and to work with dignity, to love our families, our communities, and our God."

One may wonder, however, if these common aspirations are experienced in the same way. Are the principles to which the President appealed in fact held in common? Do all of the devout accept human nature, human rights, and progress as guiding principles? This is a question for devout Christians as well as devout Muslims. In his speech, the President appealed for cooperation between the United States and the Islamic world by saying that we have the ability "to reimagine the world, to remake this world." But if, as the Bible teaches, God made the world and saw that it was good, why would humans need to remake it? To the devout, will not such an aspiration seem impious?

No doubt, many devout Christians and Muslims would agree with the principles and approach President Obama enunciated in his speech. However, in speaking from the tradition of liberal Protestantism (see Document 19), the President demonstrated in his Cairo speech that religion may have an unsettling effect not just in American but also in world politics.

I am honored to be in the timeless city of Cairo and to be hosted by two remarkable institutions. For over a thousand years, Al-Azhar[1] has stood as a beacon of Islamic learning, and for over a century, Cairo University has been a

---

[1] Founded in 970, Al Azhar University is often described as the leading center of Islamic learning in the world.

source of Egypt's advancement. And together, you represent the harmony between tradition and progress. I'm grateful for your hospitality and the hospitality of the people of Egypt. And I'm also proud to carry with me the good will of the American people and a greeting of peace from Muslim communities in my country: *As-salaamu alaykum.*[2]

We meet at a time of great tension between the United States and Muslims around the world, tension rooted in historical forces that go beyond any current policy debate. The relationship between Islam and the West includes centuries of coexistence and cooperation, but also conflict and religious wars. More recently, tension has been fed by colonialism that denied rights and opportunities to many Muslims and a cold war in which Muslim-majority countries were too often treated as proxies without regard to their own aspirations. Moreover, the sweeping change brought by modernity and globalization led many Muslims to view the West as hostile to the traditions of Islam.

Violent extremists have exploited these tensions in a small, but potent minority of Muslims. The attacks of September 11, 2001, and the continued efforts of these extremists to engage in violence against civilians has led some in my country to view Islam as inevitably hostile not only to America and Western countries, but also to human rights. All this has bred more fear and more mistrust.

So long as our relationship is defined by our differences, we will empower those who sow hatred rather than peace, those who promote conflict rather than the cooperation that can help all of our people achieve justice and prosperity. And this cycle of suspicion and discord must end.

I've come here to Cairo to seek a new beginning between the United States and Muslims around the world, one based on mutual interest and mutual respect and one based upon the truth that America and Islam are not exclusive and need not be in competition. Instead, they overlap and share common principles, principles of justice and progress, tolerance and the dignity of all human beings.

I do so recognizing that change cannot happen overnight. I know there's been a lot of publicity about this speech, but no single speech can eradicate years of mistrust. Nor can I answer in the time that I have this afternoon all the complex questions that brought us to this point. But I am convinced that in order to move forward, we must say openly to each other the things we hold in our hearts and that too often are said only behind closed doors. There must be

---

[2] A traditional greeting, "May Allah's peace be upon you."

a sustained effort to listen to each other, to learn from each other, to respect one another, and to seek common ground. As the Holy Koran tells us: "Be conscious of God and speak always the truth." That is what I will try to do today, to speak the truth as best I can, humbled by the task before us and firm in my belief that the interests we share as human beings are far more powerful than the forces that drive us apart.

Now part of this conviction is rooted in my own experience. I'm a Christian, but my father came from a Kenyan family that includes generations of Muslims. As a boy, I spent several years in Indonesia and heard the call of the *azaan*[3] at the break of dawn and at the fall of dusk. As a young man, I worked in Chicago communities where many found dignity and peace in their Muslim faith. As a student of history, I also know civilization's debt to Islam.

It was Islam, at places like Al-Azhar, that carried the light of learning through so many centuries, paving the way for Europe's renaissance and enlightenment. It was innovation in Muslim communities that developed the order of algebra, our magnetic compass and tools of navigation, our mastery of pens and printing, our understanding of how disease spreads and how it can be healed. Islamic culture has given us majestic arches and soaring spires, timeless poetry and cherished music, elegant calligraphy and places of peaceful contemplation. And throughout history, Islam has demonstrated through words and deeds the possibilities of religious tolerance and racial equality.

I also know that Islam has always been a part of America's story. The first nation to recognize my country was Morocco. In signing the Treaty of Tripoli in 1796, our second President, John Adams, wrote: "The United States has in itself no character of enmity against the laws, religion, or tranquility of Muslims." And since our founding, American Muslims have enriched the United States. They have fought in our wars; they have served in our government; they have stood for civil rights; they have started businesses; they have taught at our universities; they've excelled in our sports arenas; they've won Nobel Prizes, built our tallest building, and lit the Olympic Torch. And when the first Muslim American was recently elected to Congress, he took the oath to defend our Constitution using the same Holy Koran that one of our Founding Fathers, Thomas Jefferson, kept in his personal library.

...Just as Muslims do not fit a crude stereotype, America is not the crude stereotype of a self-interested empire. The United States has been one of the greatest sources of progress that the world has ever known. We were born out of revolution against an empire. We were founded upon the ideal that all are

---

[3] The call to prayer.

created equal, and we have shed blood and struggled for centuries to give meaning to those words, within our borders and around the world. We are shaped by every culture, drawn from every end of the Earth, and dedicated to a simple concept: E pluribus unum—"Out of many, one."

Now, much has been made of the fact that an African American with the name Barack Hussein Obama could be elected President. But my personal story is not so unique. The dream of opportunity for all people has not come true for everyone in America, but its promise exists for all who come to our shores, and that includes nearly 7 million American Muslims in our country today, who, by the way, enjoy incomes and educational levels that are higher than the American average.

Moreover, freedom in America is indivisible from the freedom to practice one's religion. That is why there is a mosque in every State in our Union and over 1,200 mosques within our borders. That's why the United States Government has gone to court to protect the right of women and girls to wear the hijab and to punish those who would deny it.

So let there be no doubt, Islam is a part of America. And I believe that America holds within her the truth that regardless of race, religion, or station in life, all of us share common aspirations to live in peace and security, to get an education and to work with dignity, to love our families, our communities, and our God. These things we share. This is the hope of all humanity.

Of course, recognizing our common humanity is only the beginning of our task. Words alone cannot meet the needs of our people. These needs will be met only if we act boldly in the years ahead and if we understand that the challenges we face are shared and our failure to meet them will hurt us all. For we have learned from recent experience that when a financial system weakens in one country, prosperity is hurt everywhere. When a new flu infects one human being, all are at risk. When one nation pursues a nuclear weapon, the risk of nuclear attack rises for all nations. When violent extremists operate in one stretch of mountains, people are endangered across an ocean. When innocents in Bosnia and Darfur are slaughtered, that is a stain on our collective conscience. That is what it means to share this world in the 21st century. That is the responsibility we have to one another as human beings.

And this is a difficult responsibility to embrace, for human history has often been a record of nations and tribes and, yes, religions subjugating one another in pursuit of their own interests. Yet in this new age, such attitudes are self-defeating. Given our interdependence, any world order that elevates one nation or group of people over another will inevitably fail. So whatever we think of the past, we must not be prisoners to it. Our problems must be dealt with through partnership; our progress must be shared.

Now, that does not mean we should ignore sources of tension. Indeed, it suggests the opposite. We must face these tensions squarely. And so in that spirit, let me speak as clearly and as plainly as I can about some specific issues that I believe we must finally confront together.

The first issue that we have to confront is violent extremism in all of its forms. In Ankara, I made clear that America is not, and never will be, at war with Islam. We will, however, relentlessly confront violent extremists who pose a grave threat to our security, because we reject the same thing that people of all faiths reject: the killing of innocent men, women, and children. And it is my first duty as President to protect the American people....

[N]one of us should tolerate these extremists. They have killed in many countries. They have killed people of different faiths, but more than any other, they have killed Muslims. Their actions are irreconcilable with the rights of human beings, the progress of nations, and with Islam. The Holy Koran teaches that "whoever kills an innocent, it is as if he has killed all mankind." And the Holy Koran also says, "whoever saves a person, it is as if he has saved all mankind." The enduring faith of over a billion people is so much bigger than the narrow hatred of a few. Islam is not part of the problem in combating violent extremism, it is an important part of promoting peace.

...America will defend itself, respectful of the sovereignty of nations and the rule of law, and we will do so in partnership with Muslim communities, which are also threatened. The sooner the extremists are isolated and unwelcome in Muslim communities, the sooner we will all be safer.

The second major source of tension that we need to discuss is the situation between Israelis, Palestinians, and the Arab world. America's strong bonds with Israel are well known. This bond is unbreakable. It is based upon cultural and historical ties and the recognition that the aspiration for a Jewish homeland is rooted in a tragic history that cannot be denied....

Around the world, the Jewish people were persecuted for centuries, and anti-Semitism in Europe culminated in an unprecedented Holocaust. Tomorrow I will visit Buchenwald, which was part of a network of camps where Jews were enslaved, tortured, shot, and gassed to death by the Third Reich. Six million Jews were killed, more than the entire Jewish population of Israel today. Denying that fact is baseless, it is ignorant, and it is hateful. Threatening Israel with destruction or repeating vile stereotypes about Jews is deeply wrong and only serves to evoke in the minds of Israelis this most painful of memories while preventing the peace that the people of this region deserve.

On the other hand, it is also undeniable that the Palestinian people, Muslims and Christians, have suffered in pursuit of a homeland. For more than 60 years, they've endured the pain of dislocation. Many wait in refugee camps in the West Bank, Gaza, and neighboring lands for a life of peace and security that they have never been able to lead. They endure the daily humiliations, large and small, that come with occupation. So let there be no doubt, the situation for the Palestinian people is intolerable, and America will not turn our backs on the legitimate Palestinian aspiration for dignity, opportunity, and a state of their own.

For decades then, there has been a stalemate: two peoples with legitimate aspirations, each with a painful history that makes compromise elusive. It's easy to point fingers, for Palestinians to point to the displacement brought about by Israel's founding and for Israelis to point to the constant hostility and attacks throughout its history from within its borders, as well as beyond. But if we see this conflict only from one side or the other, then we will be blind to the truth. The only resolution is for the aspirations of both sides to be met through two states, where Israelis and Palestinians each live in peace and security....

Too many tears have been shed. Too much blood has been shed. All of us have a responsibility to work for the day when the mothers of Israelis and Palestinians can see their children grow up without fear, when the Holy Land of the three great faiths is the place of peace that God intended it to be, when Jerusalem is a secure and lasting home for Jews and Christians and Muslims and a place for all of the children of Abraham to mingle peacefully together as in the story of Isra, when Moses, Jesus, and Muhammed, peace be upon them, joined in prayer.

The third source of tension is our shared interest in the rights and responsibilities of nations on nuclear weapons.... For many years, Iran has defined itself in part by its opposition to my country, and there is in fact a tumultuous history between us.... Rather than remain trapped in the past, I've made it clear to Iran's leaders and people that my country is prepared to move forward. The question now is not what Iran is against, but rather what future it wants to build....

The fourth issue that I will address is democracy. I know there has been controversy about the promotion of democracy in recent years, and much of this controversy is connected to the war in Iraq. So let me be clear: No system of government can or should be imposed by one nation on any other.

That does not lessen my commitment, however, to governments that reflect the will of the people. Each nation gives life to this principle in its own way, grounded in the traditions of its own people. America does not presume to know what is best for everyone, just as we would not presume to pick the outcome of a peaceful election. But I do have an unyielding belief that all people yearn for certain things: the ability to speak your mind and have a say in how you are governed, confidence in the rule of law and the equal administration of justice, government that is transparent and doesn't steal from the people, the freedom to live as you choose. These are not just American ideas, they are human rights. And that is why we will support them everywhere.

Now, there is no straight line to realize this promise, but this much is clear: Governments that protect these rights are ultimately more stable, successful, and secure. Suppressing ideas never succeeds in making them go away. America respects the right of all peaceful and law-abiding voices to be heard around the world, even if we disagree with them. And we will welcome all elected, peaceful governments, provided they govern with respect for all their people.

This last point is important, because there are some who advocate for democracy only when they're out of power. Once in power, they are ruthless in suppressing the rights of others. So no matter where it takes hold, government of the people and by the people sets a single standard for all who would hold power. You must maintain your power through consent, not coercion; you must respect the rights of minorities and participate with a spirit of tolerance and compromise; you must place the interests of your people and the legitimate workings of the political process above your party. Without these ingredients, elections alone do not make true democracy.

The fifth issue that we must address together is religious freedom. Islam has a proud tradition of tolerance. We see it in the history of Andalusia and Cordoba during the Inquisition. I saw it firsthand as a child in Indonesia, where devout Christians worshiped freely in an overwhelmingly Muslim country. That is the spirit we need today. People in every country should be free to choose and live their faith based upon the persuasion of the mind and the heart and the soul. This tolerance is essential for religion to thrive, but it's being challenged in many different ways.

Among some Muslims, there's a disturbing tendency to measure one's own faith by the rejection of somebody else's faith. The richness of religious diversity must be upheld, whether it is for Maronites in Lebanon or the Copts in Egypt.[4] And if we are being honest, fault lines must be closed among Muslims as well, as the divisions between Sunni and Shi'a have led to tragic violence, particularly in Iraq.

---

[4] Maronites and Copts are Christians.

Freedom of religion is central to the ability of peoples to live together. We must always examine the ways in which we protect it. For instance, in the United States, rules on charitable giving have made it harder for Muslims to fulfill their religious obligation. That's why I'm committed to working with American Muslims to ensure that they can fulfill *zakat*.[5]

Likewise, it is important for Western countries to avoid impeding Muslim citizens from practicing religion as they see fit, for instance, by dictating what clothes a Muslim woman should wear. We can't disguise hostility towards any religion behind the pretense of liberalism....

The sixth issue that I want to address is women's rights. I know— [applause]—I know, and you can tell from this audience, that there is a healthy debate about this issue. I reject the view of some in the West that a woman who chooses to cover her hair is somehow less equal, but I do believe that a woman who is denied an education is denied equality. And it is no coincidence that countries where women are well educated are far more likely to be prosperous.

Now, let me be clear: Issues of women's equality are by no means simply an issue for Islam. In Turkey, Pakistan, Bangladesh, Indonesia, we've seen Muslim-majority countries elect a woman to lead. Meanwhile, the struggle for women's equality continues in many aspects of American life and in countries around the world.

I am convinced that our daughters can contribute just as much to society as our sons. Our common prosperity will be advanced by allowing all humanity, men and women, to reach their full potential. I do not believe that women must make the same choices as men in order to be equal, and I respect those women who choose to live their lives in traditional roles. But it should be their choice. And that is why the United States will partner with any Muslim-majority country to support expanded literacy for girls and to help young women pursue employment through microfinancing that helps people live their dreams.

Finally, I want to discuss economic development and opportunity. I know that for many, the face of globalization is contradictory. The Internet and television can bring knowledge and information, but also offensive sexuality and mindless violence into the home. Trade can bring new wealth and opportunities, but also huge disruptions and change in communities. In all nations, including America, this change can bring fear. Fear that because of modernity, we lose control over our economic choices, our politics, and, most

---

[5] Obligatory charitable giving.

importantly, our identities, those things we most cherish about our communities, our families, our traditions, and our faith.

But I also know that human progress cannot be denied. There need not be contradictions between development and tradition. Countries like Japan and South Korea grew their economies enormously while maintaining distinct cultures. The same is true for the astonishing progress within Muslim-majority countries from Kuala Lumpur to Dubai. In ancient times and in our times, Muslim communities have been at the forefront of innovation and education....

Americans are ready to join with citizens and governments, community organizations, religious leaders, and businesses in Muslim communities around the world to help our people pursue a better life.

And the issues that I have described will not be easy to address, but we have a responsibility to join together on behalf of the world that we seek, a world where extremists no longer threaten our people and American troops have come home, a world where Israelis and Palestinians are each secure in a state of their own and nuclear energy is used for peaceful purposes, a world where governments serve their citizens and the rights of all God's children are respected. Those are mutual interests. That is the world we seek, but we can only achieve it together.

I know there are many, Muslim and non-Muslim, who question whether we can forge this new beginning. Some are eager to stoke the flames of division and to stand in the way of progress. Some suggest that it isn't worth the effort, that we are fated to disagree and civilizations are doomed to clash. Many more are simply skeptical that real change can occur. There's so much fear, so much mistrust that has built up over the years. But if we choose to be bound by the past, we will never move forward. And I want to particularly say this to young people of every faith in every country: You, more than anyone, have the ability to reimagine the world, to remake this world.

All of us share this world for but a brief moment in time. The question is whether we spend that time focused on what pushes us apart, or whether we commit ourselves to an effort, a sustained effort to find common ground, to focus on the future we seek for our children, and to respect the dignity of all human beings.

It's easier to start wars than to end them. It's easier to blame others than to look inward. It's easier to see what is different about someone than to find the things we share. But we should choose the right path, not just the easy path. There's one rule that lies at the heart of every religion, that we do unto others as we would have them do unto us. This truth transcends nations and peoples, a belief that isn't new, that isn't black or white or brown, that isn't Christian or Muslim or Jew. It's a belief that pulsed in the cradle of civilization and that still beats in the hearts of billions around the world. It's a faith in other people, and it's what brought me here today. We have the power to make the world we seek, but only if we have the courage to make a new beginning, keeping in mind what has been written.

The Holy Koran tells us: "O mankind! We have created you male and a female, and we have made you into nations and tribes so that you may know one another."[6] The Talmud tells us: "The whole of the Torah is for the purpose of promoting peace."[7] The Holy Bible tells us: "Blessed are the peacemakers, for they shall be called sons of God."[8] The people of the world can live together in peace. We know that is God's vision, now that must be our work here on Earth.

Thank you, and may God's peace be upon you.

---

[6] Koran 49:13.

[7] The Talmud is a collection of commentaries on the Torah, the first five books of the Bible.

[8] Matthew 5:9.

Appendices

Study Questions

For each of the Documents in this collection, we suggest below in section A questions relevant for that Document alone and in section B questions that require comparison between Documents.

1. John Winthrop, "A Model of Christian Charity" (1630)

A. What does Winthrop mean by "charity"? How does this principle relate to his understanding of the way that God has "disposed of the condition of mankind" so that "some must be rich, some poor, some high," etc.? In what ways is the principle of charity intended to shape the new political community?

B. How is Winthrop's vision of the Massachusetts Bay colonists' covenant with God similar to or different from John Quincy Adams' account of America in Document 7 or FDR in Document 21? How does his understanding of "charity" relate to later understandings of social justice and religion presented in Documents 17, 22, or 23, for example?

2. Laws, Rights, and Liberties Related to Religion in Early America (1610-1682)

A. How do the authors of these laws understand human nature? How do they understand the role of religion in public life? What is the difference between religious toleration and freedom of conscience as presented in these laws?

B. Which of these laws, if any, would be compatible with the view of "civil liberty" presented by Henry Ward Beecher in Document 13?

3. Cotton Mather, *A Man of Reason* (1718) and Jonathan Edwards, *A Divine and Supernatural Light* (1734)

A. Are the distinctions in these sermons merely matters of emphasis, or is there a genuine problem of incompatibility? What are the implications of the shift from a more socially-oriented approach to religion to a more individualistic one?

B. How does Mather's view of reason relate to or diverge from the account of reason given by later thinkers such as Palmer (Document 11), Hall (Document 16), or Schaeffer (Document 23)? How would Lincoln evaluate Edwards' claims about the importance of supernatural light, based on Documents 10 and 12?

4. Jonathan Mayhew, *A Discourse Concerning Unlimited Submission and Non-resistance to the Higher Powers* (1750)

A. Explain Mayhew's argument: how does he reconcile the command to Christians to "be subject" to civil powers with their duty to "resist the Devil"? Is this a paradox? How does he address the criticism that his position will lead to anarchy?

B. Given that Mayhew's sermon was delivered in celebration of the Puritan revolution in England, and that Winthrop wrote regularly in support of that revolution from Massachusetts, discuss the relationship between Winthrop's vision of civil society (seen in Document 1 and in the Massachusetts Laws and Liberties, Document 2) and Mayhew's. In what ways is Mayhew's argument for the legitimate resistance to tyranny similar to that presented in the Declaration (Document 5) or Schaeffer (Document 23)? In what ways does it differ?

5. Excerpts from Founding Documents (1776–1798)

A. What is the significance of "nature" in the Declaration of Independence? If instead of the phrase "the separate and equal station to which the Laws of Nature and of Nature's God entitle them," the Declaration read simply "the separate and equal station to which the laws of God entitle them," would that change its meaning? What is the connection between morality, knowledge and education made in the Northwest Ordinance and Washington's Farewell Address? Would it be right to say that religion is necessary to preserve the rights enumerated in the Declaration? If so, why does the Declaration not mention this? Is Jefferson's understanding of nature in Query VI of *Notes on the State of Virginia* the same as in the Declaration? How are nature and Providence connected in the Declaration? How do Jefferson and Rush differ on the issue of religion in education?

B. In Document 14, E. L. Youmans argues that the theory of evolution calls into question the existence of a Creator God, at least as such a God is presented in the account of creation in Genesis. If this is true, does it call into question the claim of the Declaration of Independence "that all men are created equal" and "that they are endowed by their Creator with certain unalienable Rights"?

6. George Washington, Letter to the Hebrew Congregation of Newport, Rhode Island (1790)

A. What is the difference between toleration and religious freedom? Would tolerance be acceptable given the argument of the Declaration of Independence about the rights that men are endowed with?

B. How is Washington's view in his letter to the Hebrew Congregation similar to and different from the views expressed in the Colonial laws excerpted in Document 2?

7. John Quincy Adams, An Address … Celebrating The Declaration of Independence (July 4, 1821)

A. What is the connection that Adams sees between the Reformation and the American Revolution? According to Adams, how is the United States distinguished from all previous government? How has religion contributed to this distinction?

B. Are the views Adams expresses about reason and its role in human life similar to or different from those of Cotton Mather (Document 3)?

8. Lyman Beecher, *A Plea for the West* (1835)

A. What is the connection between religion, education, and liberty for Beecher? Why does he fear Catholicism, and what does it tell us about the types of religions that he believes will be compatible or incompatible with the American way of life?

B. How is Beecher's vision of American expansion related to Winthrop's "city on a hill" (Document 1)? How does it relate to the Northwest Ordinance (Document 5) or Adams' July 4 Address (Document 7)? In what ways is Beecher's understanding of religion and liberty similar to or different from that presented by Obama (Document 25)?

9. Edward Beecher, *The Nature, Importance, and Means of Eminent Holiness Throughout the Church* (1835)

A. What is holiness, according to Beecher? How is the holiness movement connected to the "regeneration of the world"? What does Beecher mean when he speaks of the regeneration of the world? What is the view of man, God and nature in the holiness and reform movements?

B. Compare Beecher's views on God's relationship to man with those expressed by Mather, Edwards (Document 3), and Moody (Document 15). In what ways do they differ? How are they similar? How might their views affect attitudes towards politics?

10. Abraham Lincoln, The Temperance Address (1842)

A. Does Lincoln see a political problem with the Temperance movement? Does he see a problem with religion in a political order based on human equality? Does he see problems with only a certain kind of religion? What characteristics of religion make it a problem for a government based on human equality?

B. How do you think that Lincoln would respond to Edward Beecher's sermon on holiness (Document 9)?

11. Benjamin Morgan Palmer, "Baconianism and the Bible" (1852)

A. Does Palmer's article draw a connection, even implicitly, between science and the Declaration of Independence? If so, what is the connection? How does Palmer argue that the Reformation and modern science are alike? What is the status of the Bible for Palmer?

B. Compare Palmer's account of science and religion to Youmans' and Hall's (Documents 14 and 16). How do they differ? Are they alike in any ways?

12. Abraham Lincoln, Second Inaugural Address (1865)

A. Is Lincoln's view of God's relation to man the same in the Temperance Address and the Second Inaugural? How would you characterize that view?

B. Is there a similarity in the view of Southerners in the Second Inaugural and the view of drunkards in the Temperance Address (Document 10)? Is this the same view or attitude expressed toward sin in Beecher's sermon on holiness (Document 9)?

13. Henry Ward Beecher, "The Moral Theory of Civil Liberty" (1869)

A. What does Beecher mean by civil liberty? Why does he say that "self-government" is a better term than liberty? How is self-government connected to morality? What is the connection between religion and morality for Beecher? How does Beecher understand nature? What does he see as the connection between nature and self-government? Does Beecher's argument require the existence of God or any of the teachings of the Bible?

B. Would A. C. Dixon (Document 18) or Fosdick (Document 19) accept Beecher's argument? Would Mather (Document 3)?

14. E. L. Youmans, "Herbert Spencer and the Doctrine of Evolution" (1874)

A. Why does Youmans believe that Spencer is important? What is the connection between Spencer's view of nature, as described by Youmans, and Spencer's views of morality and social relations?

B. How is the view of nature in Spencer's work, as Youmans describes it, different from nature as understood by Palmer (Document 11)? How is the view of society and government in Spencer's work, as Youmans describes it, different from the views expressed by John Winthrop (Document 1) and Henry Ward Beecher (Document 13)?

15. Dwight L. Moody, "On Being Born Again" (1877)

A. What does it mean to be "born again," according to Moody? How is the born again person supposed to act in their society?

B. In what ways does the concept of being "born again" seem similar to or different from the experience described by Mather or Edwards (Document 3)? How does Moody's view relate to the vision of social engagement presented by Addams (Document 17) or King (Document 22)?

16. G. Stanley Hall, "Philosophy in the United States" (1879)

A. What is Hall's attitude toward religion? Does he see philosophy as the antagonist of religion? What explains this attitude?

B. How do the views expressed by Youmans (Document 14) and Hall (Document 16) differ from those expressed by Palmer (Document 11) and Henry Ward Beecher (Document 13)?

17. Jane Addams, "Religious Education and Contemporary Social Conditions" (1911)

A. What type of religious education does Addams see around her, how does she want it to change, and why? How would you describe her understanding of religion and its relationship to human nature?

B. Is Addams' vision of religious education similar to or different from that presented by Beecher (Document 8)? How would she respond to Mather (Document 3) or Dixon (Document 18), both of whom seem to be more concerned about teaching proper theology than engaging in social reform per se? In what ways can we connect Addams' vision of religiously motivated social reform to Winthrop's vision of Christian charity (Document 1), if at all?

18. A. C. Dixon, "The Bible at the Center of the Modern University" (1920)

A. What are the key characteristics of what Dixon calls German thinking? Why is he so concerned that it will gain influence in the United States? How is it related to evolution? Is what Dixon describes as German thinking compatible with the principles of the Declaration of Independence? Why is Lincoln important to Dixon? What is Dixon's attitude toward science? What is Dixon's attitude toward the Bible?

B. Would Dixon consider Spencer, as described by Youmans (Document 14), as "German thinking"? What would Dixon say about Spencer's social and ethical philosophy?

19. Harry Emerson Fosdick, "Shall the Fundamentalists Win?" (1922)

A. What is Fosdick's attitude toward science? Toward the Bible? What does Fosdick mean by progressive revelation? Is there a connection between progressive revelation and evolution? What is the greater authority for Fosdick, the Bible or science?

B. What would Fosdick say about Dixon's claims about the strong mistreating the weak (Document 18)? Would he object? If so, on what basis?

20. J. Gresham Machen, "The Bible," *Christianity and Liberalism* (1923)

A. What does Machen mean by the inerrancy of the Bible? Why is it important to him?

B. How does Machen's view of inerrancy differ from Fosdick's (Document 19)?

21. Franklin Delano Roosevelt, Address to the National Council of Catholic Charities (1933)

A. What does Roosevelt mean by social justice? What is the connection between religion and social justice? What does Roosevelt understand to be the roles of government and the churches with regard to social justice?

B. How are Roosevelt's views of religion and politics different from those expressed by Dixon (Document 18), Fosdick (Document 19) and Spencer (as described by Youmans in Document 14).

22. Martin Luther King, "Can a Christian Be a Communist?" (1962)

A. How does King portray America in relation to the divine? In what ways does he suggest American religion has failed in regard to Civil Rights? What remedies does he recommend for these failures? How did the religious rhetoric of the Civil Rights Movement affect its ability to dissent from the established political and cultural order? What does King suggest Christians can learn from communism and how should they apply those lessons to America's ongoing racial, cultural, social, and economic problems?

B. In what ways are King's views of Christianity and politics and how human beings should treat one another similar to or different from those of Winthrop (Document 1), Dixon (Document 18), Fosdick (Document 19), and Schaeffer (Document 23)?

23. Francis Schaeffer, "A Christian Manifesto" (1982)

A. What is Schaeffer's "manifesto" – that is, to what course of action is he calling American Christians? What does Schaeffer mean by "Humanism" and why does he see it as such a threat?

B. Is Schaeffer's understanding of civil disobedience similar to or different from that presented by Mayhew (Document 4)? How would Schaeffer respond to Palmer (Document 11) or Hall (Document 16)?

24. Ronald Reagan, Remarks at the Annual Convention of the National Association of Evangelicals (1983)

A. What is the connection Reagan sees between religion and liberty? What does Reagan mean by secularism? Why does he see it as a threat to America?

B. Is the connection Reagan sees between religion and liberty similar to or different from the view expressed in the Northwest Ordinance and Washington's Farewell Address (Document 5)?

25. Barack Obama, Address at Cairo University (2009)

A. What is the "new beginning" that Obama sought in Cairo? What is it based on? Is it based on a religious precept or a principle evident to all human beings? Is the "new beginning" more likely to succeed if it is based on one or the other? In his speech, the President said that "freedom in America is indivisible from the freedom to practice one's religion." What does this mean?

B. Are Obama's views of religion most similar to Dixon's (Document 18) or Fosdick's (19)? Are Obama's views of the relationship between religion and freedom similar to those of Beecher (Document 13) or Reagan (Document 24)? If they differ, how do they differ?

Suggested Reading

Ahlstrom, Sydney E. *A Religious History of the American People*. New Haven: Yale University Press, 1972; 2nd edition, with a chapter by David Hall, 2004.

Bonomi, Patricia U. *Under the Cope of Heaven: Religion, Society, and Politics in Colonial America*. New York: Oxford University Press, 1986; updated edition, 2003.

Bozeman, Theodore Dwight. *Protestants in an Age of Science: The Baconian Ideal and Antebellum American Relgious Thought*. Chapel Hill, North Carolina: University of North Carolina Press, 1977.

Gaustad, Edwin S. and Leigh Schmidt. *The Religious History of America: The Heart of the American Story from Colonial Times to Today*. New York: HarperOne, 2004.

Evensen, Bruce J. *God's Man for the Gilded Age: D. L. Moody and the Rise of Modern Evangelicalism*. New York: Oxford University Press, 2003.

Hall, David D. *A Reforming People: Puritanism and the Transformation of Public Life New England*. New York: Knopf, 2011.

Kidd, Thomas S. *God of Liberty: A Religious History of the American Revolution*. New York: Basic Books, 2010.

———. *The Great Awakening: The Roots of Evangelical Christianity in Colonial America*. New Haven: Yale University Press, 2009.

Larsen, Edward J. *Summer of the Gods: The Scopes Trial and America's Continuing Debate over Science and Religion*. Cambridge: Harvard University Press, 1997.

Marsden, George M. *Understanding Fundamentalism and Evangelicalism.* Grand Rapids, MI: Wm. B. Eerdmans Publishing Company, 1991.

————. *The Soul of the American University: From Protestant Establishment to Established Nonbelief.* New York: Oxford University Press, 1996.

————. *Fundamentalism and American Culture.* New York: Oxford, 2006.

Miller, Randall M., Harry S. Stout, and Charles Reagan Wilson, eds. *Religion and the American Civil War.* New York: Oxford University Press, 1998.

Miller, Steven P. *The Age of Evangelicalism: America's Born-Again Years.* New York: Oxford, 2014.

Murphy, Andrew R. *Prodigal Nation: Moral Decline and Divine Punishment from New England to 9/11.* New York: Oxford, 2008.

Noll, Mark A. *America's God: From Jonathan Edwards to Abraham Lincoln.* New York: Oxford, 2005.

Porterfield, Amanda. *Conceived in Doubt: Religion and Politics in the New American Nation.* Chicago: University of Chicago Press, 2012.

Smith, Christian (ed.). *The Secular Revolution: Power, Interests, and Conflict in the Secularization of American Public Life.* Berkley: University of California Press, 2003.

Swartz, David R. *Moral Minority: The Evangelical Left in an Age of Conservatism.* Philadelphia: University of Pennsylvania Press, 2014.

West, John G. *The Politics of Revelation and Reason: Religion and Civic Life in the New Nation.* Lawrence, Kansas: University Press of Kansas, 1996.

White, Ronald C., Jr. *Social Gospel: Religion and Reform in Changing America.* Philadelphia: Temple University Press, 1976.

Worthen, Molly. *Apostles of Reason: The Crisis of Authority in American Evangelicalism.* New York: Oxford, 201